Land Cinema in an Age of Extraction

Land Cinema in an Age of Extraction

Becca Voelcker

UNIVERSITY OF CALIFORNIA PRESS

University of California Press
Oakland, California

© 2026 by Becca Voelcker

All rights reserved.

Cataloging-in-Publication data is on file at the Library of Congress.

ISBN 978-0-520-41644-4 (cloth)
ISBN 978-0-520-41645-1 (pbk.)
ISBN 978-0-520-41646-8 (ebook)

GPSR Authorized Representative: Easy Access System Europe,
Mustamäe tee 50, 10621 Tallinn, Estonia, gpsr.requests@easproject.com

34   33   32   31   30   29   28   27   26   25
10   9   8   7   6   5   4   3   2   1

For my parents

CONTENTS

Acknowledgments ix
Note on Language xiii

Prologue 1

Introduction 7

1 · Poets of the Land: The Subjects of Landscape-Portraits 34

2 · Farmer-Filmmakers, Fieldwork, and Growth 65

3 · There Is No Countryside: The Anti-Pastoral 100

4 · Companion Planting in Wounded Land 129

5 · On the Picket Line, on the Television: Representation, Empathy, and Distance 162

6 · Extraction Is Stealing, Relationships Give Meaning 193

Selected Filmography 219
Notes 221
Bibliography 249
Index 273

ACKNOWLEDGMENTS

I was able to write this book because of many other people's generosity, time, and care. The book began as a PhD dissertation, which I was fortunate enough to complete with the guidance of Giuliana Bruno, who became an inspiration, mentor, and friend during my time at Harvard University. During the time spent earning my PhD I was also honored to work with Haden Guest, who made the Harvard Film Archive feel like a second home. I am also indebted to Dennis Lim, who introduced me to wonderful films, filmmakers, and festivals during our five years teaching together in Harvard's Department of Art, Film, and Visual Studies.

During the course of this project, I felt encouraged and calmed in the very special presence of Laura Frahm, with whom I shared many Friday writing sessions, and Jennifer Coates, who became a brilliant mentor and friend. Thank you both for an extraordinary amount of care.

Thank you also to everyone who discussed the project with me as it grew, including Siobhan Angus, Jenny Chamarette, Tom Conley, Kieron Corless, Ed Dimendberg, Kirsty Sinclair Dootson, Gareth Evans, Aneela Ferdinand, Asako Fujioka, Jorie Graham, Ros Gray, Raphaël Grisey, Itsushi Kawase, Paulina Kolata, Mame Kurogouchi, Stephen Johnstone, Okamura Keiko, Rob Knipe, Jie Li, Scott MacDonald, Suhail Malik, Ricardo Matos Cabo, So Mayer, Koki and Miyoko Muroi, Markus Nornes, Clive Nwonka, Colin Perry, Lucy Reynolds, Jake Subryan Richards, Julian Ross, Jackie Stacey, María Vélez-Serna, Owen Sheers, Jeremy

Till, Nina Wakeford, John Williams, and Alex Zahlten. Thank you to my students at Goldsmiths for learning and thinking with me.

Thank you to the Daiwa Anglo Japanese Foundation for originally enabling me to move to Japan in 2013, a decision that changed my life, and to numerous initiatives that supported my research at Harvard, especially the Reischauer Institute for Japanese Studies. Thank you to the many curators and conservationists who made archival research so accessible and transformative: Mark Johnson at Harvard Film Archive; Philippe-Alain Michaud at Centre Pompidou; Benjamin Cook and Charlotte Procter at LUX; Steven Ball at Central Saint Martins' British Artists' Film & Video Study Collection; Yamashita Koyo at Image Forum; Yoko Sawada at Osiris; and the archival team at Channel Four. During my research, many people answered film-specific questions and provided images and material. Many thanks to Enzo Camacho, Ana Vaz, Zhang Mengqi, Rose Lowder, Cinema Action's Ann Guedes, Ogawa Pro members Iizuka Toshio and Fuseya Hiroo, and Anne Charlotte Robertson's sister-in-law Rebecca Robertson and friend Susan Hardy-Brown.

Thank you to producers at the BBC for giving me the opportunity to shape ideas explored in this book on the radio, especially Robyn Read, Jayne Edgerton, Ann Fôn, and Luke Mulhall. I am also very grateful to curators at the Barbican Centre in London for helping me transform this book into a public film program; thank you Tamara Anderson, Matthew Barrington, and Alex Davidson.

I am extremely grateful to my editor at the University of California Press, Raina Polivka, for believing in this project from an early stage. Thank you also to the anonymous peer reviewers who offered such generous and encouraging feedback. And thank you to Sam Warren and everyone behind the scenes at the press as well as Yvonne Ramsey, copyeditor, who all helped bring this book to fruition.

Last but not least, I feel deep gratitude to friends, family, and loved ones. Thank you, Ben, for Film Club. Thank you, Lucy and Kai, for that wondrous spring when all our worlds changed. Thank you to my brothers for lifelong friendship. Thank you, Sherah, for accompanying me in life like a big sister, no matter the geographic distance. Thank you, David, for your immense kindness and love. And thank you to my parents for always listening and caring. I'm so glad you went back to the land.

NOTE ON LANGUAGE

Japanese, Chinese, and Vietnamese names appear with surname first. The names of authors of works in English, however, follow the order and orthography used in their publications: Trịnh Thị Minh Hà, for example, is referred to as Trinh T. Minh-ha or Trinh, following convention in her own books. Macrons have been omitted from common place-names such as Tokyo but retained for other words such as *fūkeiron* (landscape theory). Where generative of meaning, Japanese characters are provided in addition to Romanized versions and their English translations. French, Gaelic, Hiligaynon, Mandarin, Navajo, Scots, Spanish, Tagalog, and Welsh words are italicized and translated into English.

Prologue

IF YOU STAND STILL TOO LONG, you will sink. Holding my father's hand we cross, feeling land clot, and resettle as we keep our pace and retrieve our feet. Beyond the peat moor, a fox flashes through the basalt outcrop that we call the Airplane Rocks. If you climb those rocks, you feel yourself flying over a patchwork land below: green pasture, reddish heather, honey gorse, and rusty banks of bracken. Farther up the mountain in the boulder fields that tumble into steep cliffs, sheep look as small as flecks of feldspar. Some days the mountain's peak hides in mist; other days, it is ablaze with sun.

Some 650 million to 450 million years ago, this mountain was a volcano. It was part of a chain of underwater volcanoes, initially scattered near the South Pole. Over millions of years drifting northward, these submarine eruptions deposited layers of ash, lava, and mud onto the seabed and formed islands. The squiggly fossils I found as a child are the remains of ancient marine life that lived in the warm, shallow seas back then. Around 420 million years ago continental plates collided, compressing layers of rock into folds and transforming mudstones into the slate for which the land grew famous, roofing the world in the nineteenth century. Some 2.6 million years ago glaciers carved deep, jagged valleys that catch clouds and hold them for days. This is Eryri, or Snowdonia, a National Park in northwest Wales.

Four hundred fifty years ago basalt and granite rocks were dug, rolled, and hoisted from this land; oak trees were cut; and slate was split to build a house. Nestling in a mossy hollow on the edge of the moor that climbs up to Mynydd Graig Goch (Red Rock Mountain) (Figure 1), the house seems to have grown from this unfathomably old landscape. I was born upstairs under the oak eaves and roof slates. My body, my mother's body, the house, the landscape: we nested inside each other in different scales of time and movement and change.

My parents moved to Wales before I was born, leaving city life in the 1970s. "We didn't want to participate in the system," my mother says. My parents grew vegetables, kept chickens, learned Welsh, and worked as local sustainability and conservation architects. "You can call it a retreat. You can call it political. I'm going to turn the compost." My mother is off, pushing the wheelbarrow, busy before the rain starts again. Time is multiple in this place. There is the moment-by-moment pace of chasing sunlight and clouds. There is also the cycle that pushes crocuses through the earth each longed-for spring. And then there is deep time: A house that has weathered 450 wood-smoky winters and twenty generations of births and deaths (the gravestones are in the cemetery at the foot of the mountain) and a landscape that has endured and transformed for 625 million years.

Y filltir sgwâr, they call it, "the square mile" in which you're born that shapes who you become. I say they, and I suppose I include myself, hovering at the threshold (probably marveling at the granite lintel above my head and feeling foreign to the Joneses, Robertses, and Williamses in the room). Born to incomers cultivating a greener lifestyle and hating Margaret Thatcher, I was raised bilingually in a community suspicious of back-to-the-landers. English colonialism and its industrial spoils lingered in the abandoned slate quarries, the reservoir that was once a village and is now Liverpool's drinking water, and the summer roads clogged by caravans. When my parents first arrived, nationalists were setting fire to cottages they saw English tourists buy; my parents put Welsh-language books in the windows of our house to show that they were joining the community long-term. And long it was for the community to stop asking "where are you visiting from?" Outsiders have a bad reputation in Wales, taking coal, slate, farmland, scenic views, and vacations.

My interest in aesthetic and political representations of marginalized places and people in this book is accentuated by my growing up in this rural Welsh context and then moving to live in large cities across the world—the most thrilling contrast being, without a doubt, Tokyo. Many of the filmmakers discussed in this book occupied insider/outsider perspectives on the places they filmed, complicating ideas of emplaced identity and belonging as well as distinctions between the country and the city. In positioning myself in relation to them and their aesthetic and political work, I take my cue from Raymond Williams, whose rural Welsh background imbued his exploration of cultural attitudes to land, particularly in his 1973 book *The Country and the City*, with a sense of personal commitment and lived urgency. Half a century on, I write with both my background in mind and an eye on the very pressing, contemporary foreground of climate crisis. This foreground, perhaps better described as an atmosphere engulfing the entire scene, colors the lens through which I look at history and sharpens my focus on how extractive practices, developed over centuries of capitalist and colonial activity, drive climate breakdown and climate injustice today.

Echoing Williams, I can therefore say that before I had read about changes to ways of life produced by and in resistance to extractivism and before I had watched them play out in the films and photographs that are the subject of this book, I saw them on the ground. I saw them in the ways a rural Welsh-speaking community resented outsider encroachments that scarred the land and in the ways "outsiders" such as my parents went "back to the land" with both a green, socialist politics and a measure of rural romanticism. But my inquiry encompasses more than aesthetic and political forms of retreat and resistance; it also connects ideas of ruralism to questions of climate justice, identifying in both a shared set of concerns for access, agency, and representation.

Extractive capitalism's violations of climate justice are omnipresent, playing out in what Rob Nixon has called the "slow violence" of land dispossession and abject poverty and in the flash points of wars fought over territories and resources.[1] I write from within universities in the Global North, where I analyze and teach photographed and filmed *perspectives*.

Today, surrounded by divisive images and misinformation regarding climate breakdown and land rights, scrutinizing perspectives is paramount. Photographs and films variously labeled as non-fiction or documentary are often treated as evidence because of their mechanical and apparently objective manufacture: *This happened; here's photographic documentation of it.* As I explore in the chapters that follow, numerous theorists of documentary film and photography have cautioned against such assumptions, arguing that documentary images' claims to authenticity assert authority over places and stories. The task at hand, then, is to ask whose perspective we are seeing and whose is being overlooked. Why was this image made? Every image proposes a narrative, a politics, a demand. Asking how an image—and therefore an idea of a land or people—was made and for what political purpose is central to this book.

Rather than focus on divisive images—what T. J. Demos calls "burning aesthetics" of climate emergency (forest fires, famines, floods)—*Land Cinema in an Age of Extraction* gathers oppositional and propositional images.[2] Made in resistance to extractive predation and in creative and practical approaches to the future, images that belong to a genre I am calling "land cinema" activate a space of mediation between pragmatic demands for eco-political change and its speculative prefiguration. Working with film, photography (and often land itself, through farming and gardening) practitioners in this book produced images that are political in both the way they look and the way they were made and shared.

Although several of its visionary projects also contained blind spots and living under extractive capitalism posed contradictions and entailed complicities for its makers, land cinema's legacy is its critical and creative commitment. As with my parents' move to Wales, land cinema's approaches to places and communities raise questions concerning socioeconomic privilege, emplaced identity, and pastoral romanticism. Land cinema's power is in foregrounding perspectives as partial, embodied, emplaced, and historical. This foregrounding exposes inequalities of access and agency, inviting audiences' critical reflection.

Like my parents' forty-year investment into land ("This is true wealth," I can hear them say. "Just look at all these saplings."), land cinema proposes an alternative future characterized by diversified values and practices of repair and being in relation. Though *Land Cinema in an Age of Extraction* is, on one level, a book about film, on another level it reads as a history of experiments in sustainable living that constructs an economic argument against financialized measures of "value," "growth," and "progress" and for alternative ethical and ecological metrics. Put differently, land cinema shows that alternatives can exist and have existed. Whereas emergency images often lack critical context regarding causality, present misery as if there was no alternative, and leave audiences in paralyzed alarm, land cinema advances land- and lens-based approaches to climate justice as possible blueprints for the future.[3]

If, as Amitav Ghosh has written, climate crisis is a crisis of imagination, then land cinema's intervention is in imaging—imagining, enacting, filming, screening—perspectives that value non-extractive modes of being and look beyond the dominant and deadly present.[4] I have written *Land Cinema in an Age of Extraction* for my peers and students: largely a generation born after 1980, now wondering what happened in the decades immediately preceding our births to so widen a rift between humans and nature and between dominant actors and their objects of exploitation and wondering also *who resisted this.*

Here are ten filmmakers and collectives who resisted. Here also is a new term and field, "land cinema," that I propose as a rubric and framework for analyzing other works of film and visual culture in other regions that operate in similarly oppositional and propositional ways. I hope that this new field of land cinema, which grows from work undertaken before me in environmental justice, film and documentary history, and ecological art, holds space for critical and creative flourishing to come.

FIGURE 1. Mynydd Graig Goch (Red Rock Mountain). Photograph by Becca Voelcker.

Introduction

IMAGINE A SHIMMERING RICE PADDY reflecting the sky in silver stripes through bright green seedlings. A man holds a microphone low above the earth and turns to the camera. "Our harvest is growing," he grins. Cut to a close-up of leaves, the camera at ankle height, leaf height. The man has been here with his filmmaking collective, some two hundred miles north of Tokyo, since 1975, learning how to grow rice and film rural land and labor.

Picture a woman sitting on the ground, legs in a V-shape, arranging broken glass and shells in a circle. The air is dusty from the demolition, the image grainy on the 16mm black-and-white film. It's 1979, and she's here with two friends and a camera, collectively mourning and blessing a neighborhood bulldozed for a Los Angeles highway.

These images pose questions: How has land come to look this way? Whose land is it? Whose perspective? All images of land require political and ecological decoding. These images foreground their own perspectives and material production to invite us to look carefully and ask questions. They belong to a genre that I call "land cinema."

Building on work in fields of environmental justice, film and documentary history, and ecological art, I propose land cinema as a coinage to describe lens-based media that represent complex relations with lands and the lifeworlds they contain. Land cinema understands political, ecological, and aesthetic aspects of land as a web of related concerns. Land cinema is oppositional in the way it documents territorial expansion, material extraction, and labor exploitation. And land cinema is

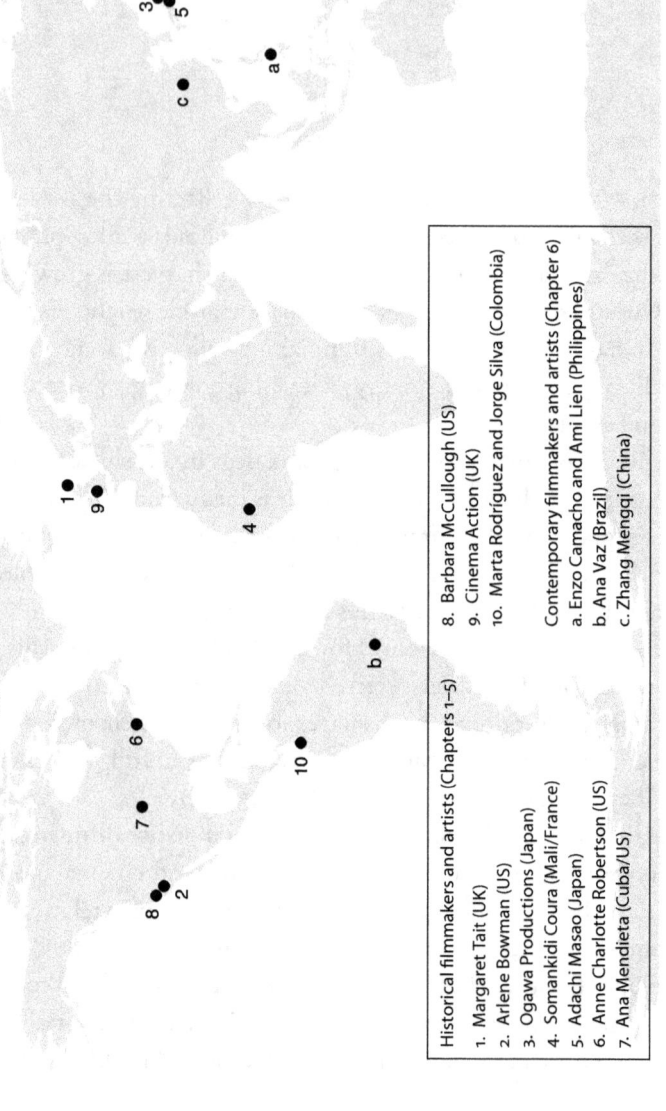

MAP 1. Locations of the book's filmmaker case studies.

propositional in its presentation of grassroots and collective possibilities for ecological and social repair. Recognizing the camera's historical imbrication with imperial and industrial projects of objectifying communities and landscapes as resources for extraction, land cinema reappropriates lens-based media as tools for resistance and responsiveness, reframing land as a locus of eco-ethical responsibility.[1]

Today we are surrounded by divisive images and misinformation regarding land rights and climate change. Theorizing land cinema is an urgent task for imagining, imaging, and enacting climate justice. This book is a history of land cinema's development, written with an eye to future possibilities for the genre. Its focus is the 1970s and 1980s, a period characterized by an intensification of material extraction under neoliberal drives for economic growth and forms of activist resistance to it guided by green and socialist movements, and by the influence of feminist and anticolonial struggles. Much has been written about activist and participatory forms of cinema in the 1970s, particularly documentary's social function. *Land Cinema in an Age of Extraction* contributes an eco-political focus to this body of work.[2] Examples I explore range from activist farmer-filmmaker collectives in rural Japan and Mali to a gardener-filmmaker in Massachusetts and from film portraits of women farmers in Orkney and the Navajo (Diné) Nation to participatory documentaries about Indigenous land dispossession in Colombia. There are also eco-feminist films decrying highway construction and agri-business in California and Iowa and essay films that apply Marxist frameworks to denounce industrialization in Tokyo and Wales. This geographic spread is important, illustrating a global trend toward environmentalism in the 1970s.

BACK TO THE LAND

In 1968, NASA published the first photographs of Earth taken from space. Humans had come a long way from hunting and gathering to be able to travel so far and capture such images. Yet the images also rendered the fragility of humankind and the planet more visible. The year

1968 was one of the high points of the Cold War. Many people feared nuclear annihilation. NASA's images represented more than the Space Race: here was a planetary perspective, an overview like never before. On the ground, meanwhile, globalization's space-time compression proffered ever more lucrative and technologized systems, and the news was awash in stories of oil spills, water poisoning, and species extinction. All was not well on planet Earth.

On April 22, 1970, over twenty million people took to the streets across the United States with placards imploring the public to "Save the Trees" and "Vote for Clean Air, Pure Water, Healthy Land." This was the first Earth Day, a mass uprising for climate care. Some protesters had read *Silent Spring*, Rachel Carson's 1962 account of pesticide pollution. Others marched with new ideas about ecosystems on their minds. That year, James Lovelock presented research suggesting that all organisms work symbiotically for the preservation of life in the biosphere. He called this the Gaia hypothesis, borrowing from ancient Greece, where the mother of all life on Earth was Gaia, meaning "land." The Gaia hypothesis inspired new green movements denouncing capitalism's damages to the environment and depletion of natural resources.

Awareness of fossil fuel depletion grew as oil crises in 1973 and 1979 disrupted the global price and availability of petroleum. Meanwhile, neoliberalism was assuming a position of global dominance, spreading from its origins in inter- and post-war Europe to rapid adoption in the United States, and a series of euphemistically titled "developments" useful for suppressing communism in Latin America and East Asia. Defined as the extension of competitive markets into all areas of life, including economics, politics, culture, and land use, neoliberalism is based on the belief that maximizing entrepreneurial individual freedom, private ownership, and global trade best advances human well-being.[3] Neoliberalism's "development" of lands depends on intensified cycles of extraction and waste. Every Earth Day since 1970 has protested this ideology, and every land cinema image critically responds to it.

While some environmentalists took to the streets in the 1970s, others left them, moving "back to the land" alone or collectively. Some gardened or farmed, produced artisanal goods, bought organic produce, and practiced yoga, meditation, and New Age religions. Henry David Thoreau's 1854 book *Walden: Or, Life in the Woods* and Aldo Leopold's 1949 collection of essays, *A Sand County Almanac*, were among the books that inspired people to move to rural areas and observe what Leopold called a "land ethic." As fulfilling as they may have been for individuals, such lifestyles did little to confront systemic issues; retreats to nature hardly tackle the multinational corporations and state bodies responsible for chemical pollution, carbon emissions, and biodiversity loss. Some well-meaning behaviors (buying do-it-yourself goods advertised in *Whole Earth Catalog*, for example) can even play into neoliberalism's individualizing logic, replacing structural change with consumer choice and personal responsibility. Tensions such as these play out throughout this book as I consider material and ethical commitments and contradictions in the works and lives of filmmakers, including those discussed in Chapters 1 and 2 who went "back to the land" in rural Scotland and Japan.

In Japan, amid a post-war boom, rapid urbanization, and increased dependency on material extraction, moving "to the wilderness" (*zaiya*) gained a positive connotation of not participating in consumerism and Americanization.[4] Although US occupation of mainland Japan ended in 1952 (and in Okinawa twenty years later), financial loans, along with subsidized wheat imports that threatened domestic rice production, illustrate how systems of Western imperialism perpetuated relations of dependency in the 1970s. Historians interpret Japan's post-war economic "miracle" as an American strategy to contain communism.[5]

Similar strategies for economic growth were deployed in Latin America throughout the 1970s. Contesting ideas of scarcity presented in the 1972 Meadows Report, *The Limits to Growth: A Report for the Club of Rome's Project on the Predicament of Mankind*, governments in Latin America held that the region's natural resources were abundant and that their task was to exploit them for "ecodevelopment."[6] Despite its green prefix, such development came at a cost. As the Colombian filmmakers I discuss in Chapter 5 documented, national and multinational "development" frequently expropriated Indigenous lands, polluted habitats, and undermined the value of agrarian epistemologies and forms of governance.[7] Addressing such violence as a form of neocolonialism, agronomist-activists across Latin America used organic agriculture as an "environmentalism of the poor and indigenous," confronting extraction with a moral economy of land relations.[8] As Paulo Freire put it, environmentalism of the poor was founded on respect for the planet and achieved through grassroots political literacy.[9]

Agrarian tradition also informed environmentalism in Japan, along with a Shinto emphasis on respecting the forces of nature and animate forms of other-than-human life.[10] Organic agriculture grew in popularity due to Fukuoka Masanobu's best-selling 1975 book *One-Straw Revolution*, which cautioned against soil disturbance and characterized nature as a field of symbiotic processes. Comparable to Carson's *Silent Spring*, Ariyoshi Sawako's 1975 study of chemical fertilizers, *Complex Pollution*, also contributed to the resurgence of interest in land and the formation of Japan's Association to Protect the Earth. In farmland outside Tokyo, farmers and environmentalists (and land cinema filmmakers discussed in Chapter 2) protested the construction of an international airport. In a village that shared a bay with a chemical factory, fishing families protested against what would become known as Minamata disease, or industrial mercury poisoning. Environmentalism spread from these locales, uniting diverse sectors of society, with farmer and fisher folk leading many struggles.

Similarly in Latin America, Indigenous and African American populations steered ecological-distributive campaigns with a keen understanding that extractive capitalism grew from colonialism as a material practice and worldview premised on separation and control. This historical attunement also characterizes contemporaneous movements for environmental justice in Africa. As multiple regions gained independence in the 1960s, national and local projects for supporting rural self-sufficiency grew.

Alongside material self-sufficiency, self-representation in political and social contexts was key. During the colonial era, France issued the Laval Decree forbidding West African people from filming themselves.[11] After independence, photography and film helped rewrite African narratives from African perspectives. As well as repairing lands and livelihoods exhausted by decades of colonial plantation agriculture, national and grassroots initiatives revitalized through film, theater, and music. Leading liberation struggles against Portugal, Amílcar Cabral emphasized the role of culture, especially cinema, alongside agriculture in nurturing Pan-African and national solidarity.[12]

Cabral helped send Bissau-Guinean filmmakers to film school in Cuba. Freire read Cabral before traveling from Brazil to support education in Guinea-Bissau. These kinds of cross-cultural influence characterize the internationalism of political and environmental activism in the 1970s.[13] Land cinema was similarly internationalist, as the following sketch makes clear.

Margaret Tait, the Orkney filmmaker discussed in Chapter 1, trained alongside neorealist filmmakers in Rome before settling in Scotland. Her fellow student in Rome, Fernando Birri, later helped shape the New Latin American or "Third Cinema" movement to which the Colombian filmmakers Marta Rodríguez and Jorge Silva, discussed in Chapter 5, contributed documentaries about land dispossession and agrarian struggle. Rodríguez studied filmmaking in Paris with Jean Rouch, who was also engaged in filmmaking in pre- and post-colonial West Africa. In Colombia, she and Silva made films with Nasa, Coconuco, Guambiano, and other Indigenous nations and met with political filmmakers in Bolivia and Chile. Silva traveled to Algeria in 1973 to participate in a meeting of "Third World Filmmakers" with Tait's colleague Birri and with Flora Gomes, one of the filmmakers Cabral sent to Cuba. In their 1969 manifesto for political cinema, Birri's Argentine colleagues Fernando Solanas and Octavio Getino cited radical Japanese film collectives as influences. One such collective, Ogawa Productions, discussed in Chapter 2, hosted members of the Black Panthers and the American Newsreel collective visiting rural Japan, later establishing an international documentary film festival there. Adachi Masao, a Japanese filmmaker to whom I turn in Chapter 3, left Tokyo for the Middle East to fight for Palestinian independence. The photographer Bouba Touré, discussed in Chapter 2, also divided his time between two continents, taking pictures in migrant hostels in Paris and on a cooperative farm in Mali to connect urban and rural, metropole and former colony. The project's west Malian location meanwhile touched the border of Senegal and Mauritania, and its membership comprised Bambara, Soninke, Pulaar, and Khassonké groups in a further cross-cultural networking of influences and ideas. Translation and place-based identity also emerge as key themes in documentaries made by Cinema Action (discussed in Chapter 5) in England, Wales, and Ireland. Before forming their collective, several Cinema Action members had worked in France alongside Chris Marker and Jean-Luc Godard, who made films in Japan, China, and the Middle East. As this cartography makes clear, through elective affinities and political solidarities forged between the local communities for and with whom filmmakers made their work and through international audiences of experimental film festivals and television, land cinema bridged regions estranged under colonialism's structural asymmetries, uniting across a shared but differential relation to extractivism.

Extraction reduces all land to material for "stealing," as Leanne Betasamosake Simpson puts it.[14] Although specific cases of material and labor exploitation vary between regions and historical instances are not equivalent, they are entangled in this overarching dynamic of expropriation.[15] The European colonization of the Americas, for example, developed into the transatlantic African slave trade, which was part of an imperial project that also reached the East Indies and China as well as colonizing "at home" through land expropriation for the industrialization of agriculture. These specific yet connected episodes fueled and funded further industrial developments in Europe and more imperial expansion across the nineteenth- and early twentieth-century world.[16] Land cinema's simultaneous local and planetary outlook addresses this entanglement, mapping what Lisa Lowe describes as extractivism's ever-shifting "convergence of asymmetries."[17]

Although this book's historical framing of land cinema identifies the period beginning in the 1970s as an age of extraction, it follows land cinema in approaching extractivism as a much older material practice and worldview.¹⁸ As Kyle Whyte writes, recent cases of land dispossession and material extraction induce a "colonial déjà vu" by repeating racialized practices across generations and centuries.¹⁹ Nevertheless, this book's framing is important in highlighting the extent to which extractive capitalism has shaped climate breakdown over the past fifty years. Since 1970, global resource extraction has more than tripled, including a 45 percent increase in fossil fuel use.²⁰ One of land cinema's defining features is its ability to connect struggles in the 1970s with deeper pasts, activating déjà vu through testimonies, archival images, and reenactments as cautionary tales for the future. Amid our current planetary crisis, learning from land cinema's capacious memory and international outlook is crucial. This book looks at history for what it can teach us in the present and the future. Though climate breakdown's effects are unequally distributed, its omnipresence demands collective action across generations and national borders.

In light of arguments put forth by Whyte and others, some scholars have argued that the Anthropocene, or "age of humans," might better be called a Capitalocene to identify specific actors and activities responsible for climate breakdown. Others have proposed the term "Plantationocene" to excavate the Capitalocene's buried past and acknowledge the human costs of colonialism's "planting" of people to work the land, as Katherine McKittrick explains, "not as members of society but as commodities that would bolster crop economies."²¹ Though land cinema predates these terms, which were all coined since 2000, it addresses the concerns they name through its interrogation of land's uses and abuses, its ability to connect past and present, and its simultaneously internationalist and local approach.

OPPOSITIONAL IMAGES: EXPOSING EXTRACTIVISM

The stories we tell about land—and how we picture it—influence our treatment of land and those who inhabit it. In turn, political and ecological changes in the land such as colonial settlement and environmental devastation affect how lands are represented in visual culture. As Raymond Williams has written, land is not a static entity separate from culture: its significance and signification vary across contexts and times. "Ideas of nature," Williams notes, reveal a great deal about the ideas and ideals of the societies that produce them.[22] In other words, what we think about when we think about land is often a reflection of ourselves and our politics.[23]

Land cinema's intersection of ecological, political, and aesthetic concerns indicates land's complexity as a concept. The term "land" can signify a terrestrial ecosystem, a field of conflict and despoliation, and a source of ideation and images. "Land" has a similarly expansive definition in other languages, and it is important to remember that not all land cinema practitioners speak English. The Japanese term for "land," *tsuchi*, also translates as "ground," "earth," "soil," and even "clay." Its written character, 土, resembles a mound of earth, a lump of clay on a potter's wheel or, at least to my eyes, a seedling sprouting from the ground as a reminder that the source of nearly all our food and life on Earth is land. No wonder *tsuchi* is one of the first characters that Japanese children learn and one of the four elements in Buddhist philosophy, alongside fire, water, and air. The term "land" in French is *terre* and *pays* and in Spanish is *tierra* and *país*. *Pays/país* derives from a Latin word for "village" or "district," indicating land's association with social belonging. Indeed, in Wales, the square mile (*milltir sgwâr*) of land (*tir*) in which a person is born is said to bestow belonging and identity. While "Wales" and "Welsh" were Anglo-Saxon settler terms for Indigenous lands and people they identified as not their own, the Welsh equivalents "Cymru" (the land) and "Cymry" (the people) derive from a word for "fellow countryman." These contrasting words for the same land demarcate a politics of perspective. Insider/outsider identifications are a recurrent theme in land cinema. Every image proposes a narrative, a politics, a demand. Asking how and why an image was made and how it came to shape ideas of a land or people is central to this book.

Reading a map often reveals clues for emplaced identification, with place-names evidencing instances of land expropriation, cultural erasure, and (neo)colonial world-building. The word "landing" conjures images of settlers disembarking from ships onto new "found" land and proceeding to enclose, name, and cultivate it as property. This territorial form of cultivation, key to the establishment of colonial plantations in the seventeenth and eighteenth centuries, dates back to the Roman legal principle of terra nullius (nothing land), which stipulated that an act of tilling land established a person's proprietary claim over it ("colony" derives from the Latin for "farm").[24] Of course, when John Locke invoked this principle in his 1689 treatise on property, he overlooked the thousands of years that Indigenous people had spent mixing their labor with the land as well as the fact that European men of property would never have to till soil themselves. They owned other people who did it.

Aesthetic representations of land offer clues to such power dynamics. In its very composition, the word "landscape" reflects the politics at stake in activities of shaping, collecting, and organizing land into a "-scape," a condition.[25] Landscape is perhaps better understood as a verb than a noun for this reason.[26] The word developed its association with aesthetic experience upon entering English from Dutch in the seventeenth century as a piece of artistic jargon and soon became central to projects of territorialization.[27] In the eighteenth-century Romantic tradition of picturesque landscape painting, for example, English colonialists' newly enclosed farmlands are depicted as verdant, Elysian idylls. The exploitation of land and people undertaken to achieve these landscapes is naturalized within their aesthetics.[28] Since the 1960s, monumental pieces of land art have been installed across the midwestern and southwestern United States, occupying land fashioned as wilderness at the cost of Indigenous communities.[29] As Nicholas Mirzoeff notes, such visuality aestheticizes the conquering of nature as beautiful and anaesthetizes viewers from the painful realities of settler colonial genocide.[30] Land cinema lays bare these realities.

Changes in the land wrought by settler colonialism, industrialization, and urbanization appear, often aestheticized and anaesthetized, in early photographs and films. The development of photographic and moving image technologies in the late nineteenth century coincided with and often produced celebratory documentation of territorial conquests. This process was not confined to the West. Film and photography flourished in Japan in the 1920s and 1930s as means to document the empire's domination of East and Southeast Asia. Verdant landscape images meanwhile forwarded an ethnic essentialism at the expense of Indigenous cultures in Hokkaido and Okinawa whose difference was forcefully assimilated.[31] As in Europe, imaginaries centered on "homeland," nation, and blood served projects of expansion and assimilation. Several land cinema practitioners in this book grew up in these troubled contexts, absorbing representations of land and identity that they later called into question.

Many examples of land cinema also critique landscape's gendered history, understanding, as Jill Casid writes in her study of colonial landscaping practices, *Sowing Empire*, that gender- and race-based violence hide in one and the same space of political and aesthetic domination.[32] In eighteenth- and nineteenth-century artistic representations and literary accounts, landscape is commonly personified as female; panoramic views present land as a passive body available for exploration by a presumptively male gaze. The word "rape" sometimes features in these accounts, deriving from a term for the violent seizure of property—the rape of the countryside is its despoliation. Land continued to be characterized as female in the twentieth century. In his recent study of Japanese earth art, Bert Winther-Tamaki notes the strongly gendered practice of a post-war avant-garde of photographers, performance artists, and sculptors who identified as female the earth they captured, penetrated, or molded.[33] Land cinema repurposes genres of landscape and lens-based media as tools for looking back and looking differently.

In this oppositional approach, land cinema speaks to an eco-feminist turn in political theory and environmental activism in the 1970s.[34] First coined by Francoise d'Eaubonne in her starkly titled 1974 book *Feminism or Death*, the term "eco-feminism" connects the oppression of marginalized groups (not only women but also people of color and the poor) to the oppression of nature under patriarchal capitalism.[35] Though the term "eco-feminism" pre-dates the widespread use of the term "extractivism" since the 1990s, its arguments shed light on extractivism's techniques of domination that result in irreversible environmental damage and injustice.[36] Women are disproportionately affected by climate breakdown, because, as Vandana Shiva has argued, it is women who are responsible for collecting food and water even in the midst of environmental emergency, forced displacement, or war.[37] Meanwhile, extractive capitalism favors a narrowly defined category of scientific "expertise" in its approach to nature and dismisses Indigenous and predominantly female epistemologies—despite the fact that 80 percent of the world's biodiversity is safeguarded by Indigenous people. Many land cinema films celebrate Indigenous women as community leaders and defenders of human rights and the rights of nature.

In championing drives for human and environmental protection, land cinema of the 1970s contributes Indigenous and eco-feminist insights to an that idea Karl Marx developed some one hundred years earlier that is known as "metabolic rift." Marx diagnosed a rift between the natural world and humankind when capitalist imperatives for growth exhausted both "the soil and the worker."[38] Extracting fossil fuels made from decomposed plants and animals as well as any other part of the ecosystem deemed profitable relies on distinguishing nature from humankind. Marx cautioned against such a division, reminding readers that "man is a part of nature" and therefore impoverished by its plunder.[39] As Val Plumwood later put it, the separation of nature from culture is a disavowal of humankind's reliance on it; ecological crisis signals (some) human's failure to respect their "material and ecological support base."[40] In other words, behind environmental degradation is a worldview that fails to picture climate care. Amitav Ghosh simply writes that climate crisis is a crisis of the imagination, a failure to envision our world differently.[41]

Land cinema addresses this crisis through moving images, inviting audiences to turn from extractive worldviews and realize humanity's place within, not above and against, nature. This turn anticipates a recent resurgence in ecological Marxism, led by John Bellamy Foster and Kohei Saito, for example, that uses metabolic rift to understand extractive capitalism's role in driving climate breakdown.[42] Saito is among several theorists who propose degrowth as an economic antidote. Land cinema proposes something different.

Presenting non-extractive ways of being through its own creative experiments on land and film, land cinema asks what if "growth" and "progress" meant multispecies abundance? What if "development" signified a social movement toward solidarity? Our current understanding of such terms is conditioned by extractivism. Other economies would support these other expanded definitions. Rather than degrowth, then, land cinema proposes alternative growth measured with ethical and ecological metrics.

PICTURING CRISIS DIFFERENTLY

Land cinema's critique of extractivism and imperial or patriarchal forms of visual representation embedded in photographic media entailed neither a retreat from land nor an iconoclastic rejection of landscape images. As well as naming the ideologies and processes of territorial land dispossession and exploitation responsible for climate injustice, many land cinema filmmakers proposed alternative worldviews and material practices, reframing agriculture, for example, as a project to repair genocidal and ecocidal damages wrought by terra nullius thinking.[43] Land cinema's images of ecological and social repair teach ways of seeing and doing that identify crisis as an opportunity for change, evoking the original medical definition of "crisis" as a turning point in an illness from which a patient may recover.

My understanding of land cinema's combined critical and creative potential derives both from arguments constructed within films and writings by their makers and from contemporary discourses of extractivism that shed new light on them. I am particularly interested here in recent work by Kathryn Yusoff, Anna Tsing, and Marisol de la Cadena.[44] These scholars propose a critical and future-oriented way of addressing climate crisis that resonates with land cinema's approach. Although writing from fields of anthropology and geography, Yusoff, Tsing, and de la Cadena emphasize the potential of artistic and activist work in doing "otherwise," as Tsing puts it, on the "unruly edges" of extractive capitalism.⁴⁵ Land cinema provides a vivid example of such doing in its land- and lens-based work, which establishes what de la Cadena calls an "a-grammatical" relation of responsibility with the other-than-human world. Rather than perpetuate power relations whereby humans are subjects who act upon nature as an inert object, this a-grammatical relation proposes alliances across species so that "plants-rocks-soils-animals-lagoons-humans" flourish together.⁴⁶

To better understand land cinema's contribution to the establishment of non-extractive relations, I draw on a second body of literature, emerging from anti-colonial and intersectional feminism, that studies how places and people subjected to extractive violence are represented (or misrepresented) in visual culture. It is no coincidence that several of the theorists I discuss in this context write as women filmmakers working in cross-cultural contexts that both span and interrogate Global North and Global South divisions. Their theoretical inquiries map onto their experiential perspectives in a way that complements the highly personal, internationalist, and interdisciplinary practices of land cinema.

Trinh T. Minh-ha's 1991 essay collection *When the Moon Waxes Red: Representation, Gender and Cultural Politics* constructs a critical framework for understanding how creative works made within and about experiences of colonial dispossession and epistemological violence can be appreciated less for resolving a "problem" than for resisting reductive analyses. Although my focus here is Trinh's theoretical output, her filmic projects also reveal the problematics of documentary and ethnographic film's claims to truth through devices such as the long take, the narrative arc, and voice-over. Against what she calls "the totalizing quest of meaning" apparent in much film designated "non-fiction," Trinh embraces the complex perspective of an "insider/outsider" position in relation to lands and peoples, expressed through devices such as contradictory temporalities, unreliable narrators, and non-synchronous soundtracks—devices that destabilize documentary's claims to transparency.⁴⁷

Trinh's hyphenated vocabulary describing women filmmakers in postcolonial contexts as insiders/outsiders influences both Fatimah Tobing Rony's and Pooja Rangan's work on the visual and sonic "biopolitics" of filming marginalized subjects. Also combining theoretical and filmmaking perspectives, Rony's books *The Third Eye: Race, Cinema, and Ethnographic Spectacle* (1996) and *How Do We Look? Resisting Visual Biopolitics* (2021) investigate how women filmmakers of color have developed a kind of double consciousness or third eye to critically examine others' gendering and racializing gaze. Similarly, Rangan discusses forms of visual and sonic expression that perpetuate (or resist) neat resolution. In *Immediations: The Humanitarian Impulse in Documentary* (2017), she cautions against "essentializing stereotypes" that purport to "give voice" to marginalized people while concealing structural inequality under a banner of authenticity and inclusion.[48] In more recent work Rangan focuses on sound and voice in film, using the term "audibilities" to describe aspects of a documentary that participate in racial, gendered, and classed discrimination.[49] Like Trinh and Rony, Rangan emphasizes the possibility of shifting dynamics when filmmakers look or speak back. Trinh's, Rony's, and Rangan's discussions of emplaced identity, tropes of representation, and the possibilities of looking back influence my understanding of land as a politicized arena of identification and exclusion and of land cinema as a critical and creative intervention in it.

These theorists' discussions also help situate land cinema's development alongside a reconsideration of documentary's privileges and protocols, led by non-fiction filmmakers in the 1970s. As Jonathan Kahana has written, this reconsideration occurred on multiple levels.[50] In addition to Trinh's critique of documentary's claims to truth, the reconsideration of documentary included re-evaluating the ethics of representing marginalized subjects (a topic Brian Winston has discussed by analyzing the "tradition of the victim").[51] Documentary's relationship to performance also came under scrutiny, as ethno-fiction approaches destabilized documentary's objectivity, in both French and Japanese New Waves and a self-reflexive turn in feminist filmmaking and video.[52] The place of subjective and diaristic modes in documentary's registers was also reconsidered not only in feminist filmmaking but also in documentary's adjacency to experimental filmmakers such as Jonas Mekas.[53] Finally, documentary's activist potential for moving audiences through what Jane Gaines calls "political mimesis" was debated and tested, with filmmakers contributing to industrial disputes, anti-war protests, and independence struggles, often critically reflecting on cinema's development in propaganda and educational slideshows and newsreels in the 1920s and 1930s.[54] Land cinema develops arguments in each of these discursive areas. Its agency is in bringing eco-political activism into this wider nexus of political and aesthetic concerns, its specific alchemy, in the mutual support that its argumentation and practice provide in forwarding climate justice as an anti-colonial, eco-feminist, and non-extractive exigency.

THERE IS NO VIEW FROM NOWHERE

In addressing aesthetic representation, land cinema also addresses political representation. Produced by and with people excluded from formal arenas of decision-making and yet most affected by decisions to seize, "develop," or plunder their lands, land cinema treats aesthetic and political representation as a combined requirement for climate justice. Refusing a "view from nowhere" position of authority in its films, land cinema defamiliarizes perspectives to emphasize point of view and also foregrounds its material imbrication with extractive practices as an additional form of emplaced recognition.

Through such recognitions, land cinema connects the history of documentary representation, film and photography's industrial production, and extractivism. This connection concerns what Siobhan Angus calls an "extractive gaze" that sees the world in terms of its availability for capture and profit.[55] As scholars have noted, the language of lens-based media betrays their extractivist and instrumentalizing origins: the photographer or filmmaker aims, shoots, takes, and captures.[56] The filmic material used to capture subjects as sources of meaning/suffering/intrigue/beauty meanwhile is itself mined, slaughtered, harvested, and processed.[57]

Several land cinema practitioners highlighted their medium's extractive and laborious origins by emphasizing the celluloid materiality of the film stock, thereby also implicating themselves in a web of emplaced and historical relations.

I use the term "cinema" throughout this book (as opposed to "film," for example) to invoke the capaciousness that the filmmakers under discussion demonstrate in such material and perspectival awareness. The term "cinema" has its roots in the Greek *kinein*, "to move," which elucidates land cinema's many moving parts. The definition of cinema that land cinema invokes encompasses the audiovisual technologies of analog materiality with which filmmakers worked; the fields of institutional, social, and professional production in (or in tension with) which they operated; the communities they represented and served; and the physical spaces in which they projected and discussed films. Sometimes land cinema practitioners pushed the definition of "cinema" further, incorporating still images within films, presenting photographic slideshows, and reproducing photographs in print publications. Each medium, distinct in form and historical significance, contributes to land cinema's expansive visual culture. Expanding cinema's disciplinary boundaries in this way, filmmakers also played on film's fundamental composition as multiple photographic frames projected at speed to produce a moving image. Invoking the origins of cinema like this was political because it encouraged audiences to become aware of cinema's inherent artifice and was *eco*-political because it recalled cinema's early application in actuality and travelogue formats that celebrated imperial and industrial land use. In highlighting how film was made as a material and social construct, land cinema also invited audiences to imagine the many ways in which images—and politics—might be re-made differently.

Land cinema's critical approach to its own materiality and manufacture, combined with its interest in participatory production and viewing, speaks to a wider socially engaged turn in non-fiction filmmaking of the 1970s that has variously been described as oppositional, militant, and committed and is often discussed in the context of Third Cinema—the leftist movement of vibrant underground filmmaking cultures to which Rodríguez and Silva, among many others, contributed.

Third Cinema emerged in the mid-1960s and early 1970s in countries including Cuba, Chile, Argentina, and Brazil, with a commitment to working-class perspectives.[58] Third Cinema challenged right-wing dictatorships and denounced US and European support of neoliberal "development." Coining the term "Third Cinema," Solanas and Getino rejected both "First Cinema," the Hollywood model that produced film as profitable entertainment, and the "Second Cinema" of the auteurist and predominantly European avant-garde.[59] Third Cinema plays with the designation "Third World" but, from its outset, encompassed marginalized sites and subjects within economically developed countries, as did land cinema.

Land cinema, like Third Cinema, was highly participatory, with subjects of films often involved in their production and with films sometimes paused mid-way so that audiences could debate what they had just seen. Filmmakers were not precious about their products—the process of bringing people together was more important. This was a cinema of imperfection.[60] Films could seem unfinished aesthetically, in other words, because the political formations to which they contributed were also still in progress. This urgency, combined with a desire to make films within a wider and ongoing struggle for political representation, continued beyond the 1970s in a "Fourth Cinema" identified with Indigenous film and video-making, also seen in several examples in this book.[61]

Land cinema adds an ecological dimension to this history of Third and Fourth Cinema by directing audiences back to the land in a reminder of our dependencies on Earth's natural systems. Yet unlike much recent environmental cinema and photography labeled "green" for its representation of issues such as deforestation and insufficiently scrutinized for the material emissions and cultural extraction its production and dissemination incur, land cinema attempts to reconcile aesthetics and politics. Like the Third and Fourth Cinema movements with which it developed in conversation, land cinema treated pictures and production in tandem: images had to be political in the way they looked and in the way they were made and shared.

INSIDER/OUTSIDER

Whether focusing on rural or urban land, or challenging these very distinctions, land cinema practitioners exposed the divisiveness of designating some regions as centers and others as peripheries. Valuing places for their ecological and social worth, instead of measuring them with financial metrics, helped advance an important argument: if the center is found wanting, then it should no longer define (and thereby suppress) the margins.[62] I take this argument seriously in this book because it also speaks to theoretical work.

With a rejection of a conventional locus of authority and its canon comes a decentering of perspectives. Learning from filmmakers' turns to overlooked or exploited places, this book multiplies frames of reference for thinking about political cinema and environmentalism. Drawing on theoretical works developed in European and North American "centers," alongside those from East Asia often confined to area studies, those labeled "Global South" and, finally, those critical of the colonial echoes of such distinctions, my aim is to treat theory as an historical and emplaced activity—in other words, as a verb. Practitioners in this book teach this in their emphasis on the *making* in filmmaking, and their treatment of landscape as a verb-like formation of power relations and perspectives.

As I discuss in the Prologue, my own perspective is emplaced, historical, and politically motivated: not a view from nowhere but an argument that every image is a perspective, a narrative, a politics, a demand. My theory-making is itself a way of being in what Max Liboiron calls a "land relation," sharing a concern for climate justice with the filmmakers I discuss, as well as a methodological problem of how to represent people and places without perpetuating epistemological and representational forms of extraction.[63]

Approaching theory-making as a view from somewhere resists framing research as an objective and authoritative procurement of hidden treasure available for cultural extraction. As Usha Iyer, Erika Balsom and other feminist film scholars point out, the visibility of a film varies between cultures, disciplines, and regions, and assuming a film has been forgotten can overlook the work of committed, situated film cultures that operate outside the canon.[64] Filmmakers I discuss in rural Japan and Colombia, for instance, long maintained centers independent from commercially dominant ones. Rather than perpetuate discovery dynamics, then, I write with Chandra Talpade Mohanty's alternative approach to history in mind, examining the past as a plurality of perspectives that can catalyze critical engagement with the present.[65] In place of a proprietary claim over under-studied films made from overlooked perspectives, this book proposes a corrective for the erasures of one dominant form of history that should be specified as a primarily white, masculinist, and anthropocentric narrative from the Global North.

In its decentering approach, *Land Cinema* has a recuperative mission similar to that articulated by Alexandra Juhasz and Shilyh Warren in the context of feminist filmmaking, whereby paying scholarly attention to understudied films contributes to their becoming more available to the public.[66] Ecological artists, activists, and filmmakers today know less about the diverse history of eco-political film than they might do because many films are difficult to access. We need examples of past alternatives as guides for future action, and for this we need—as Lis Rhodes has argued, again in the context of feminist film—a different history.[67] I hope that my attention to "counter-histories" in this book helps counteract a frequent exclusion of women and people of color from histories of avant-garde artistic practice and documentary and presents their perspectives as important focal points for climate action.[68]

The idea of counter-history often accompanies discussions of land and rural labor. Counter-history was central to Raymond Williams's studies of cultural imaginaries, assembled from the spoken, literary, and artistic accounts of rural and working-class lives slighted and excluded by many historians.[69] Williams, perhaps unsurprisingly, was involved in the production of a film Cinema Action made in rural working-class Wales, discussed in Chapter 5. Similarly to the way in which Williams and Cinema Action paid attention to aspects of everyday experience that history's grand narratives neglect, many land cinema filmmakers foregrounded subjective experience in their work, understanding the personal and political as one.

Such is the case with Massachusetts gardener-filmmaker Anne Charlotte Robertson (Chapter 4), whose ecological and political surroundings infused her sense of identity and her life's work with personal-political-environmental details that cannot easily be separated. In assessing together the lives and works of filmmakers such as Robertson, we can see their representations of landscapes as also portraits. I offer the term "landscape-portrait" throughout this book to emphasize the extent to which places condition peoples' senses of self and vice versa.

Approaching films as complex, personal, and politicized as Robertson's requires a kind of open engagement that Eve Kosofsky Sedgwick describes as "reparative reading." Engaging with several discourses in a non-dualistic manner, reparative reading respects differences and values moments of affinity.[70] Rather than drawing conclusions as a stable authority, the reparative reader connects with her body and lived experiences and is open to being taken in unanticipated directions by the text at hand.[71] My reparative reading of films in this book is also, I hope, mindful of the ethical responsibility of research conducted with sensitive material. Robertson's lifelong struggle with mental illness deserves respect, as does the generational trauma that the Navajo/ Diné filmmaker Arlene Bowman documents as she explores settler colonial genocide, land dispossession, and structural discrimination (Chapter 1). Watching these women's films (and, in the case of Robertson, consulting thirteen boxes of writings, drawings, hospital discharge forms, garden plans, and environmental protest letters) requires appreciating filmmakers as people with hopes, dreams, desires, and sorrows as valid and vulnerable as anyone's.

Robertson filmed her garden diary for sixteen years. Ogawa Pro stayed for eighteen years in Yamagata's mountains and rice paddies in a project that far exceeds most environmental and artistic endeavors labeled "site-specific."[72] The psychological and material demands of long-term immersion in a social and spatial site are numerous—and many Ogawa Pro members quit over the years—but something about this extended, iterative, and collaborative mode of working is fundamental to land cinema. Perhaps the endeavor's unrushed character resonates with nature itself. Land cinema, like organic farming, respects the speeds of Earth.

Much has been written about the ecological potential of "slow cinema" as an alternative to commercial films' fast-paced action and linear plots.[73] Land cinema is aligned with slow cinema's desire for alternative forms of representation but is neither necessarily slow nor long. Though Robertson's thirty-six-hour film and Ogawa Pro's three-hour documentaries are extensive, others in this book are short. Barbara McCullough's lasts barely five minutes, and Ana Mendieta's last only three minutes. Long or short, the films are attentive and curious in their looking.

The distinction between slowness, duration, and attention is important, as it avoids popular associations of natural processes with slowness and global modernity with accelerated rhythms. Ecological breakdown, after all, is rapid—and political institutions are often slow to respond. Practicing arts of noticing, over three hours or three minutes, land cinema not only attends to what So Mayer calls "the textures and scents of the so-much-larger-than-us-world" but also notices, exposes, and decries the paces of extractive capitalism.[74]

A reparative reading of filmmakers' works and lives is also appropriate for their multidisciplinary approaches. Perhaps better described as filmmaker-artist-activist-farmer-gardener-writer-theorist-revolutionary-organizers, those discussed in this book challenged the idea of a film project as having a single output and end. Community workshops, strikes, protests, and discursive screenings were equally important to nurturing eco-political solidarities. In this open-ended multi-disciplinarity, land cinema activates a space of mediation between pragmatic demands for eco-political resistance and its experimental aesthetic prefiguration. As Caroline Levine writes, such mediation has significant implications for understanding the connection between political and aesthetic knowledge.[75] Aesthetic forms such as a chorus of voices on a soundtrack and political forms such as the democratic gathering of people can share a set of motivations and work together toward change.

STRUCTURE

Land Cinema in an Age of Extraction considers three main topics: films that complicate ideas of rural retreat; films that propose the anti-pastoral as a form of environmentalism attuned to polluted, urbanized, or industrialized land; and films that use non-extractive methods of production and distribution to foster political and ecological solidarities. While each chapter constructs independent arguments, read together the chapters reveal land cinema's simultaneous entanglement in extractivism and potential for resistance, shedding light on possibilities for eco-political action today.

Chapter 1, "Poets of the Land: The Subjects of Landscape-Portraits," compares Margaret Tait and Arlene Bowman as figures exemplifying what Trinh calls "insider/outsiders," having familial connections to the rural places they film and a sense of estrangement due to physical and social distance. Learning from Rony's and Rangan's work on the visual and sonic biopolitics of filming marginalized subjects, I explore how Tait's and Bowman's films question perspective and ask what it means to be an insider/outsider to a place, a generation, and its (agri)culture. By foregrounding their own positionality, both filmmakers critically deploy film as a perspectival medium imbricated with histories of settler colonialism. Being in a place and filming it, their works suggest, is a political act of positioning.

Rural estrangement and return also feature in Chapter 2, "Farmer-Filmmakers, Fieldwork, and Growth," which is written around photographs of the farmer-filmmaker collectives Ogawa Pro in Japan and Somankidi Coura in Mali as a visual seedbank of ideas. With a framework that understands growth in terms of ecological and social flourishing rather than financial gain, these experiments in post-colonial West

Africa and boom-time Japan appear both distinct and linked, offering timely insight into what Tsing describes as possibilities for collaborative survival on the edges of capitalism.

Land cinema is not an exclusively rural endeavor, as Chapters 3 and 4 make clear. Seen today, the representations of non-pristine nature discussed here speak to the continued problem of climate injustice, whereby neocolonial states and corporations outsource extractive activities to the Global South and into pockets of racialized, gendered, and classed inequality in the Global North, thereby insulating the centers of power that bear greatest responsibility for climate breakdown.[76] Continuing an emphasis on tactile images introduced in the book's first two chapters, Chapters 3 and 4 consider how affective techniques such as close-ups, blurs, rapid pans, and stuttered editing forward an idea of land as an embodied, relational choreography of emplaced responsibility rather than a static topography and of film as being a kind of body itself, photochemically exposed to the environment as a witness.

Chapter 3, "There Is No Countryside: The Anti-Pastoral," studies a group of Tokyo-based filmmakers, photographers, and theorists who pioneered their own highly politicized "landscape theory" (*fūkeiron*) around 1970. Steeped in Marxism, *fūkeiron* argued that post-war capitalist expansion had desecrated nature, with their work anticipating Saito and others by cinematically illustrating the "rift" Marx identified in industrialized societies. Continuing to draw from Tsing's approach to finding seeds of resistance in the ruins of capitalism as well as Japanese philosophical traditions that regard nature and culture as an integrated climate, the chapter argues that polluted landscapes must feature in conversations about land if we are to address climate justice adequately. To borrow a phrase from Donna Haraway, *fūkeiron* "stays with the trouble," inviting audiences to view landscapes as crime scenes, with extractive capitalism as the perpetrator.[77]

Staying in non-pristine environments, Chapter 4, "Companion Planting in Wounded Land," examines three experimental films that present the female body in a North American landscape to explore intersectional violence and climate justice. The chapter's focus is Anne

Charlotte Robertson, whose filmed form of eco-therapy and protest against social dislocation and environmental pollution decenters documentary's anthropocentric gaze and re-centers Robertson as an organic body responsive to and responsible for many others.[78] I compare Robertson's embodied and earthed work with short films by Ana Mendieta, in which she lies submerged in landscapes in Iowa and Mexico, and by Barbara McCullough, in which a woman dances in a razed lot earmarked for a Los Angeles highway. Reading the films as acts of mourning and blessing, I consider how reclaiming corporeal connections with places made inaccessible by gendered, raced, and classed discrimination can transform terra nullius thinking into land stewardship, and counteract the monumental scale and machismo of land art with an eco-feminist lightness of touch.

In the book's final two chapters, I consider land cinema's contribution to structural change by discussing methods of making and broadcasting films that bridge particular and planetary perspectives. Chapter 5, "On the Picket Line, on the Television: Representation, Empathy, and Distance," explores relationality, or what Elizabeth Povinelli calls "being together in difference," by looking at the co-creation and dissemination of films by Cinema Action in Wales and by Marta Rodríguez and Jorge Silva in Colombia.[79] Made about and in long-term collaboration with rural and Indigenous women experiencing land dispossession and strike action, the filmmakers used their insider/outsider perspectives and skills in organizing to denounce climate injustice. Hoping to increase their impact in the 1980s, both collectives transitioned from grassroots filmmaking and distribution to international public television broadcast. Exploring this transition, the chapter considers the potentials and risks of land cinema that is made to raise consciousness across long distances, drawing on arguments by Trinh, Rangan and Jade E. Davis concerning the representation of suffering and differences between empathy and action.[80]

Chapter 6, "Extraction Is Stealing, Relationships Give Meaning," borrows Leanne Betasamosake Simpson's phrase for condemning extraction and celebrating meaningful relations with and on land over time. With Simpson's ideas of connection and longevity in mind, this shorter and more projective final chapter asks how land cinema from the 1970s and 1980s resonates today, tracing political and aesthetic characteristics of land cinema in three contemporary examples from the Philippines, Brazil, and China. Reflecting on these examples, combined with those from previous chapters, I argue that land cinema's critical and creative work is proof that there *is* an alternative to extractive capitalism. It's there in land cinema's images as a workable blueprint for the future.[81]

ONE

Poets of the Land

THE SUBJECTS OF LANDSCAPE-PORTRAITS

"I HAD TO GET NEARER THE SKY," wrote the filmmaker, poet, and medic, Margaret Tait, "for the city was too full of rooms."[1] In 1968 as she was turning fifty, Tait returned to Orkney, a windy archipelago off the far northeast of Scotland where she was born and raised. Like many filmmakers in this book, Tait took to the land, to "the last of the wilderness" as she called it, to align herself with what she identified as a traditional rural lifestyle under threat.[2] Urban tourists and industrialists interested in North Sea oil and nuclear power were encroaching on Scotland's Highlands and Islands with persuasion vocabularies of development and modernization. As if by some polar magnetism, Tait was drawn north, out into the landscape. "I can't be content with a window," she wrote in a poem, referring to the city life she left behind in Edinburgh.[3]

Energized by the "electric explosions" of storms "lashing on the untamed earth I live on," Tait gained "limb wisdom" and "bone knowledge" of what it meant to be a human member of an "infinite" web of life in Orkney's ancient landscape.[4] She "wished for a storm to test my strength" and "the magic stillness of a wet evening after rain."[5] As Orkney's huge skies lay in its looking-glass lochs, Tait would wander, composing lines or sequences. Her poems were as visual as films, her films as lyrical as verses. A "film-poem or poem-film," she wrote, should express "presence, let's say, soul or spirit, an empathy with whatever it is that's dwelt on, feeling for it."[6]

Expressing love of Orkney and an empathetic anxiety over its modernization, Tait's 1981 film *Land Makar* portrays her neighbor, an elderly woman farmer. Tait described the film as a "landscape study with a figure very much in the picture."[7] *Land Makar* characterizes a hybrid landscape-portrait genre that Tait developed in more than thirty films made between the 1950s and her death in 1999, most of which were short, edited in associative sequences of color or movement, and many of which observed everyday life in Orkney.

The thirty-two-minute film opens with a wide landscape shot of an oat field. The composition and watery color of the 16mm film resemble a painting. Bundles of grain stand on end before a squat stone building with a thatched roof. A loch shimmers in the mid-distance, banked by sea-salty pale, treeless slopes. Then there is a black-and-white sequence of haymaking, a small tractor, and a woman yanking sheaves from the tractor's baler. Next is an inter-title written in chalk:

a film by MARGARET TAIT featuring MARY GRAHAM SINCLAIR

Cows are lowing. Next, is a medium shot in color: this must be Mary Graham Sinclair (Figure 2). Her cheeks glow from seventy years of weather. Wisps of white hair curl around the rim of her woolly hat. She inspects the landscape beyond the camera, and then there is a title card:

LAND MAKAR

"*Land makar?*" asks Sinclair on the soundtrack.

Tait, who is never seen but is heard throughout the film in conversation with Sinclair, answers in a lilt that is part Orkney, part Edinburgh: "Yes. *Land makar*, 'poet of the land.'"

Makar is the Scots word for "poet." The English word poetry comes from *poiesis*, "to make." *Makar*, poet, maker. Tait's opening sequence establishes an association between the subject of the film and the subject making the film, one land *makar* cultivating the soil and another making a cultural representation of it.

"Poet of the land?" Sinclair queries.

Tait confirms: "I sort of see you as creating the beauty of the place."

"Some beauty," Sinclair comments.

FIGURE 2. Mary Graham Sinclair working her croft at West Aith, in *Land Makar*. Frame enlargement.

Sinclair's retort occurs barely two minutes into the film and calls its elegiac pastoralism into question, establishing tension between two women, two generations, and two perspectives. This moment of divergence introduces an important aspect of land cinema, which is its juxtaposition of different perspectives to indicate land's varying ecological, political, and cultural significances. In this chapter, I explore the political power of such tension by looking at instances in which a filmmaker portrays an older rural woman as a means to examine her own situated—or estranged—relation to land. Such perspectives, which Trinh T. Minh-ha identifies with the complex positionality of an "insider/ outsider" filmmaker, are key to land cinema and recur throughout this book.[8]

ISLAND

By the time she returned to Orkney, Tait had studied medicine in Edinburgh; served as a wartime medic in Sri Lanka, India, and Malaysia; and learned filmmaking in Rome. In Scotland from the mid-1950s, she combined filmmaking, poetry, and work as a locum tenens doctor, traveling between patients and clinics in a little van with "Ancona Films" painted on its side and her wind-up 16mm Bolex camera in the back beside her doctor's bag. Ancona Films was named after Via Ancona in Rome, where Tait had lived. She printed "Rome, Edinburgh, New York" on her letterhead in proud indication of her international connections (she began the company with fellow students Peter Hollander, later based in the United States, and Fernando Birri, who later returned to Argentina as a key figure in Latin America's Third Cinema movement for political and cultural liberation, a subject to which I turn in Chapter 5). Though Ancona Films began as a collaboration, Tait carried it, operating at a loss from her studio flat in Edinburgh and later from the studio she kept in an old church in Orkney.

Filmmaker, poet, and medic, Tait combined an artistic sensibility for the close-at-hand with scientific precision, finding "a whole country at the foot of the stone / If you care to look."[9] She liked to train her bright, beady eyes and Bolex lenses on what convention overlooked, quoting Federico García Lorca, who argued that an apple was no less intense than the sea. Made for herself, for her neighbors, and for anyone further afield—so long as they cared to look—Tait's films are visual odes to places and people, made when a "word has to go too, being inadequate / And only my eyes are left / For saying it all."[10]

Saying it all, from her own angle (Tait was fond of Emily Dickinson's poetic project to "tell all the truth but tell it slant"), her films practice what Anna Tsing calls an art of noticing.[11] They pay careful attention to people, stones, heather blowing, a hand (her mother's) turning the page of a book or unwrapping a sticky boiled sweet, a rainbow, a calf, a tractor, and a shadow (her own). While such quotidian, domestic, botanical, and personal subjects have often been trivialized as feminine and amateur topics for cinema, Tait championed them.[12]

Telescoping between the macro and the micro, issues of agrarian demise and industrialization hover rather than dominate within Tait's films and poems. Modern science and technology are equal but not superior to other ways of knowing—and the delight, for Tait, was often in the unknowing. "Express the doubt too," she wrote.[13] Modern technologies of vision (cameras, telescopes, microscopes) were tools for humble curiosity rather than scopic means to dominate. Tait photographed flowers in time lapse, marveling at their opening. An imperceptible movement to the human eye, the flowers' unfurling signaled time's relativity and the manifold paces of life operating alongside human and mechanical ones.[14] Holding her camera by hand or on a tripod with its pan and tilt loosened, Tait imbued her films with her own presence, looking, learning, telling it slant.

Tait's presence is palpable in *Land Makar*, as we hear her speaking with Sinclair. In other films too, Tait emphasizes the relationship between filming and filmed figures by including her own reflection in a mirror or catching the eye of a passing neighbor. One of her earliest films, *A Portrait of Ga* (1952), features a voice-over in which Tait affectionately describes "Ga" (her mother, the subject of this four-minute film) as one of her many relations and ancestors dwelling in "the windy Orkney isles." Tenderly following Ga around her house and garden, the film establishes Tait's sense of self within this so-much-larger-than-us world, crystalizing before the camera as landscape-portraiture.[15]

By filming Orkney and grandmotherly custodians such as Ga and Sinclair and screening her films for the Orkney community (often advertised by word of mouth and served with a pot of coffee), Tait anchored herself on the island. In ancient times, Orkney formed part of a sub-Arctic trade route whose cultural traces appear in dialect words derived from Old Norse and Viking archaeological remnants. Tait admired these traces because they centered her in a context pre-dating settler colonial encroachments from the mainland and England and before modern industrialization and tourism.

When Tait's studio was cleared after her death—her husband ferrying boxes of reels to the mainland for the Scottish Film Archive to dry and de-mold—many notebooks surfaced that offered insight into projects she planned that would explore this archipelagic anchoring and allegiance. Tait's working method entailed developing several films concurrently, each flowering whenever she had enough footage or time to complete it or saved for reuse in future projects. She planned an "album" of "mini-portraits" for neighbors called *Kent Faces* (*kent* is the Scots word for "known") and a project called *Heartlandscape*, combining "portraits of people who live in the place" with landscape sequences of ancient, modern, and natural Orkney (an old mill, modern turbines, bird habitats, peat land).[16]

Orkney's human-made, natural, traditional, and modern elements also converge in *Place of Work* (1976) as Tait observes the busyness of drilling a road, delivering a letter, and making a film. Humans are not the only ones at work either. Cats watch birds, birds build nests, and even clouds rush somewhere. Like *A Portrait of Ga* and *Land Makar*, this film celebrates kinship on the island, less as a diary (a term "the London Filmmakers seem to love") but more as a "film-poem" for a community of many generations and species.[17]

Tait's film-poem, which was not unlike Maya Deren's substitution of linear plot for "particular moments" of vertiginous emotion, combined "empathy with whatever it is that's dwelt upon" with a suspicion of conventional representation.[18] The result was an unusual form that resists narrative closure. In a 1964 film lasting barely nine minutes, for example, Tait portrays her friend, Hugh MacDiarmid, who reads his poem "You Know Not Who I Am" on the soundtrack. Tait's free-flowing close-ups never rest long or show MacDiarmid's face in full. As if anticipating the camera work, MacDiarmid remarks that "it is in vain" that "you'll try to hold me."[19]

"Breathing with the camera" is how Tait described such movements. In between poems in the three books of verse she self-published in a flurry around 1960, she printed an electrocardiographic impression of a heartbeat as a fleuron. Like heartbeats, like breaths, Tait's written lines and filmed shots created rhythms. Bending over her Moviola upright editing machine to inspect her reels, Tait memorized images until she spotted a visual association (akin to a rhyme) between two shots, "cutting on colour" to splice into sequence (sound was incorporated later, with local pipe music, poems, and riddles adding further cadence).[20]

The filmmaker Nathaniel Dorsky has described this kind of poetic, associative editing as synaptic, synapses being structures that allow neurons to communicate with target cells inside the brain.[21] Tait would no doubt have enjoyed this medical analogy. "Synapse," from the Greek, *haptein* ("junction, join") shares its etymology with "haptic," a quality of being tactile. Tait filmed to engage the senses in haptic acts of looking. "Rhythmical movement," she wrote, "is the inherent/ essence of all things."[22] In *Land Makar*, the camera ranges in close-up over coals glowing in Sinclair's stove, and a clutch of swan eggs smooth and cool beside the loch. These are sense images of how it feels to be immersed in the heart landscape, to be grounded, rooted, at home.

Tait's associative editing appealed to the poetically inclined (MacDiarmid admiringly described her as "ploughing a lonely furrow"), but programmers at the BBC viewed her work as "technically inadequate."[23] Like many women filmmakers of her generation whose work was labeled haphazard (yet influenced male counterparts celebrated as avant-garde), Tait longed for greater exposure.[24] She resolved to make films "as seriously as if they were major productions or works of poetry," self-financing most through medical work and securing funding for her first and only feature as late as 1992.[25]

But Tait had long known that filmmaking could be realized on a budget. Studying at Rome's Centro Sperimentale di Cinematografia, she observed the depth of feeling that Italian neorealism achieved shooting on location, in real places, with non-professional actors. Such methods seemed so free compared to filmmaking in Scotland. There, the documentarian John Grierson, and the Films of Scotland Committee over which he presided seemed stultifying.

Tait called Grierson a busybody and rejected his advice to edit and shorten one of her films into "a tak-tak-tak natty little short film."[26] Assuming what Pooja Rangan has called a paternalistic approach to filmed subjects, Grierson produced films for state and industrial sponsors with the aim of promoting national interests and social responsibility.[27] His employers included the Empire Marketing Board, established by the British Conservative Party to bolster trade. Although Grierson is widely praised for his dignified portrayals of working-class life, in Tait's eyes he was instrumentalizing, presenting subjects as examples of what Brian Winston calls "suffering humanity."[28] This was not how Tait wanted to portray Orkney. She both loved her subjects and wanted them to retain their strangeness. "I didn't want you to be cosy and neat and limited," she wrote in a poem titled "To Anybody At All." "I didn't want you to be understandable."[29]

RESERVATION

Though Tait extols Sinclair as *Land Makar*'s eponymous poet, her inclusion of the women's differing understandings of beauty foregrounds a level of self-awareness that animates the film with a strange, tense energy. From this moment, *Land Makar* becomes a film about different subjective positions. As Michael Renov puts it, in instances such as this the *subject* in film becomes the subject *of* film.[30] Arlene Bowman, to whom I now turn, filmed her Navajo (Diné) grandmother to examine her own cultural dislocation from rural reservation life. In this sense Bowman's 1986 film *Navajo Talking Picture*, like *Land Makar*, is as much about its maker as its purported subject. But in Bowman's film, divergent perspectives lead to an antagonism far greater than Tait's and Sinclair's awkwardness. If *Land Makar* is about making, *Navajo Talking Picture* is about taking.

Bowman was plucky, not yet thirty and living in Los Angeles when she embarked on the film. She intended to document a day in the life of her grandmother, who lived some six hundred miles east, on a Navajo reservation in the northern Arizona desert. Bowman visited the reservation three times between 1981 and 1983. On her third visit she was asked never to return. *Navajo Talking Picture* emphasizes this traumatic rupture by combining sequences on the reservation with footage shot later in Los Angeles as Bowman reflects on the uncomfortable pictures and decisions she has taken. Early in the forty-minute film, a man chases sheep in a pen, with Bowman filming as a metaphor of her own attempts to capture the Navajo identity that eludes her.

Rather than propose intergenerational female allyship (or the somewhat forced allegiance that Tait explores), Bowman is openly confrontational with her *másání,* her maternal grandmother. Grandmothers play a central role within matrilineal and matrilocal Indigenous communities, imparting traditional values of reciprocity and harmony to their grandchildren. In turn, grandchildren should fill their *másání's* lives with "peace, happiness, and beauty."[31] Bowman's film disrupts this.

Born in 1955, Bowman was of a generation of Native Americans whose lifeways and lands were fundamentally damaged by federal policies to terminate agrarian and tribal economies along with Indigenous languages and traditions.[32] Such policies followed a livestock reduction program aimed at tackling soil erosion in the 1930s that Bowman's grandmother, Ann Ruth Biah, would have witnessed firsthand. In that program, the Navajo-Churro sheep, so beloved to Navajo communities, were rendered "scrubby," expendable material, and Navajo farmers were forced to slaughter their own flocks.[33] Federal agents consulted all-male tribal councils on the issue, despite the fact that it was Navajo women who oversaw much animal rearing (as Bowman mentions in her voiceover, her grandmother is "a strong and independent traditional Navajo woman"). Livestock reduction severely restricted women's economic power at the same time that it terminated Indigenous sovereignty.[34] Amid impending famine, many Navajo people had to seek wage work off the reservation.

Alongside federal drives to assimilate Indigenous nations within a white, urban, Anglophone version of the United States, the government had an additional motive: land. Emptying Navajo territory cleared the way for its industrialization. Between 1942 and the mid-1980s, large amounts of radioactive ore were extracted from Navajo land, supplying uranium for Cold War atomic weapons and nuclear energy. Uranium corporations paid Navajo miners little, kept land prices artificially low, and concealed catastrophic health and environmental dangers. As Traci Brynne Voyles puts it, uranium extraction relied on visual and rhetorical campaigns that represented Navajo land as uninhabited wasteland available for despoliation.[35]

In reality, Navajo land was far from uninhabited—many Navajo people remained, taking up dangerous work in the mines or, in the case of Biah, staying to tend those animals that had survived. But rural populations did plummet, as Navajo communities were relocated en masse to cities (including Los Angeles, which itself is sited on Tongva land). Like many, Bowman spent most of her childhood in what she called the "white world" of Phoenix, Arizona. As a young adult she shuttled around the United States, only occasionally visiting her grandmother's depleted community.

Urban relocation and forced assimilation deepened a rift in both Indigenous and non-Indigenous imaginaries between "rez" (reservation) and "city" Native Americans. Such binaries became barometers for measuring value—forcing Indigenous people to appear as either authentically rooted (though backward) on the reservation or modernized and hence diluted in the city.[36] Bowman and Biah wrestle with this binary themselves, projecting what Raymond Williams describes as social and political stereotypes onto each other and the land.[37] Bowman can't even speak Navajo, her grandmother complains. Bowman comes from "the ocean" (Los Angeles) and will hopefully return there sharpish. Meanwhile, Bowman ambushes her grandmother with distressing persistence.

In foregrounding these vexed spatial and linguistic divides, Bowman invites audiences to consider the difficulties that urban Indians can have in connecting with family members living on reservations. As Kent Mackenzie understood in *The Exiles*, his 1961 documentary about Indigenous communities in Los Angeles's Bunker Hill, Bowman explores a bind in which she is both disconnected from her heritage and othered in her urban surrounds. *Navajo Talking Picture* becomes a place of exile where Bowman speaks out, with the film's focus on domestic discomfort enacting a kind of "felt theory" to articulate Indigenous trauma.[38]

"I want to film confrontation," Bowman announces midway through the film. She knows that she is not supplying audiences with a typical image of Navajo women. "I'm supposed to be extinct," she remarks, "or wear my hair in long braids." As Beverly Singer notes, it was perhaps Bowman's refusal to conform to expectations "of how Indians look and act in movies" that restricted her access to mainstream media and audiences.[39] *Navajo Talking Picture* was not a big hit.

Upon release in small festivals across North America and Europe (where we can assume that the vast majority of audiences could not understand Navajo), Bowman's film was lambasted. Unsurprisingly, *Navajo Talking Picture* was not welcomed on the reservation either. The film is still distributed by Women Make Movies and, judging by IMDb reviews, continues to divide audiences. Here was a young woman filmmaker disobeying documentary ethics of informed consent and a social script requiring Indigenous American women to respect their elders.[40] Reactions tend to reflect Biah's own responses to her granddaughter. Here was a modern urbanite who looked more like an aerobics instructor than a Navajo daughter. Hollywood must have gone to her head, sending her into the desert to stalk her aged relative living peacefully without electricity in her *bikéyah*, her land. Here was an outsider. Here was how not to make film.

Despite being taught as an example of how not to make documentary in some anthropology and filmmaking classes, *Navajo Talking Picture* deserves consideration.[41] Taking my cue from Randolph Lewis's careful analysis of the film, I want to suggest that *Navajo Talking Picture* is less disaster than intervention.[42] Positioned as neither quite daughter nor tourist within the reservation, Bowman films to complicate readings of land-based identity. Working in the wake of settler colonial devastations to landscapes and communities, filming divergent perspectives was a method for refusing narrative resolution and its implied social harmony (and hidden social control). Bowman rejects a neutral "view from nowhere"—she is emplaced, often in front of the camera, often interrupting, demanding, refusing to take no for an answer. In this way, Bowman both replicates an extractive gaze and exposes—through her grandmother—its violent form of objectification.

Understanding Tait's and Bowman's positions as neither quite daughters nor tourists within the island and reservation cultures they filmed, I want to consider ways in which their films complicate readings of land-based identity and reveal shared goals for portraying landscapes as fields of conflicting perspectives. This complication anticipates similar strategies used by other filmmakers in this book, whose work ranges across distinct cultures and coincides around a set of eco-political investments in representational ethics. By shining a light on stereotypes, Tait's and Bowman's films demonstrate how binaries of rural/urban and traditional/modern are weaponized to legitimize so-called development and conceal settler colonial violence.

For Tait and Bowman, working within extractive modernity and in the wake of settler colonial devastations to landscapes and communities, filming landscape-portraits riddled with divergent perspectives was a method for refusing narrative resolution and its implied social harmony (and hidden social control). Emphasizing their own positionality was key to exploring the complex ethics of taking pictures in contexts where so many lands, livelihoods, and liberties had already been taken. Although distinct in situated context and formal approach, Tait's and Bowman's filmmaking shares a drive to disrupt the assumed authority of documentary and art historical representations of rural life.

The title of this chapter points to not only the ambiguous question of subject in Tait's and Bowman's films (who is the poet, the maker, the author, the authority?) but also a question concerning pictorial orientation. Should we hold these films up as landscapes or portraits? What is their conceptual and therefore ethical orientation? Put another way, what are the filmmakers' angles, or attitudes, to the places and people they film? Might they be replicating extractivism by taking pictures in aestheticizing or unilateral encounters, and if so how far can this medium-subject nexus be read as a performative indictment of extractivism's reach? The films' deliberate ambiguity of attitude offers a counterproposal for simplistic readings of rural lands and lifeworlds.

The landscape-portrait mode that Tait and Bowman develop is key to land cinema's eco-political power, situating and juxtaposing multiple perspectives and voices, at times replicating an extractive gaze and at other times looking back with a counter-visuality that challenges expectation.[43] Here, counter-visuality manifests as an awkwardness that performs the difficulty of being an insider/outsider to a place, a generation, and its (agri)culture. The awkwardness invites wider questions of how to represent place-based identity in anti-colonial filmmaking, which theorists including Trinh, Rangan, and Fatimah Tobing Rony have explored.

Following Trinh, I want to propose Tait's and Bowman's land cinema as a site through which particular forces of extractivism (settler colonialism, industrialization, urbanization) generate a cultural agency that destabilizes and questions. Looking at the visual and sonic "biopolitics" at play in filming marginalized subjects, Rangan and Rony analyze how filmmakers, particularly women of color, have appropriated ways of seeing and filming that are conventionally used for objectification to critique racialized, sexualized, and classed discrimination.[44] Their work is useful for understanding why Tait and Bowman foreground awkward interactions with their subjects. Awkwardness prevents a neat categorization of women as either rural or urban, traditional or modern. In turn, this refusal thwarts any presumptive perspective of omniscient comprehension and neutrality. *There is no view from nowhere*, Tait's and Bowman's films show.

In articulating their own representational difficulties, Tait and Bowman exemplify an important aspect of land cinema. They reveal the fact that knowledge of a place and people is situated, motivated, and contestable. Refusing neat passages to resolution, their films also shed light on contemporary climate injustice, which narratives of sustainability and resilience often greenwash. Comprising less than 5 percent of the world's population, Indigenous people protect 80 percent of global biodiversity— but celebrating Indigenous knowledge as a curative to the ills of climate breakdown requires caution, necessitating questions about what sustainability sustains and for whom.[45] Often emerging in contexts where Indigenous lands are enclosed, drilled, or logged for global trade, resilience narratives fail to address the extractivist forces necessitating resilience in the first place.[46] Reducing indigeneity to an instrumentalized imaginary (homogenized and converted for capitalist returns), such narratives also assume that the bearers of Indigenous knowledges are grateful to be so celebrated. Sinclair would surely be skeptical of such treatment. By including Sinclair's retort, Tait's film intervenes in resilience narratives, acknowledging Tait's differences and allegiance with Sinclair as an unresolved tension. "I didn't want you to be cosy and neat and limited."[47]

The films' focus on generational difference also opens paths for thinking about histories of extractivism as pasts that are not past and about contemporary climate breakdown as a symptom of historical causes that produce what Kyle Whyte calls a "colonial déjà vu" in island and reservation landscapes.[48] Although I attend to the materiality of analog film in later chapters, it is worth noting that extractivism also plays out across the physical body of film in much land cinema. Tait and Bowman used analog film well into the days of video, as did most filmmakers in this book. Today, photographic and film media's material and processual imbrication in extractive practices is increasingly well known. Film requires mined silver, harvested cotton, and boiled animal bones, among other ingredients.[49] Watching Tait's and Bowman's films in light of this knowledge invites considering how, through their medium's material production, these filmmakers were entangled in some of the same industrial, extractive processes they also aimed to critique.

ISLANDERS AS INSIDERS

Land Makar was filmed at West Aith, a smallholding (known as a croft in Scotland) on the main island of Orkney, not far from Tait's own home.[50] Tait shot the film over four years, chronicling cycles of seasons to celebrate both Sinclair's labor during plowing, calving, and harvesting time and the environment's aesthetic changes from bleak mid-winter to glimmering spring.

As Sinclair detected in their conversation about beauty, Tait's approach to Orkney was different to hers. For Sinclair, crofting was less a poetic vocation than a struggle for survival. Crofting is a tenure system whereby people rent smallholdings from landowners and share grazing, mooring, and harvesting rights with neighbors. Crofters such as Sinclair cultivated land in low-intensity practices, using seaweed for fertilizer, peat for fuel, and heather for making rope. In unfenced allotments, they grazed tethered animals and grew oats and barley. Crofting developed from an even earlier Indigenous system known as *dùthchas*, a Gaelic concept that describes a person's identity and sense of membership in familial and territorial lineages.[51] *Dùthchas* understood land as a common resource.

Commoning was antithetical to the capitalist tenet of private property, and as the British Empire grew, crofters were subjected to a form of domestic colonization.[52] In the eighteenth century, industrialists enriched from imperial exploits abroad began purchasing swaths of the Highlands and Islands in a process euphemistically called Clearances. They sought "to colonize at home" by subduing "the character of the native population" labeled "filthy" and "savage."[53] They burned crofts so that tenants could not return home and enclosed common lands for industrial-scale sheep grazing. As Silvia Federici has pointed out, this colonial violence was also patriarchal, razing women's rights to autonomous space that the commons provided and corralling reproductive labor for capital accumulation.[54] The Clearances displaced thousands of crofters southward and overseas or into prison (a large prison construction program accompanied the Enclosures Acts, and these combined initiatives were legalized by a Parliament composed entirely of male landowners).[55] At the same time, "colonies" of former soldiers and sailors were given crofts deemed terra nullius wasteland and were paid to "improve" them.[56]

To be one of the few remaining crofters in 1981, as Sinclair was, and to be a woman crofter, was to know this bitter history. Difficulties did not end in the nineteenth century either. Further waves of economic exodus emptied the Highlands and Islands in the early twentieth century. Britain's post-war emphasis on development saw many areas ceded to tourism, North Sea oil, and nuclear power industries. When Tait returned to Orkney in 1968, proposals to privatize the region's remaining crofts were opening old wounds. Whereas Sinclair might have feared being bought out and forced overseas or into old-age poverty, Tait belonged to a mobile class of Orcadians who chose to return to the island for the sense of well-being it afforded.

Tait was no crofter, but she was empathetic. The title *Heartlandscape* for her Orkney project indicates where her loyalty lay. Her film *The Drift Back* (1956) chronicles an early episode of migration that sees islanders "drift back" to the islands from the cities where work proved scarce or unrewarding. The islanders' return clearly appealed to Tait's Orcadian pride and growing dislike of cities. In *Caora Mor Big Sheep* (1966), she offers a sarcastically jolly account of urban tourists visiting the Highlands, "coachload after coachload, and here is the countryside they come to see, dotted with sheep." After the Clearances, sheep outnumbered people in the region. Flocking through the film, sheep no longer represent agricultural livelihood (itself an external imposition serving the international wool trade) but instead represent tourism, a new form of industry. In *Colour Poems* (1974) Tait hints at other extractive encroachments, filming a gravel quarry and featuring snatches of radio reports on North Sea oil. Beginning to film Sinclair three years later, Tait expressed solidarity with Indigenous land tenure systems and agricultural stewardship. Agri-business "insulted" land and people, she wrote in a poem, by "presenting dehydrated potato," "in packets," as products of an industry that "keeps the machines turning / and brings the money in."[57] Her political alignment was clear.

Aligned but not alike. When Tait admires Sinclair's plowed furrows, she might think that they resemble celluloid film strips (as Marjorie Keller did in her 1985 ode to agriculture, *The Answering Furrow*). Sinclair would unlikely view furrows in this way. For a farmer, the regularity of furrow height would indicate that the plow blades are working to a constant depth and creating an even seedbed (Figure 3). Tait's appreciation of West Aith was artistic. Landscape provided "the equivalent of notes," she explained in an interview, "or words, or blobs of paint."[58] In her notebook she continued this association, describing her desire at West Aith as being "to frame and *enclose* this pretty *landscape* like putting it on a canvas."[59]

Understanding the gap in perspective between Tait and Sinclair reveals the secret subject of the film. More than championing crofting as an endangered livelihood, *Land Makar* enabled Tait to celebrate her

FIGURE 3. The sky and loch at West Aith, in *Land Makar*. Frame enlargement.

own work and examine her own insider/outsider position in an oblique form of self-portrait. Her description of the film as a "landscape study with a figure very much in the picture" alludes as much: though behind the camera, *Land Makar*'s unnamed "figure" is Tait's own.

Tait admired Sinclair because she identified with her. Here was an older woman who worked alone without much modern equipment. Tait shot, recorded sound, and edited alone, using celluloid film well into the days of video. Celluloid film's cellulose basis brought further botanical association with Sinclair's agricultural work. Tait described her own practice much as she described Sinclair's: "filming in the old style, loneworker fashion!"[60] Crofter, poet, filmmaker: Tait made a unilateral identification through analogous craft and independence.

I want to linger on this reflexive politics because it characterizes a larger turn from a didactic mode of social commentary common in non-fiction film of the first half of the twentieth century. Dubbed a "father" of this earlier mode, Robert Flaherty made fanciful portraits of First Nations, Polynesian, and Irish island cultures in the 1920s and 1930s, earning the description "documentary" that established the genre. That description was offered by none other than Grierson, whom Tait began to dislike. Whereas Grierson argued that documentary was a creative treatment of actuality, Tait insisted that it lacked poetics, and film was a poetic medium.[61] Choosing lyrical observation over commentary, sensory sequencing over narrative plot, and accent-rich interviews with women subjects such as Sinclair, Tait reflects trends in documentary emerging since the 1960s that rejected Grierson's informational mode.[62]

Land Makar also anticipates a further trend in post-Griersonian documentary whereby unreliable narrators and subjects in disagreement call a film's authority and authorship into question. Whereas Grierson would surely have cut Sinclair and Tait's disagreement about beauty from *Land Makar* because it destabilizes the narrative angle, scholars such as Trinh would surely emphasize the radical potential of such moments of divergence in calling attention to a filmmaker's perspective and frustrating audience expectations for clarity.[63] For Trinh, such frustration thwarts the "totalizing quest of meaning" seen in much ethnographic and documentary filmmaking, while for Rangan, frustration refuses a philanthropic logic in which vulnerable people are silenced and packaged for a film market that trades in emergency gestures of sympathy and requires inequality for its very existence.[64] *Land Makar* intervenes in documentary tradition by negotiating its political terrain through position and perspective, with Tait neither fitting within its conventions nor shaking free of them entirely. Tait is an insider/outsider to not only the Orkney community she films but also the history of her medium.

If we take the central conflict between Tait and Sinclair seriously, then *Land Makar* refuses that Tait's sense of self, freed from its inauthentic (urban) existence, can be re-authenticated on the island and through film. Instead, *Land Makar* foregrounds problematic tropes commonly used to represent Indigenous and rural women as possessing a poetic, spiritual affinity with nature. Sinclair's gruff retort rebuffs such essentialism. She refuses to be drawn into a picturesque landscape tradition.

The picturesque landscape tradition developed at precisely the time that Clearances decimated landscapes and communities in Scotland's Highlands and Islands. The same landowning men who instigated Clearances commissioned picturesque paintings of the rolling pastures and tidy walls newly enclosed within their property. As scholars of the eighteenth and nineteenth centuries note, discursive and material practices of landscaping, whether in the form of painting, planting, or poetry, should be understood as ideological techniques of empire that developed gardens, farms, and plantations for the enclosure and accumulation of power.[65] Picturesque sculpted landscapes disavowed their own artificiality, conventionalizing nature and naturalizing convention. Seemingly tranquil landscapes concealed their designers' and makers' alienation from land as well as the violence of settler colonialism.[66] Wildness was subtly controlled, with distant ruins and raggedy peasants framed as evidence of an inevitable natural course of history.[67] Commoning was rendered backward and bygone in an aesthetics that insulated those responsible for its demise.

Tait's legacy in relation to this tradition is highly ambivalent. *Land Makar* displays painterly landscape influences that imply Tait's seduction by the genre but at the same time it features Sinclair as an outspoken critic of such romanticism and, by extension, of the imperial violence that enabled the picturesque. While West Aith is indeed poetically dilapidated, Sinclair is not silenced.

The subject of silencing and speaking out is key to both Tait's and Bowman's films. Aware of the importance of language to place-based identity, particularly within colonial contexts where English dominates Scots and Scottish Gaelic in Britain and Navajo in the United States, Tait and Bowman approached translation as a political question. Their responses could not be more different.

Land Makar contains no subtitles. When it played at a festival in England, organizers worried that audiences would miss important information spoken on the soundtrack. Tait responded that if audiences did not understand "Sinclair's vivid comments about her work and her surroundings" that added "an extra dimension" and "richness," they might simply enjoy Sinclair's voice as "incidental music."[68] Recalling Tait's love of poetry, we might liken her refusal to use subtitles to a bard's preference for the spoken word over written verse. When Tait's films were restored and screened more widely in the 2000s, in large part due to Sarah Neely's scholarship, several critics praised *Land Makar*'s lack of dubbing and subtitles on grounds of "authenticity" and for weaving spoken language into the land's soundscape.[69] Such receptions seem to go along with Tait's preference. Here was a woman who didn't want things to be "understood," "cosy and neat."[70]

But surely, given her objections to Orkney's marginalization, Tait—an Orkney person trained abroad, of independent means, and connected to international film circles—had a platform and missed an opportunity to forward audiences' awareness of Orcadian culture. In a short story Tait wrote in 1956 called "Incomers," tourists fail to understand what an Orkney boatsman tells them about local birds and resolve to "look them up in a book" upon their return to the city and, by implication, the civilized center of proper English.[71] Tait's scorn for these urban outsiders anticipates that leveled at tourists in *Caora Mor Big Sheep. I am an insider*, she implies, *because I speak the language.*

The question of how or whether to help audiences understand dialect and speech has long troubled documentary. Broadly, subtitles emphasize the possibility of understanding others semantically, appealing to theorists including Bill Nichols for their communicative and informational potential. Conversely, a lack of subtitles emphasizes the power of language as a formal element and a marker of cultural difference. This latter emphasis appealed to Trinh. In the same year that Nichols celebrated documentary's verbal and rhetorical realism, Trinh published a polemic against voice as the authoritative basis of documentary.[72] She rejected what she identified as a paternalistic, didactic, and expository voice in documentary—a Griersonian voice—that delivered a white middle-class man's perspective as an invisible yet omniscient voice of universal reason. Such a voice, Trinh argued, answers an imperialistic desire for the filmed world "TO MAKE SENSE" whereby privileged audiences view people on-screen and "WANT TO KNOW WHAT THEY THINK AND HOW THEY FEEL."[73]

Land Makar refuses audiences such clarity. Sinclair's rural, working-class, Norse-, Gaelic-, and Scots-influenced Orcadian speech is a vocalization of emplaced identity. As Angela Aguayo writes, with the increasing availability of lightweight cameras and sync sound recording since the 1960s, socially oriented documentary filmmakers could transmit "unfiltered vernacular voices of marginalized communities" in projects of empowering self-representation.[74] But Tait's use of speech complicates such emancipatory hopes.

By presenting Sinclair's voice without subtitles, Tait forwards an audible system of allegiance. Rangan has examined such systems as "audibilities," a term she uses for aspects of a documentary that participate in processes of sonic discernment. Audibilities construct systems of meaning whereby the ear ("an organ of discrimination") identifies racial, gendered, and classed difference.[75] *Land Makar*'s audibilities place Tait and Sinclair on one side, with non-Orcadian audiences on the other side: insiders/outsiders.

Yet this system of allegiance is itself a site of rupture in the film, as Tait and Sinclair disagree on definitions of work and beauty. While many experimental non-fiction films made by women in the 1970s foreground conversation (between girlfriends, mothers, daughters, neighbors) to carve out spaces of feminist solidarity, Tait's film requires that we pay closer attention to class difference.[76]

Sinclair cuts the conversation short. There is no time to stand around talking. She has work to do.

ON AND OFF THE RESERVATION

"I'm just getting tired of all this filming. What's the use? Go and catch the sheep." Biah's words are spoken by a translator because Bowman does not speak Navajo, and her grandmother does not speak English. English translations were added to the film's soundtrack in post-production. It is clear to the audience that Bowman had little idea what her grandmother was saying—though surely Biah's body language spoke loud enough. Throughout the film, Biah turns her back on her granddaughter and flees inside her hogan. "She just didn't want to be filmed," Bowman recalls on the soundtrack in performative flatness. She places unexpected emphasis on words and pauses dramatically. "Could you ask her why she thinks I'm using her?," Bowman asks a local man she has roped in as her interpreter. "Tell her ... [the film] is not to exploit," Bowman instructs him. "You know what the term *exploit* means?," she adds, seemingly oblivious to her question's condescension. "Yeah" he answers. He knows what "exploit" means.

Bowman's persistence enacts Trinh's personification of the colonial voice of documentary ("WE WANT TO KNOW WHAT THEY THINK").[77] Like Sinclair at West Aith, Biah frustrates her granddaughter's totalizing quest of meaning. Biah's refusal and Bowman's refusal to give up propel the film's odd dynamism.

Bowman's own presence is central in this dynamic. *Navajo Talking Picture* was her first film, made as her graduation project at the University of California, Los Angeles. Early in the film's voice-over, she describes her intention of portraying Biah on the land: "Understanding is what I want. Understanding between my grandmother and myself and myself and the Navajo." But from the film's opening sequences, this intention fails. Later we see Bowman driving into the northern Arizona desert in sadness and frustration. The project is not going well, she tells us in voice-over. As filming continued to raise concerns on the reservation, Bowman turned her camera on herself. The film's title tells as much—this is a project whose maker wants to speak out about Indigenous (mis)representation. If Biah wouldn't talk, Bowman would.

Unsafe and inconclusive, *Navajo Talking Picture* is not an easy watch. In the film's final minutes, Bowman drives back to Los Angeles with peers who have helped with the camera and sound. "What do you think, you guys? Are you going to say anything? I want some reaction," she demands. Though addressing her crew through the rearview mirror, her words also challenge the audience, embroiling us in the confrontation.

Inserting herself into the film, Bowman performs a complicated insider/outsider character in relation to her heritage. This awkward positionality, so reminiscent of Trinh's descriptions of the "Inappropriate Other" filmmaker, sees Bowman straddle two worlds, generations, and landscapes: white and Indigenous, modern and traditional, urban and rural to expose the settler colonial manufacture of such divisions.

Projecting her own unease onto her grandmother, Bowman reveals an achingly larger context of colonial dispossession, displacement, and representational violence. Exemplifying what Alisa Lebow has described as a characteristic slippage in "first-person film" whereby the filmmaker informs her own sense of self by portraying someone close to her, *Navajo Talking Picture* sees its maker and subject matter converge.[78] A confrontation between kith and kin ("kith" deriving from a word for knowledge of one's native land and people) presents Bowman as un-kin, un-kith, uncouth, lacking in knowledge, an outsider.

"My grandmother doesn't live like me, that's for sure," Bowman's voice-over continues. "She's unlike me in the way I grew up." Though seemingly basic, these statements invite audiences to consider the reasons for Bowman's urban childhood being so unlike her elder's. Establishing one of the film's many binaries, Bowman's "then and now," "her and me" comparison resurrects a representational trope commonly used to portray Indigenous life as bygone.

In his history of *Navajo and Photography*, James Faris surveys how white settlers, often wielding cameras, rendered Navajo people as intriguing elements in a landscape, more like archaeological fragments than living people.[79] Bowman would have been all too aware of this objectifying and ossifying gaze. She would also have known some of its most famous images, produced by Edward Sheriff Curtis in a twenty-volume photographic survey, *The North American Indian*, that was funded by the banker J. P. Morgan in the early 1900s. Curtis was also involved in making films about Indigenous communities.[80]

In *The Third Eye: Race, Cinema, and Ethnographic Spectacle* (1996), Rony identifies Curtis as an artistic accomplice to settler colonialism and industrial modernity, his misty, smoky images of Indigenous people and (inaccurately reenacted) ceremonies exemplifying an extractive gaze, or what Laguna Pueblo photographer Leslie Marmon Silko calls the look of a "voyeur/vampire."[81] Echoing Faris, Rony explains how Curtis's aesthetics excluded Indigenous people from social history by placing them within picturesque natural history tableaux where "a spectator posited as Western, white, and urbanized" examines "people portrayed as being somewhere nearer to the beginning on the spectrum of human evolution" and therefore nearing extinction.[82] She calls such aesthetics "salvage ethnography," a term associated with the anthropologist Franz Boas, who collected evidence of American cultures threatened with extinction often due to factors such as genocide, land dispossession, and mining, which were concealed by a rhetoric of modernization. Salvage ethnography's "taxidermic mode of representation," as Rony calls it, obscured the violence of settler colonialism and preserved a binary power relation whereby the "noble savage" is always already familiar, nostalgic, and defeated.[83] Activities outside of capitalism, such as daily life on Navajo land, are captured on camera and converted into financial returns (Curtis's photographs were bestsellers).

Bowman's comparisons between herself and her grandmother, city and reservation, and life now and then manufacture an "us and them" dynamic uncomfortably close to this mode of salvage ethnography. Biah no doubt feels this all to keenly. "My grandmother came out," Bowman reports in the voice-over. "She said to us in Navajo, LEAVE. And she pointed with her finger and hand out to the land. I didn't understand. I kept filming."

Continuing to film, Bowman searches for justification. "I wanted to make the film badly," she said. Her adverbial placement is telling. We might expect Bowman to have said "I badly wanted to make the film," and understood her to have dearly wanted to complete her project. But "badly" (and not dearly) is placed in a syntactical position that modifies the making of the film. She was making the film badly, perhaps by intention. She was breaking rules. Certainly for Biah, the very act of filming was taboo.

Many Indigenous people (including photographers) have understood the camera's extractive violence, describing white settler photographers such as Curtis as "shadow catchers" who extract spiritual power from their subjects.[84] As Hopi photographer Victor Masayesva writes, the camera is an invasive weapon unless it is invited; knowing when *not* to take someone's picture is paramount (such as during certain ceremonies and dances).[85] In Bowman's film, we see her consult a specialist in the Native American Studies Center at the University of California, Los Angeles, who explains why taking pictures is culturally taboo. Yet Bowman continues.

Navajo Talking Picture performs a non-consensual ambush that compels audiences to feel the violence of taking—extracting—from Navajo communities. Bowman grew up watching inaccurate and demeaning representations of Navajo people in Hollywood westerns where "cowboys and Indians" battled and white heroes won. Directors including John Ford projected frontier fantasies onto southwestern landscapes such as Monument Valley, using unnamed Navajo people as cast and crew members (or, in Ford's words, "my personal tribe").[86] Bowman would later experience cultural appropriation firsthand when she appeared in *The Dark Wind,* a box office flop produced by Robert Redford in the early 1990s, that cheaply aestheticized the werewolf aspect of Navajo skinwalker stories.

Participating in such depictions as both actor and audience, Bowman surely experienced a dilemma akin to that which Frantz Fanon describes in *Black Skin, White Masks.* Born in Martinique of African descent, Fanon absorbed a commercial cinema and magazine culture produced "by white men for little white men" and recalls the humiliation of having to identify with images that depicted Black people as inferior and savage.[87] Writing forty years on, Rony reflects on a similar experience, suggesting that she has grown a third eye, inspired by both Fanon and W. E. B. Du Bois, that enables her to look at herself as an Indonesian woman through the eyes of others, to critically examine their racialized and gendered gaze.[88]

Bowman also seems to have grown a third eye to resist simplistic schemas of spectatorship and identification. Her film asks *How do I look? Am I not (supplying) the romantic image you wanted* (no braided hair)? Breaking conventions on both sides of the camera, Bowman explores the experience of viewing herself as an object. Her third eye is her camera, a tool of resistance she uses in a way that anticipates the title of Rony's 2021 book *How Do We Look? Resisting Visual Biopolitics*. There, Rony examines the multiple meanings of "look" encompassing the experience of being looked at as an object and the political possibility of becoming a subject who looks back.

Bowman's film complicates the emancipatory hope implied in Rony's idea of looking back, however. Bowman's third eye settles on the othered version of herself she identifies in her grandmother and there she faces a dilemma. Pursuing Biah as white men pursued their Navajo ancestors with photography, film, academic exegesis, tourism, and mining, Bowman presents contemporary reality—the savage salvage—of Indigenous identity as a dislocated body that has internalized its oppressors and turned on its own kin. Performing an extractive gaze to alert us to its violence, Bowman makes us consider our own ways of looking. Even though she is the one filming, not a white documentarian or anthropologist, her camera still upsets her grandmother, and our gaze is still not welcome. Simply taking up the camera herself, Bowman implies, is not going to make right the representational wrongs inflicted on generations of Navajo people.

Throughout this book we will encounter filmmakers who use self-reflexivity to foreground extractive violence, though Bowman is an outlier in her ferocity—most land cinema filmmakers practiced kinder ways of looking. Nevertheless, Bowman's uncomfortable approach anticipates a medium-subject nexus common in land cinema whereby the filmmaker's own presence behind or before the camera enacts the difficulty of taking pictures in and about extractive contexts. Whereas Curtis's genre of salvage ethnography erased the presence of researchers and filmmakers (traces of white feet, Rony calls them) in a disavowal of the very industrial and colonial mechanisms driving their subjects to extinction, Bowman steps into the shot to announce her own troubled gaze.[89]

In troubling the emancipatory promise of taking up a camera, Bowman's work critically revisits a project infamous in ethnographic and documentary film history, *Navajo Film Themselves*, undertaken in 1966 in Pine Springs, Arizona, less than an hour's drive north of Biah's reservation in Lower Greasewood. The project culminated in a collection of seven films and a book titled *Through Navajo Eyes: An Exploration in Film Communication and Anthropology*.

As its title suggests, *Navajo Film Themselves* saw the project's initiators, the social scientists Sol Worth and John Adair, lend cameras and sound equipment to Navajo people with an invitation to film themselves. Worth and Adair hoped to discover representational and narrative strategies among these novice directors (whom they paternalistically called their "film children") that would demonstrate an authentic Navajo way of seeing the world.[90] The issue with such a project is that its designers posited their own (white, middle-class, urban, male) ways of seeing as the norm and anything other as an exotic deviation from the norm. Accordingly, the project has sparked interest among anthropologists and film theorists. Trinh criticizes it as a "charity mission," Rangan notes its "essentializing stereotypes," and Rony observes its lack of cultural sensitivity.[91]

Bowman's intrusive presence on the reservation invites comparisons with *Navajo Film Themselves* in several ways. Here is a Navajo filming herself and her grandmother, but unlike most of the films created in the 1966 project, Bowman's film bristles with anger. In this sense it recalls that of an anomalous film in Worth and Adair's project, made by a young Navajo man named Al Clah. Bowman liked Clah's film, in which an aggressive protagonist served as a self-portrait of the filmmaker. Clah had spent time away from the reservation at art school. "I am the intruder," he remarked.[92] Clah clashed with those he tried to film by insisting on culturally inappropriate close-ups. Bowman identified with Clah, wanting to speak out (to make a "talking picture") about her experience of estrangement. "I was once told that you will just get labeled as a 'troublemaker' if you speak up," she said in an interview, "[but] if you don't speak up, you get walked on or killed as bounty like our ancestors before us."[93] Bowman, like Clah, felt alienated both on and off the reservation: insider/outsider.

When Worth and Adair left Pine Springs they took the cameras with them, and none of their "film children" continued directing. In a well-documented exchange before their departure, which anthropologists have used to demonstrate Worth and Adair's insufficient social grounding in the community, an elder asks the filmmakers whether their project will do his sheep any good. When Worth and Adair admit this is unlikely, the elder retorts, "Then why make movies?"[94] Like Sinclair in West Aith and Biah on her reservation, this elder recognizes a conflict of interest between an insider and an outsider's motivations.

Navajo life (*diné bi' iína'*) revolves around community, land relation, and the special presence of the Navajo-Churro sheep, who signify companionship, warm wool, nourishing milk, and a tradition of animal and land stewardship. The fact that this elder and Biah both mention sheep is unsurprising, given this important inter-species connection and the breed's near extinction due to federal livestock reduction policies.[95] Judging by Worth and Adair's quizzical response to the elder's question, they had little idea that sheep meant so much to their subjects. Bowman's film is much more knowing. In seemingly incidental scenes of sheep in a pen and fraught exchanges about her presence with the camera, Bowman plants historical references to extractive histories of picture taking and (agri)cultural loss (Figure 4).

Ethical questions arising from misaligned perspectives and motives (for making a film, for raising sheep) lead to an important inquiry concerning who has the authority, legitimacy, or responsibility to represent others and for what aesthetic, social, or economic goal. Such questions catalyzed the development of Indigenous modes of self-representation in the following decades, including a Fourth Cinema movement that challenged dominant narratives and affirmed marginalized points of view.[96] Positioned in awkward relation with this development, Bowman's film

FIGURE 4. Capturing sheep in *Navajo Talking Picture*. Frame enlargement.

cautions audiences against rushing to conclusions. A simplistic handover of equipment, Bowman suggests, underestimates the damaging representational legacies of settler colonialism. Her grandmother's memories run deep.

Like Bowman, Trinh is circumspect about Worth and Adair's project, discussing it in a section titled "No Master Territories" in her 1991 essay collection *When the Moon Waxes Red: Representation, Gender and Cultural Politics*. "Giving voice" to Third World subjects, Trinh argues, is a device to legitimize violence under a banner of authenticity and inclusion.[97] Bowman anticipates Trinh's problematization of documentary by exposing her own attempt at territorial mastery as being as futile as chasing her grandmother's sheep (we see her catching a lamb in one scene while her grandmother evades her).

Bowman also anticipates the gendered implication of Trinh's phrase, foregrounding Biah and her discordance to undermine any master narrative that lumps women together as kindred caregivers, naturally affiliated with nature. As eco-feminists including Val Plumwood have pointed out, colocations of nature, care work, and femininity have shackled women (especially poor women of color) within patriarchal projects that legitimize assaults on women's labor and natural resources by elevating men above the rest of humanity and nature.[98] The historian Jennifer Nez Denetdale adds a Navajo perspective, describing how settler colonialism undermined Native women's power by disrupting their matrilineal systems of pastoral kinship and land relation (again, back to the sheep).[99] Presenting herself as cut off from rural lifeways and her own grandmother, Bowman visualizes how patriarchal colonialism has disrupted kinship, leaving only un-kin, uncouth relations of traumatic dislocation. In this sense, uncomfortable and unresolved, the film is an eco-feminist and decolonial strategy for talking back.

Bowman's film also talks back to debates in documentary circulating at the time concerning voice and narration. Her portrayal of herself and her grandmother, like Tait's with her neighbor, complicates both Nichols's identification of voice-over narration with documentary's "expository mode" and Trinh's dismissal of it on grounds of didacticism. As Stella Bruzzi has noted, defending the potential of voice-over in documentary, "the diversity of the form strongly suggests that an overarching definition of voice-over documentaries is distortive."[100] Bowman's own voice-over narration and Tait's off-camera conversation with Sinclair that stands in for a voice-over diversify the potential of voice-over, bringing performative, emplaced, accented, and gendered subjectivity to their films. Their voice-overs do not speak a view from nowhere. Rather, they speak in multiple voices and from several perspectives, their dissensus demanding that audiences keep thinking.

In this sense, Tait's and Bowman's films "speak nearby," as Trinh puts it, rather than "about, . . . in their place or on top of" subjects.[101] Speaking nearby, speaking back, and often in body language as much as in words, Biah evades Bowman's picture taking, and Sinclair disrupts Tait's romanticism. Perhaps there are four poets of the land in these landscape-portraits after all, each speaking her mind, none silenced by another, and all contributing to the opening of a discursive space for thinking about extractivism.

When I discuss Bowman's film, I often accidentally call it "Navajo Taking Picture," a useful mistake for thinking about the taboo of taking (stealing, extracting) a person's image, both within Navajo culture and more broadly the various extractivist contexts of appropriation and exploitation that this book explores. Taking, however, also reminds me of the emancipatory possibility of filmmakers taking up space and taking up cameras in projects of grassroots resistance, a topic to which I turn in Chapter 2.

TWO

Farmer-Filmmakers, Fieldwork, and Growth

IN A BLACK-AND-WHITE PHOTOGRAPH, a man crouches in a thicket of rice plants (Figure 5). The sun shimmers across their swaying surface. He peers through his Bolex viewfinder, expectant curiosity curling his mouth. In 1975, this man moved with his filmmaking collective two hundred miles north of Tokyo to a mountainous hamlet in Yamagata that's snowed-in most winters. Living together there, they learned how to grow rice and make documentaries about rural life.

In an 8mm color film still, a man dances on parched earth in a T-shirt bearing the acronym of an African liberation group (Figure 6). He wears branches in his hat and a grin. He's been helping thirteen friends collect adobe from a termite mound to build an irrigation channel. They came home from hostels and factories in Paris in 1977, establishing a cooperative farm on the banks of a river at Mali's border with Senegal and Mauritania. They produce millet, onions, chili, tomatoes, bananas, radio, theater, photography, and film.

These images depict members of the collectives Ogawa Productions in Japan and Somankidi Coura in Mali as they undertook long-term experiments in farming and used cameras to chronicle their activities for cultural and agricultural regeneration. Their contemporaries questioned the move. Why abandon Tokyo's subversive experimentation and leftist barricades for the woods? Why leave jobs in Paris to return to an area devastated by decades of colonial plantation agriculture, a protracted drought, and a recent military takeover?

FIGURE 5. Ogawa Shinsuke in the field. Thanks to Markus Nornes, Hatano Yukie, and the Narita Airport and Community Historical Museum.

FIGURE 6. A young Bouba Touré dancing in an 8mm film by Monique Janson, Somankidi Coura, 1977. Estate of Bouba Touré. Thanks to Raphaël Grisey.

Images in this chapter encapsulate the political and *eco*-political answers with which the collectives responded. Combining agriculture and culture, soil and celluloid, food sovereignty and self-representation, the collectives aimed "to show that there are other possible ways of development," as one Somankidi Coura member put it.[1] Following a feminist and anti-colonial tradition of film and photographic scholarship that finds registers of meaning within images as a way of reframing history to acknowledge people and places objectified, overlooked, or erased, I write with and about images of the collectives as a method for bringing their eco-political visions into focus.[2]

The photographed and filmed images with which I write were made as Ogawa Pro and Somankidi Coura adjusted to their back-to-the-land lives. Between 1975 and 1992, Ogawa Pro's membership ranged from a handful to fourteen, squeezed into a single wooden farmhouse where they slept, ate, and produced films, their wives raising the children and undertaking domestic work. Somankidi Coura, initially comprising fourteen members, built housing and a school near an existing village called Somankidi, whose occupants helped with construction, glad to see youths returning to the region with a commitment to stay. Even djinni, spirits inhabiting the earth, welcomed them.[3] Japanese farmers in Yamagata's Magino and Furuyashiki villages were initially less cordial toward their new neighbors, suspecting that Ogawa Pro were communists building explosives (in fact, the test tubes in Ogawa Pro's shed contained plant fertilizer).[4]

Ogawa Pro's lengthy documentaries about rice farming culture and the many photographic slideshows and short films produced at Somankidi Coura to document polyculture crops and collective living promoted self-sufficiency in the face of global agri-business and its neocolonial patterns of extraction. Initially produced for their own members as records of activities and achievements and for the education of farmers and workers elsewhere, the collectives' images have spread since their making, reaching film festival and arthouse film theater audiences across the world.[5] Ogawa Pro was integral to this dissemination, helping launch the Yamagata International Documentary Film Festival in 1989. Though Ogawa Pro ceased operations in 1992 when its founder, Ogawa Shinsuke, died of poor health, the biannual festival sustains the collective's jovial, down-to-earth spirit to this day.

In Figure 5, the man crouching in the field is Ogawa Shinsuke, who gave Ogawa Pro its name and presided over it with charisma and coercion. A portly, gregarious figure, Ogawa was delighted to be away from the city, up to his knees in mud and awash in farmers' stories.

Ogawa's biography and the fabrications with which he embellished it provide clues for his investment in agrarianism as a political practice.

Ogawa claimed to have studied ethnology at university, associating himself with an important center of national folk studies (he admired Yanagita Kunio, who had himself worked on film and photographic projects in the 1940s, portraying Japan through a pastoral gaze).[6] Ogawa also claimed to have dropped out of university, as was fashionable in 1960s counterculture. In reality, he graduated with a diploma in economics.[7] He also liked to declaim his poor, rural background, chatting with farmers over pickled vegetables, everyone sitting cross-legged around a stove. Lending an air of authenticity among fellow filmmaker-activists and working-class subjects, Ogawa's exaggerations helped him identify with their cause—an indication of the idealism that shaped his career. Call it a documentarian's creative treatment of actuality, he seemed to suggest, echoing John Grierson, whose social agenda and educational approach to documentary Ogawa admired.[8]

Throughout the 1960s Ogawa witnessed roads, shopping malls, and office blocks spread across the landscape, with rapid economic development after World War II indebting the nation to the United States in an asymmetrical relation. Japan provided America with a base in East Asia during the Cold War as well as a supply of natural resources and labor for the global market. Though Japan's economy boomed, laborers prospered little. Glossy images of purchasing power papered over social and environmental exhaustion. Ogawa's early documentaries chronicled the overworked and under-waged and were made independently or with Jieiso, a group he led in the late 1960s that served as a precursor to Ogawa Pro. These films contributed to a wider leftist movement for educational and labor reform and in opposition to nuclear armaments and the Vietnam War. Films were made for and about specific political struggles, aiming to move working-class audiences to activism.

Unsurprisingly perhaps, given his activism, Ogawa's pitches for television were unsuccessful. The lack of uptake further motivated his experiments in grassroots production and distribution, where self-organized screenings and the raucous discussions they provoked became central to the politicizing process. So long as at least three people showed up, Ogawa declared, he had an audience.[9] Ogawa recruited filmmakers, activists, and students as his "staff" in 1968, funding Ogawa Pro's enterprise with audience donations and loans ("we'll pay them back with films").[10] In later years audiences grew, crowding village halls, clapping, chanting, and booing during screenings and answering surveys afterward. Ogawa wanted to know: Were they active in the struggle portrayed? Did they sympathize with its philosophy? Would they organize or fundraise in the future?

Producing documentaries about laborers forgotten by Japan's economic plans, particularly in rural communities whose perspectives were also overlooked in leftist protests erupting in the cities, Ogawa Pro championed farmers from the outset. "I knew I had to film farmers," Ogawa claimed, "because I was a farmer myself."[11] Though more aspiration than fact, Ogawa's words anticipate the earthy direction his life would take.

The man in Figure 6 is Bouba Touré, then in his twenties and newly returned to the Senegal River basin region he had left as a teenager in search of work. Unlike Ogawa, Touré did not name the collective after himself and always reminded audiences that he was one of fourteen initiators. Touré is, however, the most known and international due to his role chronicling and transmitting Somankidi Coura's activities in still photographs, 8mm films, and videos. Though Touré died in 2022, the cooperative continues to this day, its membership exceeding three hundred.

Filming a self-portrait on a handheld camcorder in 2008, Touré reflects on the founding of the cooperative three decades prior and his ongoing relationship to image-making, which he describes as "walking with time." Images avert time's headlong rush into forgetting, he explains, filming the walls of his cramped apartment whose address gives this half-hour film its name, *Bouba Touré, 58 rue Trousseau, Paris, France*. Touré lives here when not in Mali. From floor to ceiling and even where he washes himself and brews his coffee, he has pasted photographs of friends in Paris and Mali and posters of heroes (Nelson Mandela, Malcolm X, Thomas Sankara, Amílcar Cabral). Cassette tapes from around the world are piled high ("music has no frontier," he says). Clocks tick on every shelf and table ("for me, time means a lot. I don't want to die and be forgotten"). The carpet is hidden under envelopes stuffed with photographic negatives. Grazing over these documents of his life, Touré repeats, like a prayer, "the struggle, the struggle, the struggle."

The camera catches Touré in a mirror. He has filled out since those early 8mm films, but his kind eyes are the same. He inspects the walls of images that fortify him. Here is a man whose parents' generation could not use cameras since France prohibited African subjects from filming themselves during the colonial era,[12] a man whose father's generation went "to die in a war he took part in without ever knowing why" and whose "great-grandfather was deported as a slave to the Americas," a man who migrated to France in the early 1960s and found himself sharing derelict factories converted into hostels with as many as three hundred men, two sinks, two toilets, and no light switches. Stoves leaked, police raided, tuberculosis spread, and Touré learned that—contrary to what the colonial regime had taught about European civilization— "a human is less important than capital" in Paris. "We lived like rats."

Between long shifts at a car factory, Touré learned to read and write (this had not been on the colonial curriculum). He also learned to use a camera and a projector. Images helped him communicate with other migrant workers. He took their photographs, gifting them or compiling slideshows. Feeding 35mm slides into a carousel, Touré fed his audiences encouragement ("strike against the slumlord," "end the slave-like conditions that have subjugated us for years").

Slideshows such as these are important to land cinema, critically recalling film and photography's early use in colonial travelogues and ethnography and evidencing cinema's politicizing potential for gathering audiences to watch and discuss what they see. Invoking cinema's fundamental composition of multiple still frames projected at speed, Touré's slideshow format also invited audiences to realize cinema's artifice. Made by someone to forward a certain perspective, films and narratives could be re-made, differently.

Migrant workers attending these slideshows came from Mali, Senegal, Guinea, Côte d'Ivoire, and Burkina Faso, but, as Touré said, borders were colonial impositions on families and tribes that pre-dated French control, and national divisions were secondary to the Pan-African unity of the hostels.[13] Scattered around Paris and particularly in the northern districts of Saint Denis and Aubervilliers, the hostels became centers for leftist activism and its aesthetic prefiguration.[14] Slideshows were lessons in history and rehearsals for its transformation.

In 1971, Touré and other migrant workers established the Cultural Association of African Workers in France, contributing to debates in a Third Worldist movement united around programs of socialism and economic sovereignty that emerged after Algerian independence and intensified with the Vietnam War.[15] Rent strikes at the hostels and liberation struggles in Angola, Guinea-Bissau, and Mozambique stimulated conversations about neocolonial exploitation. The Cultural Association of African Workers in France raised funds, sent clothes, donated blood to countries still fighting for independence, produced theater about colonial struggle, and organized screenings of militant films from regions transitioning to socialism.[16] Meanwhile, reports arrived of a terrible drought in the Sahel region that was devastating land already exhausted by colonial plantation agriculture. Touré's father wrote to him "We have nothing left to eat." Something had to be done.

Becoming "more and more conscious that we have to act locally, so that our brothers and sisters wouldn't have to come to France to sell their labor," Touré and others at the Cultural Association of African Workers in France focused their playwriting and workshops on the prospect of returning to Africa to rejuvenate land, planting ideas for what came to fruition in 1977.

Many newly independent regions in Africa received "development" aid from European non-governmental organizations at that time. The French government also tried paying migrants to return home. Touré rejected "humanitarian aid" as "just colonialism in another form." Somankidi Coura's emphasis on self-sufficiency and organic methods also resisted a wave of corporate-owned new technologies then encroaching on the Global South with high-yield monocultural species and chemical fertilizers under the banner of Green Revolution and the illusion of epistemic privilege achieved by modern biotech science.[17]

Filming verdant mixed crops, Touré chuckles to his camera and cooperative members nearby. "Perfect," he says. "It's all organic." They answer, "No pesticide, no fertilizer."

In understanding nature's limits and celebrating its abundance and life-giving power, Somankidi Coura, like Ogawa Pro, belongs to a history of oppositional movements to exponential economic growth, variously led by agrarian radicals, romantic poets, revolutionary socialists, and, more recently, eco-feminists and proponents of ecological Marxism.[18] In the contemporary context of climate breakdown and amid debates about degrowth strategies to curb carbon emissions, the collectives offer clues for how ideas of worth and progress might be re-evaluated for post-extractive futures.

Such a re-evaluation challenges an extractive logic that focuses on gross domestic product (GDP). GDP has shaped mainstream economics since the mid-twentieth century, counting economic activity regardless of its social and ecological impact. Oil spills, earthquakes, and wars boost GDP because of the costly rescue and reparation projects they entail. The often un-remunerated labor of growing one's own food, raising children, and caring for unwell and elderly people, as Marilyn Waring puts it, counts for nothing.[19] Keeping trees and oil in the ground and maintaining healthy waterways and fresh air are also invisible as GDP. Kate Raworth and J. K. Gibson-Graham are among many recent economists who criticize so-called developed nations' continued fixation on GDP, while Vandana Shiva has gone as far as describing economic growth as "anti-life."[20] Degrowth strategies have been proposed for curbing consumption and waste, but although reducing current fossil fuel dependency is important (so long as it resists the carbon colonial outsourcing of polluting production to the Global South), degrowth maintains a binary logic that centers the idea of financialized activity and its reduction, leaving little room for *different* forms of growth.[21]

Reconsidering growth fosters a different and more diverse set of values. As Anna Tsing writes, alternative economic forms open "sites for rethinking the unquestioned authority of capitalism," their diversity offering "a chance for multiple ways forward."[22] Though pre-dating the term "degrowth," the different forms of growth cultivated in Ogawa Pro's and Somankidi Coura's farming-filmmaking experiments include a proliferation of cultural engagement, a flourishing of communal green space, increased ecological and political literacy, and a resurgence in wildlife and biodiversity. With a "different growth" framework, experiences of struggle and solidarity in post-war Japan and post-colonial West Africa appear both distinct and linked, offering insight into what life beyond extractivism could be like if growth meant many things and economics stemmed from ethics and ecology.

The collectives' alternative framework for growth also transforms fields of representation. Scopic regimes that developed alongside extractive projects of colonial exploration used cameras to survey frontiers, often reducing rural people and places to sources of profit and objects of pity or exoticism.[23] Ogawa and Touré rejected such violence, training their lenses on the fruits of their collective labor. Without diversifying how wealth and growth are imagined and measured, they realized, a cold logic of financialization would prevail, seeing life, as Touré put it, as "less important than capital."

The extractive damages that Ogawa Pro and Somankidi Coura resisted belong to a global history of capitalism that Kathryn Yusoff characterizes by its desire for inhuman properties, with slavery, Indigenous genocide, and settler colonialism evidencing "total submission to the principle of extraction" and providing the bedrock for continued resource dependencies and the situated, racialized labor exploitations they entail.[24] If post-war Europe and Japan seemed cleaner and shinier in the 1960s and 1970s, then such renovation came, to borrow from Karl Marx (whose writings both collectives knew), "dripping from head to foot, from every pore, with [the] blood and dirt" of extractive capitalism accumulated over decades and centuries.[25]

Western aid packages to Japan during and after post-war occupation, along with subsidized American wheat imports that threatened Indigenous rice production in the 1970s, exemplify some of many ways that Western imperialism perpetuated extractive relations of dependency in Ogawa's day. At that same time, although a wave of independence movements around 1960 might suggest a waning of European power in Africa, with countries such as France opening their borders to newly independent nations, exploitation continued. While West African migrants such as Touré suffered in Paris, European companies continued to extract minerals and cash crops from West Africa.

In her 2018 book *A Billion Black Anthropocenes or None*, Yusoff criticizes geology and climate science for forgetting four centuries of colonialism when dating the Anthropocene age to changes in geological data caused by nineteenth- and twentieth-century industrialism. Climate change, Yusoff argues, is coeval with early capitalism's "organization of human property as extractable energy properties" in the colonization of the Americas and the forced transportation of African people to the "New World" as a workforce beginning in the sixteenth century.[26] While some theorists propose the term "Capitalocene" to better account for the specifically capitalist logic and protagonists driving that colonial project and its climate effects, others including Anna Tsing use the term "Plantationocene" to acknowledge the centrality of enslaved labor, land enclosure, and intensive agricultural practices in capitalist-driven climate change.[27] Though Ogawa and Touré precede such terminologies, they would surely applaud this critical tracing of climate breakdown to colonial conversions of land into territorialized cash crops.

Tsing's 2015 book on capitalist destruction and multispecies survival, *The Mushroom at the End of the World*, studies ecologies and economies, including small-scale farming in rural Japan and global agri-businesses, and emphasizes the damage to regions and landscapes wrought by plantation principles. Her tracing of the imperial origins of climate damage helps elucidate the eco-political and anti-colonial significance of Ogawa Pro and Somankidi Coura's back-to-the-land projects. These projects' experiments with organicism and self-sufficiency meanwhile resonate with Tsing's interest in "unruly" possibilities that emerge when multiple species form symbiotic alliances around and against capitalist systems. They also speak to Yusoff's consideration, via Sylvia Wynter, of accounts of enslaved and maroon communities establishing different "intimacies" with the earth, growing their own food and cultures, beside the

FIGURE 7. Ogawa Pro's fieldwork. Thanks to Markus Nornes, Hatano Yukie, and the Narita Airport and Community Historical Museum.

plantation's stronghold.[28] Although the plantation creates species hierarchies in which ownership over other people, animals, and the earth itself is prized, it is also a field where "the politically-and-biologically diverse potentials of the seams of global capitalism" can be realized.[29] It is in these unruly edges, in plots beside plantations, that Ogawa Pro and Somankidi Coura sowed alternative futures. What follows is a seed catalog, an album of images, for what they grew and invite us to imagine.

In Figure 7, men march toward the camera in a formation that seems military, though these plowed furrows are not trenches. They have cameras, T-shirts, and jeans from the city. Centered in the foreground and larger than the others is Ogawa Shinsuke.

Ogawa had worked hard for this position. He cut his teeth at Iwanami Productions, a public relations firm that opened a film department in 1950 to make industry and government-contracted documentaries.

Despite potential limits imposed by industrial contracts, some of Japan's most innovative filmmakers emerged from Iwanami, including Tsuchimoto Noriaki, Hani Susumu, and Haneda Sumiko. Ogawa joined a group of younger employees at Iwanami who were interested in political film and debating works in progress.[30] Collective discussion of how to shoot or edit would later become central in Ogawa Pro's methodology.

Iwanami is important to the story of Ogawa Pro's formation because it was a company invested in industrial production at the same time as being home to budding anti-capitalist and experimental documentary. Arriving relatively early in Japan, moving image technology supported the state's ideological construction of a homogenous nation in pre-war and wartime periods of imperial expansion. Documentary (usually called *bunka eiga*, or "culture film") and folk ethnography (*minzokugaku*) were deployed as visual and ideological frameworks for such projects.[31] After 1945 non-fiction filmmaking continued to serve the state, now allied with an American imperative for economic growth and depicting steel, automobile, and electrical industries.[32] Ogawa Pro emerged in complicated relation with these contexts. Iwanami was where Ogawa Shinsuke learned to make film and to dissent. Ogawa's films displayed both national pride and an anti-capitalist politics. The collective's first long-term filmmaking project saw these motivations converge, hurling its fresh-faced members into challenging fieldwork.

"Fieldwork" is a term that helps elucidate several aspects of Ogawa Pro's and Somankidi Coura's projects. On one level, the word describes practical work conducted in the natural environment rather than in a library, a laboratory, or an office and encapsulates the collectives' land-based farming and filmmaking initiatives. "Fieldwork" is also a common term in anthropology, a discipline with historical connections to colonialism that the collectives' politics certainly call into question.[33] Another definition of "fieldwork" is as a temporary fortification. In their active support of liberation movements, both collectives would welcome this militant association.

Ogawa Pro spent six years filming at temporary fortifications and lookout towers in an area to the northeast of Tokyo called Sanrizuka, centered around several hamlets and the town of Narita. They filmed as protesters and farmers chained themselves to trees and lay before bulldozers, as helmeted police arrived in wire-windowed vans and as Japan's economic "miracle" became nightmarish.

Back in 1966 the government had announced plans for an international airport at Narita, which many people feared the United States would use to refuel on route to Vietnam. Anti-American sentiment was already high due to plans to renew the Treaty of Mutual Cooperation and Security between the United States and Japan (commonly known in Japan as Anpo jōyaku, or simply Anpo). The airport seemed to serve Cold War strategies more than ordinary Japanese people. Its construction would level farmland and hamlets, with those displaced paid off and evicted. Narita was an ideological battleground between rural land rights and urban, global authorities. Farming tools became symbols of protest partly because of farmers such as Ōki Yone, who refused to leave her home at the center of the proposed runway. Ōki was foisted onto a police riot shield and carried from her house as it was bulldozed. She lost three teeth in the struggle and was dumped on the ground nearby.[34]

The seven films that Ogawa Pro shot amid such violence—its Sanrizuka Series—testify to the fervor and failure of the uprising. Supportive filmmakers and activists, including members of the Black Panther Party and the Newsreel collective from the United States, visited the farmers' and filmmakers' fieldwork. Sanrizuka resonated with liberation projects across the world, the rough urgency of Ogawa Pro's black-and-white films chiming with those made at barricades in France, in post-revolutionary Cuba, and across Latin America in resistance to US-influenced right-wing dictatorships. Ogawa Pro contributes an important agrarian perspective to this history of oppositional filmmaking and internationalism, exemplifying land cinema at its most activist and earthy.[35]

In Figure 7, Ogawa Pro members walk through the center of the field. Having filmed from the edge during their early projects, Ogawa came to realize that he should get closer to farmers' work and politics. "We needed to start using our own bodies to realize our ideals," he later announced—though, more accurately, it was his "staff" who got their hands dirty.[36] Ogawa preferred editing footage and reading indoors. In Figure 7, the men imprint their political alliance into the soil.

Ogawa's emphasis on gaining experience in the field derived in part from a chance meeting. After showing the Sanrizuka films to a farmers' association in Yamagata in 1974, a villager challenged Ogawa Pro's method: if Ogawa Pro really wanted to film farmers' struggles, shouldn't its members learn how to farm themselves? Ogawa loved this kind of provocation and its anecdotal power, later recalling that he resolved to leave Tokyo at once.[37] Thus began Ogawa Pro's experiment for collective living, rice farming, and filmmaking.

Not a single member predicted quite how much time and manual labor this experiment demanded. Eighteen years, several tons of rice, and a suite of films later, Ogawa Pro's peculiar cultural and agricultural output testified to their commitment to champion rural land and communities. The films were made about farmers for farmers—and by farmers if one believed Ogawa's interpretation—as a means of solidarity. At the time, sustained and respectful portrayals of rural life were rarely seen on large or small screens. Studios churned out *kaiju* (monster) and *yakuza* (mafia) genres, melodramas, and pornography. Documentary continued to be state- or corporate-sponsored, and experimental filmmaking was predominantly Tokyo-based.

Ogawa Pro and Ogawa's Iwanami contemporary, Tsuchimoto, were exceptional. Often compared to Ogawa, Tsuchimoto championed the plight of fishing communities devastated by industrial mercury pollution in Minamata. While Ogawa looked to the soil for evidence of Japan's painfully industrialized present, Tsuchimoto looked to the sea. Learning from their older colleague at Iwanami, Hani Susumu (who made two exquisitely observant short documentaries about elementary school children in the 1950s, engaging the children themselves in the filmmaking), immersive fieldwork, receptivity to subjects' body language, and patiently held sequences became key methodologies for both Ogawa and Tsuchimoto as they headed north and south to film farmers and fisher folk.[38] Celebrating social immersion, Ogawa described himself and his collective as "outsiders, or even worse, people from the city, surrounded by artificiality, who had completely lost the feeling for the diversity of other life forms and our relation to nature. Only close cohabitation with the peasants and the learning of work in the fields could show us the way to their essence."[39] Ogawa's words recall the photograph of the men walking (in fields that he called "our school").[40] While his focus on "other life forms" presents an ecologically attuned epistemic openness, his essentializing lyricism also reproduces a dichotomy of metropole/peasant that emphasizes Ogawa Pro's heroic immersion as a moral conversion.

Another troubling aspect of the photograph is its lack of women. Ogawa Pro's membership largely confined women to domestic and assistant roles—even Ogawa's spouse, whom members secretly likened to Mao Zedong's powerful wife, could not compete with him. Most photographs of the collective betray its gendered imbalance. Men march the fields. Men operate the cameras. Men review the day's film rushes and drink into the night. If women are present they hover in the background, pouring beer, frying meat (Ogawa's favorite), and hushing children. As inclusive as Ogawa Pro's films are when considering women farmers, the collective's own divisions of labor remained patriarchal and centered on Ogawa's leadership.[41] In hindsight, several members regretted this unfair politics, and some lost marriages to it. Member Toshio Iizuka recalls the appeal of moving to Yamagata as a collective, where family life could continue alongside farming and filmmaking.[42] Reality turned out differently. In a 2000 documentary made by Barbara Hammer about Ogawa Pro, Iizuka's former wife Hiroko summarizes the six years she spent with the collective: "every day, cooking, cooking."[43]

Applauding their collective lifestyle and visionary anti-colonial and ecological strategies, men in Ogawa Pro had blind spots. The situation at Somankidi Coura was not very different.[44] Women involved in the community eventually protested their subordinate position by striking during a chili harvest and forming a women's association to cultivate their own fields.[45] Touré later reflected that Somankidi Coura would have been "zero" but for the labor and peaceful influence of women.

FIGURE 8. Somankidi Coura's Moussa Coulibaly and Ousmane Sinaré during an agricultural internship, Haute-Marne, 1976. Photograph by Bouba Touré. Estate of Bouba Touré. Thanks to Raphaël Grisey.

In Figure 8, a young man watches another turn soil with a fork. The photograph is in portrait orientation, though its subject is a French landscape layered with stripes of furrows in the foreground receding toward a hedgerow and a lane, another field, and woodland. In the mid-distance, a third man guides a tiller attached to a tractor that a fourth man drives. The men in the foreground are young, Black, and dressed in sneakers, flared jeans, and patterned shirts typical of the mid-1970s. The others are older, white, and wearing work clothes and caps. This is a field in France's Haute-Marne region, where future members of Somankidi Coura including Moussa Coulibaly and Ousmane Sinaré, in the foreground in Figure 8, trained in agriculture for six months before returning to Mali. Although some members, including Touré, grew up farming corn and millet before emigrating as teenagers, they wanted to learn about irrigation from farmers whose low-intensity organic methods enabled self-sufficiency—when they weren't threatened by agri-business takeovers and the marketing of chemical pesticides.

Touré, Coulibaly, Sinaré, and others came to Haute-Marne in 1976 because they, like Ogawa Pro, identified a connection between soil health and political freedom. In a post-independence context, reclaiming food sovereignty through sustainable agriculture helped repair decades of colonial plantation damage and offered an alternative to rural exodus. They had already spent time in the French countryside in 1973 attending Larzac's Harvest Festival, where farmers gathered in opposition to state plans to extend a military base. Continuing the spirit of this protest, Touré described a farmer's pickax (*daba*) as his preferred "weapon" for struggle and intended his photographs as tools for the education and politicization of fellow West Africans. More recently in collaboration with the artist Raphaël Grisey, who has become Somankidi Coura's biographer and champion, Touré has made work for French and international audiences. Their collaborative film *Xaraasi Xanne—Crossing Voices* (2022), for example, recounts the founding of Somankidi Coura for viewers unfamiliar with West Africa. *Crossing Voices* also sheds light on migrant districts in Paris often only seen publicly through newsflashes about *les sans-papiers* (undocumented migrants).

The title of *Crossing Voices* encapsulates Touré's use of film and photography to vocalize experiences of alienation and to repair an estranged relation between Europe and Africa by crossing between regions. The photograph of the men turning earth in Haute-Marne is one of thousands that Touré took in France and Mali over the next forty years, many of which feature in *Crossing Voices*. Touré's images form an expanded visual archive that also includes 8mm amateur films taken on visits to

Somankidi Coura by the French farmers with whom its founding members trained and a feature film directed by Sidney Sokhona in which Touré plays a version of himself.

In Sokhona's film, *Safrana or Freedom of Speech* (1978), four West African men, who previously worked "to build cars and carry garbage bins" in Paris, travel to the French countryside, led by Touré, to train with farmers. The film opens with a quote from Mao, emphasizing the importance of assimilating knowledge gleaned through hands-on experience abroad into nation building at home. As we see in the film's staging of animated conversations across plowed furrows and kitchen tables, the French farmers' concerns resonated with their trainees' hopes of developing organic subsistence agriculture in West Africa.

While training in France and acting in Sokhona's film, Touré contacted local governments in Senegal, Mali, and Mauritania asking for land. Mali responded first, offering sixty riverside hectares in the Kayes area, which had the highest level of migration to Europe at that time.[46] Touré and his collaborators accepted.

Few people believed that revitalizing an area so damaged by colonial occupation and its aftermath was possible. The place was overgrown with baobab trees, its soil parched by drought and depleted from a French sisal plantation and factory that operated there before independence. After 1960 Mali's new government subsidized back-to-the-land projects and ran cooperative farms, but corruption and a lack of infrastructure troubled such ambitions.[47] A botched United Nations aid program to develop the factory and its surroundings had left ruins.[48] Electricity cables hung like raggedy branches. Snakes nested on the ground and in the trees. The water tower sat empty, and cows wandered through the cinema building. The area seemed to epitomize Marx's diagnosis for the combined social and ecological ills of industrialism. Intensive extractivism had simultaneously exhausted "the soil and the worker," tearing a rift between humans and the rest of nature.[49]

Sokhona's speculative film and Somankidi Coura's realized farm refused this situation. "I rejected miserablism, humanism and pity," Sokhona said, his defiance anticipating critiques of socially oriented filmmaking's paternalistic gaze by Trinh T. Minh-ha and Pooja Rangan, discussed in Chapter 1. "In *Safrana*," Sokhona explained, "I thought it was more important to show that immigrants were taking control of their own fate."[50] Resonating with concurrent films that Med Hondo made about sociopolitical struggles, Sokhona's determination to celebrate organized resistance chimes with Somankidi Coura's fieldwork. In permaculture collaboration with nature, Somankidi Coura's mutual economy shared political and ecological education as well as fresh fruit and vegetables as fortifications against extractivism's enforced dependency. Nurturing land and culture together, they worked, as Touré put it, in their "Ho Chi Minh sandals" (made from discarded tires) and knitted "Amílcar Cabral hats" in "pursuit of happiness" rather than money.[51]

In Figure 9, stooped figures transplant rice seedlings into soil beneath the water. A man pulls soil toward a levee with a hoe. A second man holds a pole, the same length as the hoe, with a camera attached to it. The camera and hoe dance above the water. Ogawa Pro member Tamura Masaki is practicing an immersive method of filmmaking that will become central to the two major feature films the collective makes in Yamagata.

In these massive, sprawling films (which Ogawa was loath to cut any shorter), filmmaking and farming are choreographed into cultural and agricultural and celluloid- and soil-based acts. *Nippon-koku: Furuyashiki-mura* (*Nippon Country: Furuyashiki Village*) (1982) runs to 210 minutes, and *Sennen Kizami no Hidokei: Magino-mura Monogatari* (*The Sundial Carved with a Thousand Years of Notches: Magino Village Story*) (1986) runs to 222 minutes.[52] Substantial time is devoted to tracking Ogawa Pro members as they plot precipitation levels and build cardboard models of irrigation systems. Often such sequences cut to pastoral scenes in which the camera pans across lush landscapes and thatched roofs, contextualizing the collective's fieldwork within a larger landscape, climate, and culture. Scripted sequences also feature, with actors playing alongside villagers to dramatize local legends. The experience of watching this assortment of genres, meandering from television documentary, community theater, and scientific study to costume drama

FIGURE 9. Ogawa Pro planting and filming rice. Thanks to Markus Nornes, Hatano Yukie, and the Narita Airport and Community Historical Museum.

and visual ethnography, perturbed audiences loyal to Ogawa Pro's earlier, more militant films.

Embodying the perspective of a farmer or even his hoe or the soil he is preparing, the films blur boundaries of vegetable, human, and technological subject in a project of immersive learning. Whether such a confusion would appeal to a farmer is of course debatable; to Ogawa, such confusions celebrated a direct, unalienated relation to land.[53]

Amid such celebration enters humorous self-reflexivity. In *The Sundial*, a farmer sits recounting local tales. Suddenly a professor of folk studies stumbles into the background, out of place in his city coat and shoes. He interrupts the farmer to impart information on local legends from his own bookish perspective. The farmer looks on in bemusement. This staging nods to Ogawa Pro's awkwardness in Yamagata and, more profoundly, to a commitment to bridging diverse perspectives. Not unlike the self-reflexivity discussed in Chapter 1 through Margaret Tait and Arlene Bowman's films, the encounter emphasizes the rift between rural and urban epistemes, echoing a student film Ogawa Shinsuke co-created in 1958, *Children Living in the Mountains*, that explored power differentials between city and country perspectives.

In the photographed paddy, the men would have seen their own reflections as they bent to hoe and film, the surface of the water mirroring them at work before the bright sky, projecting an eco-political vision for (agri)cultural and climatic harmony. The camera and hoe create long lines, pointing across the photograph and focusing our gaze downward to the soil, which signifies progress and development through its yields of rice, and by extension, films. Such an earthed definition of development was at odds with ideas of upward progress in Japan's high-growth economy. The collective's move back to the land constructed a form of environmentalism that sees rice farming as a model of socially and environmentally balanced living and sees filmmaking as an important addition that enables reflection, like the water, and dissemination, like the seedlings, of possibilities for flourishing in the seams of global capitalism.

Ogawa Pro's choice of rice farming speaks to its ecological and social interest in cooperative agriculture. Unlike wheat, rice requires scheduling irrigation and therefore coordination between farmers. Ogawa liked this contrast with wheat, associated with Western farming and global food imports. Although wet rice agriculture only developed around 400 BCE, having come to Japan from Korea, rice is viewed as a historical staple of the Japanese diet. In Shinto tradition, the god of rice, along with other deities (*kami*) who represent natural powers such as water and harvest, encourages a reverence to land and environment. There is even a term that refers to Japan as "the land of abundant rice" (*mizuho no kuni*).[54] The first written documents in Japan, commissioned by the Emperor as tools to differentiate the nation from China, appropriated rice as a sacred homegrown crop and foodway.

Seen through a critical lens, Ogawa Pro's association of rice with an ideal of Japanese cooperation tends toward ethnic environmentalism. As I explore further in Chapter 3 by looking at Watsuji Tetsurō's association of a supposedly Japanese temperament with the nation's climate, the trouble with such thinking is its exclusion of other histories and ways of living. Identifying rice with nation—seeing "rice as self," as Emiko Ohnuki-Tierney puts it—excludes those who grow other crops as well as non-agrarian people (who comprised the majority of the population by Ogawa Pro's day).[55] Feeding a common trope in Japanese branding that celebrates rice paddy landscapes and rice-centric cuisine, the filmmakers' historical research and reenactments were selective endeavors shaped by and for Ogawa Pro's political and ecological ideology.[56]

This ideology also overlooks the fact that rice farming is not itself without environmental impact, being a monoculture crop that requires significant amounts of water and releases methane, contributing to greenhouse gas emissions. Ogawa Pro's films also conceal the presence of tractors and chemical fertilizers common in Yamagata by the 1970s. Instead, the films focus on manual labor, visiting farmers in their paddies and in adjacent plots where persimmons, matsutake, daikon, and other vegetables grow as well as silkworms. Self-sufficiency and skills in traditional farming and sericulture are celebrated as antidotes to modern agribusiness and its alienating effects. Farmers are portrayed as experts in nurturing land and community cohesion. While these elements provide an important antidote to narratives of progress centered on industrial science and food imports, they only tell part of the story. Again, we might recall Ogawa's admiration of Grierson, who described documentary as the creative treatment of actuality.[57]

Rice was also integral to Ogawa Pro's social world. Ogawa liked to sit with farmers long into winter nights sharing expertise, memories, and legends, washed down with sake (rice wine) and other produce from their fields. Socializing in this way, sometimes bringing a camera into the circle as an additional interlocutor, Ogawa Pro framed rice as a communal substance activated through shared labor in the paddies and again over a shared meal, with cups of sake poured for neighbors (according to custom, one never pours for oneself) and a large pot of rice divided between everyone's bowls. As Ohnuki-Tierney writes, commensality (the sharing of food between people or between people and gods as in the practice of leaving rice as an offering at the ancestral family alcove) establishes a sense of "us" through shared acts involving rice. If rice in a bowl or cup symbolizes "us" at home, rice paddies are a "spatial equivalent, symbolizing the social group, be it family, the local community, or the nation at large."⁵⁸

Focusing on rice also enabled Ogawa Pro to concentrate on particular periods in history. Members were fascinated by the Edo period (1603–1868), for example, because of its characterization as a distinctively Japanese era isolated from foreign influences and associated with rice farming. Although rice was celebrated as intrinsically "Japanese" before then, it was during the Edo period, when Edo (present-day Tokyo) became the capital city, that rural rice paddies became idealized—especially through woodblock prints depicting harvesting scenes. As the city grew, so did its romanticization of the countryside.

Ogawa Pro was also interested in the Edo period because of its agrarian politics. Rice farmers had an important role in Edo society, occupying a higher strata of society than artisans and merchants—if only symbolically. In reality, farmers' material rewards were few, with landlords accumulating rice for profit. Revolting against such a situation, farmers organized agrarian riots called *yonaoshi* (world reformation).⁵⁹ In the twentieth century, despite post-war land reforms that saw 91 percent of farmland tilled by its owners by 1951, conflict over land development continued, and the term *yonaoshi* resurfaced to describe militant uprisings in the 1960s, including those that Ogawa Pro filmed at Narita airport's construction site. *Yonaoshi* resisted both American influence (including wheat imports) and Japanese corporate and state interventions in rural life.⁶⁰ Ogawa Pro filmed farmer protests at the airport and reenacted Edo-era riots in *The Sundial*, to resurrect *yonaoshi* for the screen and celebrate overlooked struggle.

Ogawa Pro also excavated deeper histories. Mid-way through *The Sundial*, an archaeological dig unearths some Jōmon pottery. Japan's Jōmon period (14,000–300 BCE) takes its name from striped pottery made in that era. Like the film's eponymous sundial, the shard of Jōmon pottery constitutes an index of time. We cut to a shot of an airplane's vapor trail—from the prehistoric to the contemporary. Jōmon pottery dates from the dawn of low-intensity farming, whereas airplanes date to the age of globalization. By rooting Yamagata villagers with their Jōmon ancestors, the film implies that the majority of Japan's post-war population (based in its urban areas) is out of sync with nature. Modernity is expelled from Ogawa Pro's idyll by being placed on a transnational vehicle whose vapor trail marks the sky and the film screen. The plane began and ended its journey elsewhere (perhaps at Narita), while Yamagata remained grounded in native tradition.[61]

The juxtaposition of pottery and plane also invites another comparison. The pottery is clay dug from the earth, fired, used for generations, discarded, buried, and exhumed again like a fossil. In photographic theory, film has been likened to a fossil because of its indexing of time and material composition of earth elements.[62] Ogawa Pro's filmed image of the pottery represents a fossil-like object in a fossil-like medium. The jet plane overhead, meanwhile, is burning fossil fuel. As if anticipating contemporary calls to "keep it in the ground" and end fossil fuel development, the film unearths pottery to recall time past and future generational responsibility.

Nippon also forwards visions of a future grounded in tradition. The characters *Nippon-Koku* appended before "Furuyashiki Village" in the film's title literally read "Japan-Country" or "Japan-Nation." *Koku* (nation) is written using the conventional Chinese character, 国. *Nippon* (Japan) is written in *katakana*, the domestic syllabary for foreign loan words (ニッポン). This denaturalization of "Japan" invites viewers to rethink ideas of nationhood and to associate the country not with recent economic growth but instead with what is on-screen: the traditional rural community of Furuyashiki.[63]

One way to describe Furuyashiki as it is presented in the film is as a *furusato*. The word *furusato* means "native place," comprising characters for "old" or "former" and "village." *Furusato* is a term used by both the Japanese state, for whom it functions similarly to American "family values" (indeed, one expression is *furusato famirii*), and environmentalists, who oppose the use of chemical fertilizers and pesticides and the development of roads, golf courses, and malls.[64] By incorporating, reinterpreting, and controlling nature, *furusato* serves environmentalism at the same time as it bolsters tourism.[65] As Tokyo's financial power and urban footprint grew in the 1970s, the *furusato* industry also spread. *Furusato* tourism continues today, often involving the transportation of city people to rural areas to partake in traditional activities such as transplanting rice seedlings and picking fruit and matsutake without having to depend on agriculture for a living. Since tourism is more lucrative than small-scale farming, villagers no longer depend on agriculture either. Japan National Railways (JNR, privatized as JR in 1987) played an important part in *furusato*. "Discover Japan," a public relations campaign that JNR ran in the 1970s, was followed by a mail-order service for regional foods and souvenirs and a magazine combining information about domestic tourism, rural real estate, farming, and green lifestyles.[66]

The Yamagata villager who first invited Ogawa Pro to the area hoped that the collective would help revitalize the region into a youthful cultural center. In turn, Ogawa Pro hoped that Yamagata's old-style culture could lend their films a rural "essence." Even Furuyashiki village's name was perfect, containing the same character (*furu*, "old") as that of *furusato*. The irony is hard to miss. In connecting the country and the city by rail and film, JNR and Ogawa Pro's *furusato* initiatives reinforced the romanticized "difference" of rural areas, despite how economically useful these initiatives may also have been.

Ogawa Pro's films associate *furusato* with embodied experience. Muddy and grinning in their fieldwork, Ogawa Pro members admired Mao's emphasis on physical experience (*taiken*, or *tiyan* as it is rendered in Mandarin). In speeches in the early 1920s, Mao claimed that unless people investigated a problem by "learning from the experience of real life" (*tiyan shenghuo*), they had no right to speak about it.[67] Ogawa replicated such rhetoric: "If you don't live in the region, you can't film it."[68] Iizuka spoke similarly: "You can't simply think about rice. You have to do it. . . . Living communally, these values displace profit and personal gain."[69]

The emphasis on empirical, embodied learning recalls a common phrase in Japanese for "learning a skill," *mi ni tsukeru*. Ogawa Pro aspired to learn farming skills so well that they became affixed (*tsukeru*) to the body (*mi*). Farming skills and climatic conditions would imbue filmmaker, film, and audience as a form of political and environmentalist immersion. Several years into their project in Yamagata, Ogawa declared that "the feeling of the sun was documented (was filmed, was imprinted) into our bodies."[70] They were learning about the environment by becoming, in a sense, human sundials while their films (including *The Sundial*) developed photochemical images alongside them. Ogawa's words liken filmmaker to filmstrip, with the skin of the (plant-based celluloid) film and the skin of the filmmaker reacting to sunlight through growth.

Filtering definitions of growth and profit through the sunlight, air, paddies, seedlings, and politics of their fieldwork, Ogawa Pro aimed for an ecologically expansive economy of shared learning and sustenance. This expansive approach required learning to hear the "voices of the rice plants."[71] Through their lenses, Ogawa Pro learned how to judge rice quality from the color and texture of its leaves. They kept a weather record to measure changes in temperature, humidity, wind direction, and precipitation; inspected the soil, measuring its proportions of clay and nutrients; and studied slides under a microscope to track minuscule processes of rice bloom, pollination, and fertilization.[72] Recalling Margaret Tait's marvel upon filming a flower bloom in time lapse, Ogawa Pro used modern camera and microscope technologies to understand other forms of life, and growth. Shuttling their camera through muddy dykes and lingering with saplings swaying in the breeze, the filmmakers sensitized themselves to the land and its atmospheric conditions, anticipating—as I explore in Chapter 3—the climatic connotations of the word for landscape in Japanese, *fūkei*, which comprises characters for wind (*fū* 風) and scene (*kei* 景).

Sound amplifies this focus. Whereas *Nippon* contains synchronous sound recorded with one microphone on a boom, *The Sundial* features Foley sound that simulates the rustle of rice ears, the squelch of wet soil, and the chirruping of birds. Ogawa claimed that such creativity was only possible because we had documented the rice field for such a long time. That's why the re-enactment is flawless.... [I]t was a process of nearly thirteen years to know what reality really is.... That is what I call *document*.... It's what has been remembered from all those days for over ten years in the depth of the physiology of the body.[73]

The demands on an audience to immerse themselves in films as long and peculiar as Ogawa Pro's replicate this emphasis on committed labor. The sheer length of Ogawa Pro's sojourn in Yamagata also plays into it, tending toward tropes of authenticity that Trinh criticizes as territorializing strategies in documentary filmmaking.[74] And yet, Ogawa Pro's commitment was radical. Expanding perspectives beyond metropolitan and anthropocentric fields, their work anticipates the many permaculture practices that Tsing celebrates for forming "livable collaborations" "amidst the trouble" of capitalist extraction and climate change.[75]

Watching the man in the photograph pull soil into the levee, opening space for the seedlings, we might think of Somankidi Coura building irrigation channels with soil from a termite mound without harming the queen, who was still inside and could regenerate it. As Grisey has written, these activities signify the collective's understanding of ecosystems. Whereas colonial plantation agriculture and its continued separations of humans from nature would associate such care with primitive animism, Somankidi Coura cultivated a post-extractive project for ecological (and geopolitical) respect in which animals, soils, and humans co-produce abundance and diversity.[76] One of Somankidi Coura's broadcasts on the regional radio it established in 1988 is dedicated to farmers' other-than-human friends, because "forever, our elders have collaborated with the termites," the host explains, knowing that "permacultures of the Sahel" encompass "the collective intelligence of soil, plants and animals."

In Figure 10, light is fading on a day of harvesting bananas. A young man presents a bushel of them to the camera, perfect in their green-yellow skins. They'll sell these bananas at the cooperative market tomorrow to buy fuel for the river pump, along with anything else needed beyond what they grow for themselves.

FIGURE 10. First banana harvest, Somankidi Coura, Mali, 1979. Photograph by Bouba Touré. Estate of Bouba Touré. Thanks to Raphaël Grisey.

Unlike the sisal produced here for rope making a century earlier as part of what Romain Tiquet calls a colonial coercion economy,[77] these bananas do not represent a "banana republic," that is, a politically unstable state dominated by a single export economy controlled by foreign capital. These bananas will not feed the story of how Europe underdeveloped Africa through extraction, export, and debt.[78] Instead, these bananas symbolize ripening communities and food-sovereignty, having grown in twenty-five riverside hectares of polyculture gardens fed by a common irrigation system, alongside adjacent land used alternatively for pasture in the dry season and permaculture farming during the three-month monsoon.

The photograph recalls the words of one of the cooperative's revered teachers, Amílcar Cabral (whose poster decorated Touré's wall in 2008). Cabral described culture as the "fruit" of history as well as its determinant in resisting the "implantation" of "foreign domination."[79] Culture was key to Cabral in leading liberation movements in Lusophone Africa. Touré did not know Cabral's writings on agronomy in the 1970s but admired his speeches on the importance of culture in driving political resistance.[80] According to Cabral, imperialism encompassed both formal colonialism and socioeconomic neocolonialism. "National liberation" was "an act of culture," he said, and cinema could help establish "a strong indigenous cultural life."[81] Literacy therefore included visual literacy, and Cabral supported several filmmakers from Guinea-Bissau in trips to Cuba's revolutionary film school to learn how to document struggles for land and freedom.[82]

Between 1949 and 1950, Cabral worked as an agronomist for the Portuguese regime while secretly helping anti-colonial organization. Conducting experiments in pedology on the colonial farm, he came to understand plantation logic from the inside, recognizing the toll that over-intensive farming took on soil vitality as inextricably linked to the toll that colonial capitalism took on its subjects (he too read Marx's work on metabolic rift, which derived in turn from soil science).[83] As if reclaiming colony's etymological connections with farming, which it shares with the word "culture," Cabral developed an anti-colonial argument for the importance of simultaneously helping lands and labor forces exhausted under imperialism through cultural and agricultural work. "Every land has its own natural wealth," he declared.[84] "Progress" (a word Cabral used multiple times in his speeches) was a combined ecological and social movement toward liberation.[85]

This democratic and environmental understanding of progress contrasts with that of the French colonial administration in West Africa, whose project for "creating value" (*mise en valeur*) attempted to develop supposedly "vacant" lands and "lazy" Africans (lumped together within a category of "Indigenous people") by using forced migration from "labor reservoirs" in other regions including present-day Burkina Faso.[86] *Mise en valeur* stocked France with cotton, peanuts, cacao, minerals, and sisal. Extractive practices continued in the post-war period, packaged within verbiage that replaced *mise en valeur* with a persuasion vocabulary of development and modernization, steeped in all the prejudice these terms imply. Touré's photograph refuses such prejudice, presenting instead the fruit of collective cultural and agricultural labor.

Taking his camera into the field and overturning its plantation logic through mixed crops and cooperative labor, Touré also resists the historical twinning of cinema and city within a thesis of modernity that privileges the urban factory (not least the Lumière brothers' own factory in Lyon). Urban modernity, Touré suggests, began not in the factory or the street but instead in the rural plantation upon which the metropole's wealth depends. As Debashree Mukherjee has recently explored, an archival tracing of early photography reveals this underacknowledged connection in its depictions of plantations as exotic curiosities.[87] Intervening in this extractive history, Touré takes the camera back to the plantation, this time in African hands, to reframe land as local sustenance and cinema as a source of anti-colonial solidarity.

In Figure 11, a van parks outside a thatched farmhouse with a banner announcing an Ogawa Pro screening. This is grassroots distribution, the dissemination of images and ideas to help marginalized farmers and a burgeoning environmental movement. By the 1970s, Japan's common forestlands of red pines and matsutake had given way to monoculture cedar and cypress plantations for the timber trade. Villagers increasingly used kerosene and electricity and farmed with tractors (despite what Ogawa Pro's films suggest).[88] Amid such decline and against a tide of industrial construction, several environmentalists looked toward ancient methods of low-intensity land cultivation to develop more sustainable forms of agriculture. Ogawa Pro followed their work with interest and contributed to it with film.

Organicism and a no-till method of farming received increasing attention due to the popularity of Fukuoka Masanobu's 1975 book *One-Straw Revolution*. Ariyoshi Sawako's study of the impact of chemical fertilizers also impressed Ogawa Pro members when it was serialized in Japan's major newspaper and published as a book. Much like Rachel Carson's *Silent Spring* (1962), Ariyoshi's book contributed to raising environmental awareness. This was a moment of budding green politics when many activist groups formed, including Japan's recycling movement and the Association to Protect the Earth. It was also a moment

FIGURE 11. Ogawa Pro films on tour. Thanks to Markus Nornes, Hatano Yukie, and the Narita Airport and Community Historical Museum.

when many artists and filmmakers went "back to the land" to challenge notions of center and periphery. Being *zaiya* (in the wilderness) gained a positive connotation of not participating in institutional systems.[89] As Bert Winther-Tamaki notes, much Japanese earth art of the time, particularly lens-based work, contrasted country and city so that urban audiences could consume images of soil as an antidote to their crowded, consumerist, and polluted surroundings.[90]

Ogawa Pro's screenings attempted to offer audiences similarly earthy experiences. The farmhouse in the photograph anticipates a temporary mud and thatch theater that Ogawa Pro would build near Kyoto to screen *The Sundial*. Unlike some cinemas in Tokyo that hushed audiences into black-box screenings, Ogawa Pro gathered people under one roof to sit on straw bales surrounded by objects from the films, local food stalls, and dance troops. The van in the photograph is a metaphor for film as an interlocutor, in transit between locations and audiences.

Ogawa thrived on audience interactions and loved inviting other filmmakers to the collective's farmhouse. Yamagata International Documentary Film Festival continued this hospitality, hosting filmmakers including Safi Faye, Haile Gerima, and Kidlat Tahimik. Made in 1976 and 1977, Faye's *Letter from My Village*, Gerima's *Harvest: 3000 Years*, and Tahimik's *Perfumed Nightmare* present portraits of rural land and communities suffering foreign impositions of DDT, monoculture, and consumerism. Made at a time when television was fast spreading, these films and Ogawa Pro's thatched theater constitute an anti-TV model of documentary.

In Paris, meanwhile, Touré was developing a similarly direct and discursive approach to screening.

In Figure 12, eleven men occupy a hostel room. One man helps another read from a book, following words with his pen. Some wear prayer caps. Some talk, and others listen. Two single beds have more mattresses pushed beneath them. Luggage piles above a cupboard, and plastic bags holding clothes hang on hooks. Images line the walls, several taken in the fields at Somankidi Coura and brought here with Touré on one of his many trips between Mali and France ("smuggling ideas, seeds, photographs, modes of resistance, and farming methods from one continent to the other").[91]

Touré describes all of his images as photos "of our actual life" (never "my life" or "their life"). His collective pronoun refuses divisions of homeland and exile, constructing a poetics of relation, to borrow from Edouard Glissant, or an internationalist localism, to echo Kuan-Hsing Chen.[92] Rejecting both the universalizing approaches of globalization and a rhetoric of localism that can disguise parochial oppression, Touré communicates shared but differential relations to extractivism and reveals routes to justice.

Touré's images are not always celebratory or comfortable. Although this photograph speaks of solidarity, literacy efforts, and connections with families back home, it also reveals the financial and legal precarity of migrant workers. Some of these men are sleeping on mattresses that

FIGURE 12. Room 5, with photographs of the fields of Somankidi Coura on the walls, Foyer Pinel, Saint-Denis, 2003. Photograph by Bouba Touré. Estate of Bouba Touré. Thanks to Raphaël Grisey.

their fathers used before them, experiencing reruns of dispossession, exodus, and racism as a past that is not past. Yet Touré's photographs are not what Trinh scathingly calls "'feed the poor' images of Africa" and its migrants. They do not serve a missionary appetite and "ease the consciences of the rich" while hiding ties between world hunger and imperialism.[93] Touré's images hide nothing. Here are tired workers, solidarity meetings, and seeded, sprouting fields. Hunger doesn't need a handout, Touré suggests, but does need healthy soil in which to grow sustenance, sustain independence, and render emigration a choice, not a necessity. Somankidi Coura's establishment reconfigured colonial centers and margins, its growing archive of images circulating across borders as an ongoing project for spatial justice. These are oppositional and propositional images, made in resistance to extractive predation and in creative and practical approaches to the future.

FIGURE 13. Fortieth anniversary of Somankidi Coura, Mali, exhibition of the photographic archive of Bouba Touré, January 2017. Stills from Raphaël Grisey. Estate of Bouba Touré. Thanks to Raphaël Grisey.

In Figure 13, men, women, and children gather around images pinned to the gable of a farm building. Goats and chickens flock through the center of the photograph and along the village path. This is an installation shot of an exhibition of Touré's photographs hung in Somankidi Coura to celebrate its fortieth anniversary in 2017.

The displayed photographs depict Somankidi Coura's development, including its construction and harvests; the production of a play Touré wrote in 1977 to explore issues of migration; Somankidi Coura's radio station, a regional farmer's network, educational programs held in Bambara, Soninke, and Fula languages; and the growth of the community over three generations. Cultivating democracy, film, vegetables, and goats in this multifunctional way, Somankidi Coura re-paired estranged species and regions, nurturing a future around and against the Plantationocene. Fieldwork fortified the struggle against emigration, with soil and political literacy growing through practice to produce yields not of GDP but instead of agronomic health, sustainable food sources, cooperative employment, community education, and, not least, a panoply of cultural productions made by the workers, for the workers, and for sharing internationally.

The images that Somankidi Coura and Ogawa Pro produced are historical documents and future-oriented ideologies. Although the rice paddies that Ogawa Pro once cultivated have grown into jungle and wild monkeys occupy the thatched farmhouses, the collective's films continue to draw audiences with their unusual forms and contexts of political commitment, influencing contemporary filmmakers (including several I discuss in Chapter 6). Viewed today amid escalating social inequality and climate breakdown, Ogawa Pro's and Somankidi Coura's ecological experiments present compelling alternatives to financialized definitions of growth and progress. Both projects transformed the idea of subsistence farming from a minimal support for survival to the word's original sense of continuing to exist and standing firm: to set, to settle, to sit, to subsist. "To subsist" and "to sustain" share a root word, meaning "from below." Re-routing (and re-rooting) themselves in the soil, Somankidi Coura and Ogawa Pro stood firm, staying with the social and ecological trouble of extractivism.[94] Subsistence re-centered them through slow processes of farming and solidarity, absorbed like nutrients from the soil, like light on the skin of the film.

THREE

There Is No Countryside

THE ANTI-PASTORAL

"THE SYSTEM OF CONTROL is there wherever you look as you walk around, starting with things like the signs in train stations warning people, 'Danger! Please walk to this side.' It may be done in a polite way, but everything is monitored."[1] These are the words of the filmmaker, activist, and self-described anarchist Adachi Masao (b. 1939). Around 1969, Adachi began monitoring how everything was monitored.

If you met Adachi, who was barely thirty, peering at the world with angular intent from under thick eyebrows and jet-black hair, you might ask what exactly he was filming. Likely he would be standing with his tripod at a railway crossing or road junction—some nondescript, functional space of transportation and manufacturing infrastructure. He'd tell you he was making a landscape film. But his film would represent nothing like the rice paddy landscapes discussed in Chapter 2 that his contemporaries at Ogawa Pro cultivated. Adachi trained his camera on "incongruous groups of tidy buildings" that "sprouted and shot off into the horizon," on crash barriers bolted to curbs, on workers' housing, and on "villages where citizens had made their daily lives" that had been "replaced with concrete and turned into highways." "Even in the landscape of pre-harvest fields," he'd say, pointing to rows of sunflowers or radishes, "there hovered a suffocating air of efficiency and mass production."[2] Though these mundane images were the only visuals that Adachi's film would contain, its title would point toward something else: *A.K.A. Serial Killer.*

LANDSCAPE = POWER

Adachi was one of several leftist filmmakers in the late 1960s and early 1970s who represented Japanese landscapes as banal, urban expanses of commerce and transportation. This loosely formed group, which also comprised photographers and writers, called their ideas landscape theory, or *fūkeiron* (風景論). "All the landscapes which one faces in one's daily life," Adachi explained, "are essentially related to the figure of a ruling power."³ Adachi's collaborator and co-director on *A.K.A Serial Killer*, the film critic Matsuda Masao (b. 1933), put it even more starkly: "*fūkei* = power."⁴

The power that Matsuda and Adachi identified as dominating Japan in the 1960s was capitalist. Although US occupation of mainland Japan ended in 1952 (and in Okinawa twenty years later), Article 9 of the postwar constitution forbade rearmament. All emphasis was placed on manufacturing and consumerism in a project serving America's Cold War strategy to suppress communism. By 1969, Japan's economy was growing at a rate three times that of the United States and Britain. The world's largest advertising company was Japanese. "Consumption is a virtue" became a catchphrase. The nation's population exceeded one hundred million, with Tokyo becoming the most populous city in the world with over ten million.⁵ But as Adachi saw, focusing his lens on shabby housing and rivers paved over with roads, economic, technological, and infrastructural growth came at a cost, exhausting workers and polluting landscapes.

Heedless to such problems, in 1970 Japan hosted a flashy World Expo in Osaka (billboards promoting Expo appear in *A.K.A. Serial Killer*). Tokyo had already hosted the Olympics in 1964, parading its economic recovery and Western affiliation. The Olympics and Expo appeared as GDP triumphs due to the resource-intensive infrastructure projects they entailed. The trickle-down effects of the Olympics and the Expo were meager if not devastating, as Tsuchimoto Noriaki's *On the Road: A Document* (1964) painfully reveals by portraying overworked taxi drivers navigating construction work, unprecedented congestion, and accidents in the lead-up to the Olympics. The Olympics and the Expo construction sites also displaced hundreds of low-income Japanese and migrant families and saw a boom in security and surveillance industries with the introduction of closed-circuit television cameras.[6]

Pointing his own camera at this bleak situation in 1969, Adachi filmed roads, railways, ferry ports, factories, office blocks, workers' housing, and shopping malls as evidence of the regulatory power of state, corporate, and global alliances. Rather than champion endangered images of agrarian life as Ogawa Pro and Margaret Tait did, Adachi aimed to disrupt associations between land and aesthetic pleasure by exposing the political and economic underpinnings of space. As Yuriko Furuhata writes, in *fūkeiron*'s rendering, landscape conditions everyday experience by controlling spatial mobility and social relations.[7] Commerce is encouraged, and political gathering is suppressed. Such regulation "may be done in a polite way," Adachi noted, but everything and everyone is monitored—even radishes and sunflowers look orderly in *A.K.A Serial Killer*. Unlike the rural imaginaries discussed in preceding chapters, *fūkeiron* presents an anti-pastoral aesthetic in which there is no countryside left.[8] Land has become a concretization of capital.

As a counternarrative to the rural and pastoral, *fūkeiron* wields significant eco-political power, rooting itself in the city and the fast-urbanizing regions that Adachi described as "Tokyo-copies."[9] Lodging themselves in centers of industry, consumption, and waste, *fūkeiron* practitioners created films, photographs, and essays that critiqued the present from within. In so doing, *fūkeiron* proposes an alternative definition of landscape and nature to that which Anna Tsing describes as colored by a "patina of romance" and associations with purity, wilderness, and a separation from modern culture.[10] *Fūkeiron* presents entanglement.

In *The Mushroom at the End of the World: On the Possibility of Life in Capitalist Ruins* (2015), Tsing advances an alternative understanding of nature to that patinaed one. She describes "third nature" as that which "manages to live despite capitalism" (if the first nature signifies balanced ecological relations and the second signifies capitalist extractivist

FIGURE 14. Accelerated landscape in *A.K.A. Serial Killer*. Frame enlargement.

transformations of that environment). Tsing is thinking not of *fūkeiron* when she offers examples of what can thrive within third nature but rather the Japanese forest mushroom, or matsutake. Her analysis, however, is useful for considering forms of visual culture such as *fūkeiron* that grow within and against capitalist conditions. Tsing is interested in the way matsutake withstands pollution and circulates inside and beyond commodity chains. Matsutake behavior inspires her to consider the creative possibility of "contamination"—of living in close proximity to diverse substances and growing with them.[11] Produced within a contaminating context of economic growth and its social and ecological destruction, *fūkeiron* images and texts circulated as records of injustice. Applying Tsing's understanding of third nature to *fūkeiron*'s politicized photographs, films, and texts produces a kind of environmentalism that dissolves the patina of the pastoral (Figure 14).

This chapter and Chapter 4 go in search of the ecological potential of the anti-pastoral as I explore what it means to engage with non-pristine nature as a form of environmentalism. Learning from Leanne Betasamosake Simpson's articulation, I define this kind of environmentalism as one that includes ecologically damaged land as opposed to just that which is considered beautiful, wild, or picturesque.[12] Writing during the hottest summer on record, with the news reporting lethal climate symptoms, I welcome the anti-pastoral for developing an environmental relation with land that is parched, flooded, fracked, filled with electronic waste, ring-fenced for financial speculation, or colonized by a carbon offsetting industry profiting from continued emissions. My focus in this chapter on *fūkeiron*'s proposition of land as a contaminated site of capitalist entanglement—and eco-political expression—feels as urgent now as it did to Adachi, filming at the roadside in 1969. Adachi continues to film Japanese landscapes today, though no one foresaw his trajectory in the interim.

ENTANGLED ECOLOGIES

Around 1970, *fūkeiron* ideas and aesthetics came to be known among left-leaning student and artist audiences via the photography and film journals *Film Quarterly* (*Kikan firumu*) and *Film Criticism* (*Eiga Hihyō*), where Adachi and others used the term *fūkeiron* to discuss the anticapitalist potential of documenting spatial homogeneity as social oppression. Another key *fūkeiron* figure contributing to these journals was Nakahira Takuma (1937–2015).

An elfin poet and essayist, Nakahira emerged as one of Japan's most important photographers in the late 1960s. Photography's possibilities for representing somatic experiences of modern urban life enthralled him. Through his camera, he could catch life on the fly in a blurry, headlong rush of movement. His images of roadsides, office blocks, and alleyways capture mundane spaces in glimpses made strange by grainy shadows and blurs. Nakahira's photographs and writings would come to define this moment of politicized urban creativity alongside a small but significant cluster of films.

Four *fūkei eiga* (landscape films) epitomize *fūkeiron*, though they were little known at the time beyond their makers' descriptions in journals and occasional screenings at underground filmmakers' spaces in Tokyo in the early 1970s. Each is a feature film that elides documentary and fiction. *A.K.A. Serial Killer* was the first, made in 1969 by Adachi and Matsuda in collaboration with the screenwriter Sasaki Mamoru and a small crew.[13] The film's title in Japanese is *Ryakushō: Renzoku shasatsuma*, literally "Abbreviation: Serial Shooter." Its sporadic voice-over reveals the origin of its title as it relays facts about the capture of a real-life murderer. We never see the film's eponymous killer, however, only the landscapes he would have witnessed as he fled police across Japan.

Made the following year, Ōshima Nagisa's *Story of a Man Who Left His Will on Film* (its Japanese title translating as "The Secret History of the Post–Tokyo War Period"), also involves fugitivity and death. The film presents footage of quotidian urban landscapes as mysterious evidence found on the camera of a student activist after his suicide. Hara Masato's 1973 film *The First Emperor* originally ran close to seven hours and was entirely composed of generic location shots intended as backdrops for an unmade film about Japanese history. Takamine Gō's 1974 film *Okinawan Dream Show* comprises landscape footage taken across Okinawa in the aftermath of US occupation, presenting a critique of neocolonial and militaristic oppression. In each film, landscape is the protagonist. Landscape (*fūkei*) = power.

My focus here is *A.K.A. Serial Killer*, which provides a model of *fūkeiron*'s political aesthetics and influenced photographers including Nakahira, who identified with its fugitive killer "wander[ing] about from place to place."[14]

No one knew the motive of Nagayama Norio, the nineteen-year-old upon whose story *A.K.A. Serial Killer* is based. He was a migrant laborer from Hokkaido, Japan's most northerly area and, at least historically, a socioeconomically and ethnically marginalized one that is home to the Ainu people. In late 1968 Nagayama broke into a US military base, stole a gun, and shot four civilians before going on the run.

Young Nagayama's extremism, Adachi suggested, was a symptom of his "threatened sense of existence," his actions provoked by a larger codified form of structural violence embedded in a "landscape being expropriated by power."[15] "Certainly it was not only Nagayama," Adachi explained, but also "all the people who lived in these transformed places" who felt angry and alienated, "so we were convinced that Nagayama, with gun in hand, kept firing at this landscape itself."[16] This was not the last time Adachi would be drawn to crime.

Using Nagayama's story as a vehicle to drive a political message, Adachi and Matsuda traveled through Japan in 1969 with their crew and camera to trace the fugitive's route. On the trip, Adachi recalled that "every place you went in Japan was turning into small urban zones modelled on Tokyo, and even the historic scenery of famous places was transformed into commercialized tourist spots through catchphrases used in television campaigns, like 'Discover Japan.'"[17] Matsuda was similarly cynical toward rural tourism on the trip. His essay "The City as Landscape," included in his major film-theoretical book, provocatively titled *The Extinction of Landscape* (1971), questions the very existence of rural place:

> Whether in the center, the countryside, the city or the periphery, ... now there is only a homogenized landscape.... We must recognize that at the end of the 1960s the schematic opposition between "Tokyo" and "homeland" [*furusato*] can no longer have currency. The rapid growth of Japanese monopoly capital blatantly makes clear its aim of the increasing homogenization of the Japanese archipelago as one gigantic city.[18]

Matsuda uses the word *furusato*, which we encountered in Chapter 2 as an important concept and industry that ignites imaginaries centered on home, rural tradition, and nationhood. *A.K.A. Serial Killer*'s depictions of Japan are an affront to *furusato*'s pastoralism.

Adachi explained that "precisely because [shots in *A.K.A. Serial Killer* resemble] picture postcards, I realized that this was the source of our suffocation."[19] The allusion to postcards is surprising if we imagine picturesque *furusato* images but not if we understand Adachi to mean generic, reproducible views. Seen today, *A.K.A. Serial Killer* does contain quaint scenes, including clothes hanging to dry between workers' houses and provincial train stations at sunset. Not every landscape is dull or ugly. But the landscapes are generic. Together they comprise a catalog of normativity. Schoolchildren in immaculate navy and white uniforms cycle along tidy roads, the slow beat of a drum on the soundtrack signaling their controlled procession and their formation prefiguring that of the somber uniform-clad riot police who line Tokyo's streets at the end of the film, suppressing political demonstration. The cumulative effect of such images is that our recognition of them as unremarkable becomes a form of complicity through normalization.

Scenes such as these, I argue, reveal *fūkeiron*'s specifically *eco*-political significance. Building on existing studies of *fūkeiron*'s anti-capitalist politics by scholars including Furuhata and Franz Prichard, I want to bring Tsing's metaphor of contamination to a conceptualization of environmentalism appropriate to third nature's landscapes.[20] *Fūkeiron* and *A.K.A. Serial Killer* present a form of eco-political resistance that refuses pastoral imaginaries and exposes their normative function.

Indications of this eco-political potential lie within *fūkeiron* practitioners' own statements. Nakahira, for example, summarized *fūkeiron*'s goal in a 1972 essay as being "to crack open" landscapes "in a deeply practice-based way" using photography, film, and text. "I am like a scrawny dog," he wrote with characteristic flair, "sniffing about for a weak crevice" or "a single crack in this complete landscape" that was "uniformly sealed-up [and] sustained by power itself."[21]

Nakahira had also traveled through Japan at the turn of the decade, documenting "the expanse of a uniform landscape" and noting his own insider/outsider position as both alienated from the environment and unable to escape it.[22] He recalled feeling "forced to confront this [landscape ... and the fact that] all that passes through it are accomplices to the crime."[23] Capturing the built environment in shaky snatches as he walked or ran, Nakahira was fascinated by the contingencies of taking a photograph, finding in them an important critique of individual artistic "expression," which he associated with capitalist modernity's emphasis on an auteur, artist, or author's "style."[24] Being grainy, blurred, and out of focus (literally *"are bure boke,"* a phrase now synonymous with Nakahira's work and Japanese photography of the era) was not about being at the vanguard of a new photographic style, he argued. Being grainy, blurred, and out of focus were qualities of experience.

To consolidate his ideas and images, Nakahira began a photographic journal called *Provoke: Provocative Materials for Thought* in 1969 with a group of critic, poet, and photographer friends.[25] *Provoke*'s subtitle gestures at the fact that the images and essays gathered in the journal's three editions were conceptual, not just stylistic. Nakahira's thinking about being grainy, blurred, and out of focus was political.

For Nakahira, the embodied experience of visual perception and the experience of being a body in a world of geopolitical and sociohistorical transformation were experiences of entanglement with a larger condition or ecology of forces ("Ecologies of Japan" was the title of a series of photographs Nakahira published in *Asahi Camera* in 1969). There is no stable view from nowhere in Nakahira's images. "Rather than the world as a statically completed space," he wrote, "the world has been transformed, becoming a flowing, transfiguring, and endlessly mutating nebula that changes shape with each shifting vantage point."[26] "Ecologies of Japan" contained images taken aboard late-night commuter trains as drunken passengers dozed under a ceiling hung with advertisements. Nakahira used a low angle and a slow shutter speed to retain the sense of being a seated passenger "shaken and blurred together" on the train.[27] His aesthetic disrupted any sense of superiority (as in being able to see and therefore control from above). *Are bure boke* visualized *fūkeiron*'s emphasis on entanglement.

Tireless in his experimentation, Nakahira did not stick to *are bure boke* for long, as the aesthetic was soon appropriated by the very media economy he aimed to resist. Even the "Discover Japan" campaign that Adachi criticized for peddling touristic images adopted *are bure boke* aesthetics. In response to that campaign, Nakahira produced a series of photographs for *Asahi Camera* in May 1972 called "Discovered Japan." Titling his series in the past tense, he inserted his images as a corrective and contradiction. The series cataloged grubby alleyways, pool halls, old electric poles, and trash.[28]

By contradicting romanticized imaginaries in this way (Figure 15), Nakahira intended to dislodge "binaries of the urban-rural and the modern-native ... whereby the urban rules the rural, the modern rules the premodern, and ... [w]hat penetrates ... is the logic of Japanese monopoly capitalism itself."[29] Nakahira, Adachi, and Matsuda couched *fūkeiron* in Marxist terms derived from class struggle and alienation, but here I want to tease out the ecological potential of their approach.

FIGURE 15. Takuma Nakahira, "For a Language to Come" (from the photobook published in 1970). © Gen Nakahira © Takuma Nakahira. Courtesy of Osiris.

As John Bellamy Foster and Kohei Saito have shown, environmental concerns were central to Marx's developing thought.[30] Though some eco-socialists have emphasized Marx's interest in how the capitalist mode of production causes ecological problems due to its insatiable drive for accumulation, Saito sees much Marxist scholarship as underplaying its environmental potential.[31] Reading Marx with contemporary climate crisis in mind, Saito aims to address this oversight and in so doing celebrate the work of Japanese scholars lesser known in the West who have long focused on Marx's studies of worker exploitation and ecological degradation as related forms of social and environmental violence.[32]

Uncovering *fūkeiron*'s eco-political aspects contributes to Saito's application of Marxism to climate justice with specifically visual (and audiovisual) modes of engagement. Bringing *fūkeiron* to ecological Marxism also expands existing *fūkeiron* studies in timely eco-political directions, presenting it as an important anti-pastoral approach within land cinema.

Fūkeiron's central eco-political argument concerns extractivism, which Marx describes in terms of stealing. Within industrial capitalist societies, Marx writes, "a greedy farmer snatches more produce from the soil by robbing it of its fertility," and a factory owner "exhausts" and "robs" workers.[33] *Fūkeiron* visualizes such crimes by cataloging exhausted yet obedient landscapes of mass production. Such scenes also evidence a keen understanding of what Marx calls a "rift" driven between nature and society under intensive industrialism, whereby the balance (which Marx likens to a metabolic process) between nature and human activities is disrupted and the distance between country and city, producer and consumer, widens.[34] Far from natural, the uniform sunflower crops in *A.K.A. Serial Killer* resemble factory production lines.

Young Nagayama's unseen presence meanwhile imbues the film with a sense of threat, encouraging audiences to search each scene for him. The process of searching entertains the possibility that something greater is hiding in plain sight, hovering in the air. Perhaps it is this greater presence that is driving people such as Nagayama to violence with a menacing atmosphere of suffocation, control, and alienation.[35]

A Marxist definition of alienation identifies workers as being estranged from the object that their labor produces, from their labor power as an activity that belongs to them, from humanity's ability to labor for ends other than profit, and from other humans with whom they are forced into antagonistic competition.[36] Nagayama's situation exemplifies these aspects of estrangement, judging by his poor, isolated, and itinerant life described in the film's voice-over.

As Marx became more familiar with agronomy, he began to relate social alienation to the devastation of the natural world.[37] Similar to the ways in which factories pressured workers into long shifts of repetitive, accelerated labor, Marx noted, modern agri-business maximized plants' absorption of soil nutrition so they could be traded and exported as fast as possible. Acceleration was key. In *A.K.A. Serial Killer* the sunflower crops bob in obedient agreement: growth and progress are afforded one meaning under capitalism, which is that of financialized profit. Technological development in postwar Japan, including the adoption of monoculture varieties bred for uniformity and fast growth, and the replacement of night soil with artificial fertilizer attempted to accelerate nature's cycles.

A.K.A. Serial Killer accentuates ideas of acceleration through formal means. In the film's opening sequence, footage of trains is sped up and spliced into a concatenation of punctuality, forming a visual analog for what David Harvey describes as capitalism's "space-time compression."[38] Footage of commuters at ticket turnstiles in the subway also seems sped up, though it is not; the commuters, like the sunflower crops, help oil the machine.

Throughout the film we see different and evolving kinds of transportation infrastructure, beginning with horse-drawn carts waiting at a dock in northern Japan that give way to coal-fueled steam locomotives and, later in the film, electric trains. In scenes shot in Tokyo, the world's first high-speed train glides through the surrounding buildings on its elevated track. Launched in 1964 to coincide with the Olympics, this train and technology were new. Its shiny white units, with a continuous blue stripe and small windows, appear like a tube, a snake, an alien hybrid of animal and machine. Colloquially known as the bullet train due to its streamlined design and high velocity, the train's moniker seems disquietingly apt for its appearance in a film about a serial shooter. The bullet train's first model, featured in the film, was called the Series 0 Hikari, *hikari* being the word for "light." Shooting through the landscape, seemingly at the speed of light, the train offered Adachi a metaphor, a vehicle, for thinking about space-time compression.

Footage shot from inside a taxi in *A.K.A. Serial Killer* is sped up so fast that the sequence, extended over three minutes, is nightmarish. Cutting the standard frame rate with which we are accustomed to seeing motion, Adachi conjures a world of headlong panic. Without an over-the-shoulder perspective as a buffer, we occupy the passenger seat as a hostage with no indication of where or how our journey will end. Resembling a "phantom ride" genre popular in early cinema, where footage was shot from a vehicle moving through a city or a landscape at speed, the sequence nods at film's own modern and urban-centric, historical development.[39] But in *fūkeiron*'s lens, a political critique of urban modernity drives the sequence; this is no celebratory cinema.

Anticipating a crash, the audience is held in suspense, with the film suggesting that the capitalist metropolis will speed on farther and faster toward its own destruction. Writing at the same time as Adachi and Matsuda were hurtling through Japan, István Mészáros explored Marx's work on metabolic rift. The more capitalism "unlocks the powers of productivity," he wrote, "the more it must unleash the powers of destruction; and the more it extends the volume of production, the more it must bury everything under mountains of suffocating waste."[40] The brinkmanship that Mészáros describes characterizes what Marx sees as one of capitalism's fundamental contradictions, whereby "progress" is inseparable from destruction and "growth" cannot avoid waste. *A.K.A. Serial Killer* keeps us in the present, on the road, to enact this catastrophic refusal of consequences. It is as if the state has marginalized Nagayama so much that he has become invisible, swallowed up by the landscape that races on, unstoppable, unlivable.

FRAMING VIOLENCE

A.K.A. Serial Killer was never widely distributed, likely due to its lack of narrative progression and informational guidance. In contrast with more explanatory modes that Matsuda and others associated with documentary's early exponents Robert Flaherty and John Grierson (whose establishment values and narrative arcs Margaret Tait disliked), Matsuda described *A.K.A. Serial Killer* as "a strange work—which can only be called an 'actual-landscape film' rather than a documentary."[41] Formally, *A.K.A. Serial Killer* appears more like the actuality films of early cinema than mid-century documentary films in both sequences such as that phantom taxi ride and the film's overall lack of character and narrative exposition.[42]

In withholding narrative unity, *A.K.A. Serial Killer* aimed to provoke politicized consciousness among a leftist avant-garde audience of students, artists, writers, and countercultural figures in music, theater, and film, many of whom Adachi knew. Celebrated anti-establishment directors including Ōshima Nagisa and Wakamatsu Kōji supported the film. Adachi knew Wakamatsu well, having worked as a writer and director at his production company in the mid-1960s making political, experimental, and pornographic films.

These men fashioned themselves as agents of provocative, scandalous experimentation. They had entered university as mass protests against the Treaty of Mutual Cooperation and Security between the United States and Japan (in Japan commonly known as Anpo jōyaku, or simply Anpo) erupted across campuses and a wave of student politicization swept Japan into exhilarating unrest. Adachi began filmmaking at the Nihon University Film Study Club (better known as Nichidai Eiken) and later co-founded the VAN Film Science Research Center, an experimental cooperative with ties to Neo-Dada and anti-art scenes. Dadaism's rejection of establishment values and anti-art's emancipation from aesthetic genres was appealing. "I didn't make any categorical distinction between art and politics," Adachi declared. "Political language had been enervated by categorization, and having constructed their own cages of 'art' around themselves, artists had become complacent, so I thought the best thing was to do away with categories altogether."[43] "I think of my work in the field of cinema as a process of revolutionizing myself," he said later.[44] "The intention was to practice a method that transcends the supposed binary between film and politics, revolution and art."[45]

Early audiences of *A.K.A. Serial Killer* would have recognized this revolutionary sentiment as belonging to the "season of politics," as the late 1960s was known.[46] They would also have recognized Nagayama's story. It was not uncommon for filmmakers and artists to incorporate news stories and images into their own work. Ōshima and Wakamatsu remediated sensationalized journalism in their films, and Moriyama Daidō rephotographed and enlarged paparazzi images to comment on Japan's media economy of scandal. The irony, however, is that in their remediation, filmmakers and photographers profited from such stories themselves. Adachi's collaborations with Wakamatsu in the mid-1960s were similarly compromised.

Wakamatsu was born in 1936 into a poor family of rice farmers. "I did not want to become a farmer," he later recalled, and "I couldn't stay out in the country any longer."[47] Arriving in Tokyo, Wakamatsu worked menial construction and factory jobs and then in a bar and later for the *yakuza*. It was through this work, overseeing film shoots taking place on gang territory, that Wakamatsu learned about filmmaking. He soon found his way into soft-core adult movie production, or pink film (*pinku eiga*) as it is known in Japan, that by then was a thriving industry. Like Ōshima, Wakamatsu enjoyed using real-life incidents as inspiration for his films. Most often, he drew from news reports of violent rapes and murders. Because Wakamatsu's work existed within the make-believe world of film, he claimed, it escaped ethical concerns.[48] Wakamatsu and Adachi would meet over "cheap hooch" and plan films together that merged sleazy exploitation, gratuitous violence, and themes of political radicalization.[49]

The titles of the films they made nod at their aggressive male perspective, almost adolescent in its preoccupation with virginity, virility, and violation. *Violated Angels* (1967) dramatizes a notorious Chicago crime in which a peeping tom trapped nurses in a room to torture and kill. *Go Go Second Time Virgin* (1969) sees a young woman gang-raped, twice. *School Girl Guerrillas* (also 1969—Wakamatsu was prolific) presents radicalized students turning on their teachers—the boys wearing military uniforms and the girls, predictably, wearing nothing. Besides sexual violence, Adachi was curious about gynecology, poring over case histories that he read as allegories of Japan's damaged "socio-political landscape" after the war.[50] Combining lurid scenes of sexual violence and pseudo-gynecological procedures with radical politics sold well. Wakamatsu and Adachi even took their films to Berlin and Cannes.

As Sharon Hayashi has written, pink films were made "in dialogue with popular debates about sex, love, reproduction, women's bodies, and sexual labor," but because they depended on "the double attraction of sex and violence," they often presented a "compromised critique of sexual discourses of the 1960s," attempting to use the "genre as a form of political allegory" while continuing to exploit women.[51] Women were used as "blank canvases," Saito Ayako writes, because "revolution was often problematically envisaged to be carried out 'on' or 'through' or 'via' the female body."[52] Few other makers and scholars of pink film have sufficiently addressed this problem. Claiming that the depiction of a woman's rape highlights the powerlessness of a victim oppressed by society feels gratuitous when the scene is shot from a high angle with an eroticized male gaze that strips her of dignity and political agency. As Fatimah Tobing Rony has written in the context of visual representations of Indonesian women, putting objectifying images of sexualized suffering on the market perpetuates a visual biopolitics of gendered control.[53]

Is a more redemptive reading of Adachi and Wakamatsu possible? Furuhata offers one by suggesting that the pink films remind audiences that "if sex and revolutionary politics are associated, it is because the news media have already transformed both into spectacles."[54] Certainly spectacularized news events dominated Japanese media at the time. Just three years after *A.K.A. Serial Killer*'s release, a militant communist organization, the United Red Army, became a news sensation through a bloody purge and a hostage crisis. The crisis was televised in the first marathon live broadcast in Japan, lasting over ten hours and drawing record audiences. Whether Furuhata's assessment is generous or not, *A.K.A. Serial Killer* feels somewhat less fixated on scandal than Adachi's collaborations with Wakamatsu. The film neither involves gratuitous sex nor visualizes Nagayama as an individual perpetrator, instead implicating global capitalism and the Japanese state in a subtle yet searing landscape depiction.

The film's Japanese and English titles imply that its main topic—landscape—deserves a murderous alias itself. Crime in the film is reframed as a systemic exploitation of nature's resources and people's labor power. The Japanese landscape should *also be known as a serial killer*, the film suggests, for its ruthless post-war economic development, unfair patterns of labor migration, and circulation of standardized commodities, which kill political and cultural freedoms to fuel the so-called free market. The uniformity of this landscape, with "its suffocating air of efficiency," is shown to be the very condition that creates the radicalization threatening it. The identity of the criminal is thus called into question. Are we searching for Nagayama or for the deadly conditions of the climate in which he lived?

The film's soundtrack amplifies this sense of misidentification and searching. While a man's voice reports Nagayama's background in staccato declaratives (*Nagayama was the fourth son of an apple farmer. Nagayama fled south. Nagayama purchased a gun*), sudden sirens and bursts of free jazz (performed by the improvisatory musicians Togashi Masahiko and Takagi Mototeru) interrupt his monotonous authority. The cacophonous soundscape calls simple identifications into question.

Adachi had a slippery relationship with identity. He was suspicious of sociological accounts of personhood and their use in criminology and often used pseudonyms in his work with other filmmakers (most often De Deguchi, a name that literally translates as "Exit"). Falsified identities would eventually place Adachi on the wrong side of international laws.

But even before this legal interlude, crime scenes had attracted *fūkeiron* practitioners. Both Matsuda and Nakahira admired Eugene Atget's photographs of Paris, which appear deserted and reminded Walter Benjamin of images used for establishing police evidence.[55] Atget's images are political, Benjamin argued, because they imply that it is history itself that is on trial.[56] *Fūkeiron* prescribed to similar metaphors. "Landscape," wrote Matsuda, is "the antagonistic power itself."[57]

Even a seemingly colorful scene of a street parade in *A.K.A. Serial Killer*'s opening minutes turns out to be centered on a shrine that settler colonizers from mainland Japan brought to Hokkaido. In other words, even this regional celebration signals a violent metropolitan infiltration of rural and in this case Ainu territory. As Prichard notes, such scenes call regional identity into question: Nagayama's passage through Japan's endless urban and suburban zones ("Tokyo-copies") renders a former imaginary "rooted in an oppositional, schematic binary pairing of 'Tokyo' versus 'homeland,' or center versus periphery," to be out of step with reality.⁵⁸ Whereas directors such as Terayama Shūji celebrated rural youths fleeing village homes to the city and Ogawa Pro members celebrated themselves as city dwellers making new centers in the countryside, *A.K.A. Serial Killer* emphasizes the plight of depopulated rural communities as well as the youths who fled them. Both are demographics caught in a climate of precarity and marginalization. As an audience, our task is to identify the capitalist forces that create such precarious conditions. Adachi and Matsuda drew inspiration for this oblique approach from Hanada Kiyoteru.

Hanada was a generation older than Adachi and Matsuda and had written extensively on avant-garde forms of representation and their political potential in post-war Japan.⁵⁹ He was a Marxist and was interested in the possibilities of combining formal experimentation with mass media. Comparing surrealism and documentary journalism in his essay "Landscapes of the Land of Mirrors," Hanada cautioned against trusting one's immediate sensory perceptions, citing Marx's *Grundrisse*—"the concrete is concrete because it is the concentration of many determinations"—to remind readers that structural violence lurks beneath what seems solid and self-evident due to the influence of habit and pervasive ideology.⁶⁰ Although Adachi felt that Hanada over-emphasized the subjective role of the individual artist (whereas he equated "artist and activist" within a wider "relational movement" of politicization), *A.K.A. Serial Killer* follows Hanada's belief in the politicizing power of disrupting conventional narratives and audience expectations.⁶¹ *Fūkeiron* also drew inspiration for this intentional estrangement from Bertolt Brecht, whose politicized theater shatters the illusion of staged action with the aim of producing a distanced criticality that challenges viewers to interpret scenes and unpack their implications.⁶² Adachi described himself as a "surrealist" for this reason: he wanted to make the familiar strange again.⁶³

Familiar, regulated, and efficient, everyday Japanese life concealed what Marx would call capitalism's laborious origins and unjust accruals of value.⁶⁴ *A.K.A. Serial Killer* aimed to reveal them by cracking open the landscape. Interrupting voice-over reportage with non-diegetic sirens, the alarming squawks of a bass clarinet and tenor saxophone, and ominous drumming, the film undermines narrative authority, its soundtracks colliding with dull images to defamiliarize them.

Defamiliarization is a central concept for the Japanese Marxists whom Saito reads to focus on ecological aspects of political economy. Kuruma Samezo, for example, exposes the alienation at play when producers only relate to each other through the mediation of the products they produce.[65] Kuruma's student Otani Teinosuke identifies a "homo economicus illusion" within the capitalist exchange process when workers are reduced to being bearers of their products as commodities.[66] Exposing such systems by defamiliarizing their seemingly commonplace nature, these economists reveal how capitalism transforms social relations into transactional routine. As Marx put it, such transformation means that "things, far from being under [their producers'] control, in fact control them."[67] Saito describes this inversion of reality as producing a "false view" in which social relations and societal values such as "equality" and "freedom" are eclipsed by commodities and their exchange.[68] As a catchphrase popular in Japan in the 1960s put it, "consumption is a virtue" regardless of social or planetary boundaries. Adachi and Matsuda's flat, static, tableau-like images state the same thing: capitalism teaches that there is no alternative.

Though frequently flat, or static, *A.K.A. Serial Killer*'s images are not without point of view. In fact, they deny viewers the possibility of watching from a privileged remove. Because Adachi and Matsuda remain hidden behind the camera, viewers find themselves alone without an orienting over-the-shoulder shot to accompany and guide. Sometimes we seem to be walking in Nagayama's shoes, and other times we are ambushing him or he might be stalking us. Adachi explains this ambiguity: "The frame will be there, but, at the same time, the audience should decide ... more freely as well.... I think that each audience member should make his or her own frames."[69] The political—and *eco*-political—power of this approach is its reminder that there is no position of externality to capitalism and its climatic damages. In Marx's formulation, humans can never exit the "universal metabolism of nature," and in Saito's gloss, humans cannot produce ex nihilo but can always produce *ex materia*; even "the most high-tech goods that 'dematerialize' the economy use energy and natural resources."[70] Humanity's metabolism with nature can never be suspended. Landscape = entanglement. Film = point of view.

The word *fūkei* (landscape) within *fūkeiron* anticipates its emphasis on entanglements with unseen and inaudible atmospheres of political malaise that are nevertheless felt in the body and omnipresent in the landscape and climate that surround and condition perspectives. *Fūkei* comprises characters for wind (*fū*, 風) and scene (*kei*, 景). The character for wind also appears in the word for climate (*fūdo*, 風土), its presence in *fūkei* indicating that the idea of landscape involves an atmospheric and climate-sensitive perception of space (a common expression for someone unable to intuit a situation or pick up on a mood is someone who "cannot read the air"). *Fūkeiron* "reads the air," attuning to the affective conditions of everyday life, its alienation, anger, and anxiety.

Fūkeiron's atmospheric attunement contributes an ecological approach to contemporaneous Marxist readings of space developed by critics including John Berger and Raymond Williams, who studied landscape as an inherently classist medium whereby wealthier people enjoy prospects (both economic and visual) that are inaccessible to others.[71] Such readings emphasized the fundamentally economic nature of landscape as a concept, whether organized in space as colonial enclosures and territories or represented on canvas and paper as celebratory displays of such control. The English word "landscape" refers to land that has been shaped, collected, and organized into a "-scape," a condition.[72] Such organization implies an exertion of power. "Landscape" developed a definition pertaining to aesthetic experience and socioeconomic vantage, entering modern English from Dutch in the seventeenth century as artistic jargon closely related to the exploitation of land and people during European colonial expansion.[73] As filmmakers discussed in Chapter 1, especially Arlene Bowman, knew all too well, conventional representations of landscape, be they painted or photographed, evidence colonial conquests of land, nature's resources, and people.

In *fūkeiron*, landscape remains an economic organization of space, but unlike in romantic representations of colonial conquest, it is drained of aesthetic pleasure (Matsuda referred to this kind of landscape as a lifeless "scene").[74] *Fūkeiron* extends Marxist readings of social alienation into ecological considerations of climates and atmospheres, emphasizing landscape as a climate in which culture and nature, the social and the ecological, are entangled.

In visualizing landscape as a climate of entangled human and other-than-human relations, *fūkeiron* offers a valuable mediation for conflicting readings of Marx's concept of metabolic rift that appear in recent Anthropocene discourse. Jason W. Moore has criticized Foster's work on metabolic rift for perpetuating a dualism of "Society" and "Nature," arguing instead for the entanglement of the natural and social in a "web" of life that characterizes the Capitalocene.[75] *Fūkeiron*'s landscapes of regimented crops and road infrastructures on one hand speak to Moore's understanding that the social and the natural are so intertwined and compromised that any reference to nature as a "first nature," pristine, external to society, and untouched by humans, is by now fiction. On the other hand, *fūkeiron* also carves out space for Foster and Saito's arguments for distinguishing "between the social and the natural" in order to understand the human-made and specifically capitalist causes of climate degradation.[76] In this sense, *fūkeiron* presents an important contribution to recent Anthropocene discourse through a simultaneous understanding of the conditions of entanglement and the specifically capitalist causes of climate breakdown. When Matsuda proclaims "the extinction of landscape," this is less to challenge nature's existence (by suggesting, as some Anthropocene theorists have, that nature is a "powerful fiction") than to emphasize capitalism's deadly reach.[77] As Saito reminds readers, "while our 'knowledge of nature' is discursively mediated by scientific praxes, and 'making sense of nature' is inevitably constrained by social power relations [and] conditioned by language," this does not mean "that external nature independent of humans does not exist."[78] The spiraling events of climate breakdown are surely proof of this.

The *fūkeiron* understanding of climate as a social and ecological nexus is also important in its subversion of an older definition of landscape in Japan, which is characterized by its nationalist and imperialist uses as an aesthetic genre and a philosophical concept. Though the word *fūkei* entered the Japanese language from Chinese in the eighth century, it only became common later during intensive industrial and cultural modernization and Western influence in the Meiji period (1868–1911). The word's growing usage reflected this moment of cultural change and a combination of anxiety and excitement that manifested in a desire to frame and preserve a distinctly Japanese tradition and landscape against modernity and globalization.[79] This was Shiga Shigetaka's mission.

Shiga, a journalist and geographer who was keen on alpine hikes and world travels, was proud of his nation and adopted *fūkei* as a term that he naturalized along nationalistic lines. As Japan experienced increasing Western influence in the late 1880s and some called for complete modernization, Shiga proposed the opposite, advocating for the strict maintenance of Japan's cultural identity. Shiga's 1894 book *Japanese Landscape* (*Nihon Fūkeiron*) rooted traditional elements of Japanese culture in its landscapes and encouraged people to visit mountains to view panoramas from elevated positions. The book sold well. The First Sino-Japanese War (1894–1895) had just begun, and nationalist sentiment was strong.[80]

Nationalism also motivated Watsuji Tetsurō's philosophical work in the early 1930s. Watsuji had studied Western philosophy (Kierkegaard, Nietzsche) and found it too individualistic and so turned to Japanese culture for a curative, exploring Zen Buddhism. He proposed a dynamic connection between humans and their surroundings and was interested in Japan's monsoon climate, whose humidity promotes vegetable growth but also produces storms. Watsuji believed that Japanese people tended to be submissive because they lived with such powerful forces of nature.[81] This essentializing characterization of ethnicity and behavior based on climate appealed to many because it naturalized (and hid) ideological forces of assimilation and colonialism. Like Shiga, Watsuji used landscape to reinforce nationhood at the expense of cultural variation (including Japanese Indigenous minorities and the East and South East Asian subjects of its colonies).

Despite these essentializing and exclusionary contexts, Shiga's and Watsuji's ideas present an interesting challenge to Western modernity's understanding of the self as a being independent from its surroundings and therefore able to exploit and profit from them. As Watsuji put it, reality is never a one-directional subject-object passage of understanding but instead is an emplaced encounter in a climate of relations, perspectives, and interpretations.[82] The compact title of Watsuji's 1935 book *Fūdo* (風土, lit. *Climate*) encapsulates his project, its title in English translation, *Climate and Culture*, unpacking his combined understanding of nature and humanity as an interdependent whole. This understanding appealed to many left-leaning environmentalists in the 1960s and 1970s including Ogawa Pro. *Fūkeiron* was more ambivalent.

Fūkeiron retains and expands the idea of climate as a nexus of political, cultural, and ecological conditions, along with a belief in climate as a forcefield of influences on people. No longer focusing on mountain peaks or monsoon storms, however, *fūkeiron* looks to monoculture crops and office blocks as the landscape determinants of people's relations with each other and the environment in the 1960s and 1970s. In *A.K.A. Serial Killer*, the wake of a ferry filmed from on board propels us southward in search of Nagayama. The shot dissolves from one of a steam train, with vapor becoming sea spray. Later the air will be filled with city smog. Such scenes accumulate in a climate of logistics, an atmosphere suffocating with accelerated progress. "*Après moi le deluge*" wrote Marx, impersonating the capitalist's disregard for the social and ecological consequences of industrialism.[83] In the wake comes the material and social fallout. *Fūkeiron*'s image of Japan is formed from this compromised climate.

Steam, fog, haze, and air pollution in *A.K.A. Serial Killer* also perform a role of blocking expansive views. Depth of field is obstructed and blurred, frustrating any attempt at orientation and clarity. This device not only amplifies a sense of entanglement and suffocation but also subversively plays with a much older Japanese landscape tradition of garden design. As in the way *fūkeiron* revises landscape philosophies of climate by Shiga and Watsuji, *A.K.A. Serial Killer* takes the garden-landscaping aesthetic of *shakkei* (literally "borrowed scenery") and eco-politicizes it.

Shakkei borrows elements beyond the garden as a backdrop. Mountains, for example, lend the garden a scenic vista and feeling of expansiveness. *Shakkei* derives from a seventeenth-century Chinese book on horticulture, which influenced Japanese landscaping, architecture, scroll painting, and cinema. Ozu Yasujirō's films display *shakkei*'s influence in their deep shots through windows and doors that link interiors to gardens and distant landscapes or cityscapes. Although Ozu's films are human dramas, they draw atmospheric affect from these background landscapes. *Shakkei* also informed Mizoguchi Kenji's sense of space, particularly in his ghostly film *Ugetsu Monogatari* (1953), which borrows rural landscapes' supernatural atmospheres through long shots of deep space veiled by rolling mist and low light.

With an ecological reading of Marx in mind, whereby the environment and its exploitation condition all experience occurring within it, *fūkeiron*'s frustration of space suggests a critical adoption and adaptation of *shakkei*. "Borrowing" a contemporary scenery of alienation, anger, and anxiety through extended takes or snatches of discordant sound, *A.K.A. Serial Killer* establishes a dynamic connection between space and society, connecting foreground and background, subject and object, figure and landscape. Space is confined to shallow planes controlled by the movement of vehicles and the restrictions of barriers: there is little room for retreat or slowness in this landscape of production, consumption, and obedience to the laws of capital. Even without visible human enforcers, space is policed through its physical organization. While pictorial space is no longer deep in *fūkeiron*, blocked by smog, building sites, and billboards, the affective space of political malaise is profound.

Blocked views appear throughout the film. Static mid-distance shots confront closed doors and blank windows. When the camera moves, it pans laterally to track the movement of vehicles and the horizontal axes of walls and streets. The effect is frustrating and claustrophobic. Even crowd scenes in station concourses feel limited. The camera does not seek any individual and is not greeted with curiosity—people rush past. In a rare instance when someone does perform to the camera, it is a clownish US military officer, grimacing and wiggling in front of a strip of nightclubs. This sequence, as with shots of an airport and numerous Coca-Cola billboards, indicate Japan's background "scenery" of American military, economic, and cultural control.

A.K.A. Serial Killer's critical relation to *shakkei* is clearest at the end of the film in the wide streets of Tokyo's Shinjuku district, inside its station, and outside a department store. Riot police with shields march on roads cordoned off with "no entry" signs. In October 1968, the same month that Nagayama committed three of his four murders, mass demonstrations against the Vietnam War and Japan's provision of landing bases for US planes erupted in Shinjuku. Adachi took to the streets with his camera. The government reacted to the demonstrations by invoking the Riot Law, and police arrested and detained hundreds of protestors overnight. And matters only worsened, In 1968, police arrested 6,000 students on charges of protest. Between 1968 and 1971, this number rose to 31, 852.[84] By "borrowing" this "scenery" of protest in the film's final minutes, Adachi and Matsuda reveal how a background of capitalist order can tip into omnipresent policing, with the slow violence of economic and legalistic restriction boiling into incendiary scenes of barricades and batons. Superficially, such scenes are far from pastoral *fūdo* and *shakkei*'s spatial harmony. But on a fundamental level, the environmental and affective potential of *fūdo* and *shakkei* comes into full force in Shinjuku. *A.K.A. Serial Killer* exposes a highly politicized landscape where background socioeconomic and ecological issues are framed and shiny commodities (neat roads, Coca-Cola billboards, strip clubs) are inverted, revealing their real costs to nature and society.

CROSS-CULTURAL SOLIDARITIES

Making films *in* struggle rather than *about* struggle has remained a goal for Adachi throughout his career—though back in 1970, quite where that struggle would take him he did not foresee.

In 1971, Adachi and Wakamatsu were in Cannes presenting *Sex Jack* (1970) and *Violated Angels* (1967) at the film festival. When it came time to fly home they decided to stop in Palestine, as Adachi wanted to meet some Japanese activists there. Admiring Jean-Luc Godard's collective work with the Dziga Vertov Group in Palestine, Adachi and Wakamatsu set about filming the radicals they met, who were then forming the Japanese Red Army to help the Popular Front for the Liberation of Palestine (PFLP). Working quickly and with excitement, Adachi and Wakamatsu edited their footage into a newsreel-style film, *Red Army–PFLP Declaration of World War* (1971), that aimed to mobilize support and militant action. At Wakamatsu Pro, films were often scripted, shot, and edited within days and shown soon afterward. "Films," Adachi liked to say, "only exist to be screened."[85]

Returning to Japan, Adachi gathered a group of activists and hired a bus (they called themselves the Red Bus Film Screening Troup), and the group drove the film "across the country as a pretext for collective conversations."[86] Rejecting existing screening and media outlets, Adachi replaced auteurism with activism:

> I came up with a form of screening that included discussions with the audience after the film was finished. It was a grassroots roadshow movement ... based on the principle that because it was a newsreel film it wouldn't make sense unless we had proper debates and built solidarity between the people who brought the news and those who watched it. Wakamatsu gave us a bunch of money when we started off, but we ran out at some point and kept the screenings going while eating scraps we picked up from the morning produce markets. And then some of the people getting on and off the bus started to attract attention from the police, so on top of the 30 or 40 people riding the bus, we were followed by several patrol cars and a riot squad bus. ... [F]rom the outside it probably looked like we were going around agitating. But what I really wanted to make was solidarity, not agitation.[87]

Adachi's words resonate with the aims of political filmmakers then organizing grassroots and clandestine screenings in Latin America under the banner of Third Cinema (see Chapter 5) as well as several activist filmmakers elsewhere who were interested in audience engagement, including Ogawa Pro. But the people riding the bus were not like Ogawa's farmer supporters. One passenger, Okamoto Kōzō, was a member of the Japanese Red Army and would soon open fire on a crowd in Tel Aviv's Lod Airport, killing twenty-six people. Okamoto's brother had already hijacked a plane to North Korea. Although Adachi did not know it, *Red Army–PFLP Declaration of World War* was to be the last film he would release for thirty years.

In 1974, Adachi left Japan. Joining the Japanese Red Army in Beirut, he appointed himself as spokesperson.[88] Between sporadic guerrilla actions and during long hours waiting for intelligence reports, Adachi began filming his surroundings. *Fūkei* = power. He mainly filmed refugee camps. In 1982 Israel Defense Forces bombed Beirut, and destroyed over two hundred hours of footage Adachi had shot in Lebanon, Palestine, and Israel. In response, he paused lens-based work to focus on militancy. A decade and a half later, Adachi's life took another turn.

In 1997 police arrested Adachi for using multiple false passports, imprisoning him in Lebanon for three years. There, he shared a cell with Okamoto, his old friend from the Red Bus Film Screening Troup. Okamoto had served time in an Israeli prison, had lived in Libya and Syria, and had been arrested again in Lebanon. Upon their release, Okamoto was granted asylum in Lebanon, but Adachi was extradited. Under house arrest in Japan, Adachi began planning his next film, long-awaited. It would be about Okamoto.

Prisoner/Terrorist (2007) "tried to talk about the notion of freedom for a human being by drawing parallels between terrorist activity and state terrorism (including prison itself, security intelligence, the prison guard system)," Adachi explained.[89] Recalling his empathy for young Nagayama in *A.K.A. Serial Killer*, Adachi attempts to contextualize Okamoto's terrorism within a political landscape of state violence. Adachi's 2022 film *REVOLUTION+1* tries something similar, exploring political malaise in contemporary Japan by looking at the case of Yamagami Tetsuya, the man who assassinated former prime minister Abe Shinzo in opposition to his corruption.[90] Adachi identified with

Yamagami as an alienated individual and raced to share the film with audiences ("before the media was able to distort the situation").⁹¹ The film was released, unfinished, to coincide with Abe's state funeral, a period of official mourning that many people in Japan opposed.

Though Adachi still cannot leave Japan and his health has deteriorated with age, he frequently attends screenings around the country, voicing his concern that "neo-liberalism has corroded people's minds and co-opted the revolutionary essence of social transformation." "When I see billboards on the streets proclaiming a 'cosmetics revolution' or a 'fashion revolution,'" he says, "I wonder what the point was of fighting all those years only for 'revolution' to become a logo."⁹²

Adachi was not the only *fūkeiron* figure who shifted the locus of his work in the 1970s. Nakahira also left Tokyo, relocating to the Ryūkyū islands of Okinawa and Amami, where he would spend several years taking photographs. Like the filmmaker Takamine, Nakahira wanted to capture images of the archipelago's landscape as evidence of US military oppression. His photographs of poor farmhouses and non-descript fields where wartime atrocities had occurred explore the limits of what is visible and sayable under occupation and in its aftermath.⁹³ But only a few years later, Nakahira's ability to visualize and speak such powerful ideas would be diminished. In 1977 after a night of heavy drinking, Nakahira experienced a blackout. He woke with severe language and memory loss that affected him for the rest of his life.

CONTAMINATION AND RESISTANCE

In 2011, lethal levels of radiation spread across Japan in the wake of the earthquake, tsunami, and explosion at Fukushima Daiichi Nuclear Power Plant. The effects of the radiation were far from invisible, despite the Japanese government and the Tokyo Electric Power Company's efforts.⁹⁴ Besides Fukushima, as climate breakdown escalates, threats to safety and freedom recur. Watching *fūkeiron* films with this hindsight, it is clear that capitalism's extractive logic of financial growth, in Saito's words, "must be judged as irrational from a perspective of sustainable human development due to the ecological degradation of the world."[95]

However, an ecological Marxist perspective such as Saito's—and, I argue, such as that operating in audiovisual form in *fūkeiron*—locates a potential site of resistance in this place of degradation. "Banal" and "lifeless" "scenes" of roads and agri-businesses not only manifest capitalism's irrationality and contradictions but also invite its overturning.[96] To repeat Tsing's formulation, such resistance might thrive in the ruins of capitalism. What I most appreciate about *fūkeiron*, however, is that its images do not rush to define this work of resistance. *Fūkeiron*'s gaps, blurs, and banalities hold space for thinking. As Adachi said, "the audience should decide."

In Chapter 4, three filmmakers in urban, suburban, and agro-industrial America take up this idea of resistance as they face classed, raced, and gendered forms of violence codified and concretized in the landscape.

FOUR

Companion Planting in Wounded Land

DISCUSSING EXTRACTIVISM and climate breakdown in 2013, Leanne Betasamosake Simpson propounded "an authentic relationship with non-pristine nature" that addresses "the wounded, as opposed to just the perfect and pretty."[1] Describing polluted or over-developed land as "wounded" establishes a corporeal metaphor that runs through this chapter as I consider bodies of land in North America, the embodied experiences of three women filming these landscapes between the 1970s and early 1990s, and the bodies of work they made.

Simpson's discussion was published online with the title "Dancing the World into Being," a reference to the importance of collective dance to Idle No More, an Indigenous coalition that organized round dances in public spaces across North America in 2012. The coalition called for solidarity in resisting the colonial capitalist "extraction-assimilation system" responsible for desecrating ecosystems and communities through deforestation, mining, condo development, pipelines, tar sands, and golf courses.[2] Simpson's notion of dance as a collective and embodied form of protest and world-making also describes the kind of filmmaking considered in this chapter.

Whether actually dancing, cradling a handheld camera, or editing in flowing or staccato rhythms, Anne Charlotte Robertson, Ana Mendieta, and Barbara McCullough danced the world into being. Their filmic choreographies merged geological, botanical, and animal bodies with their own and the mechanical, material bodies of their cameras and film stock. Though unknown to each other as they worked in Massachusetts,

Iowa, and California, these women filmed their surroundings in strikingly similar ways. Primarily filming for themselves as records of their love of nature and anguish over its degradation, they expressed senses of empathy and entanglement in polluted, industrialized, and territorialized lands. Their films chronicle both American landscapes undergoing transformation, and their makers' dancerly, playful cultivation of relationships with non-pristine nature.

Hoping to engage audiences in artistic and experimental film circles (which they eventually did, though due recognition was slow to come in circles stagnant with white patriarchy), Robertson, Mendieta, and McCullough represented landscapes in ways that refused exterior or superior perspectives. Sometimes appearing on-screen or holding the camera in one hand and seeds or soil in the other, these women wanted to re-pair estranged places, communities, and species.

Like the Orcadian and Navajo films discussed in Chapter 1, those discussed here exemplify land cinema's capacity for landscape-portraiture, whereby people appear in relation to the climate that shapes them and refuse separations between humanity and the rest of nature. In this chapter, the human presence within the landscape-portrait is intensified into embodied, sensual expressions of land relation, and films make their materiality visible as physical celluloid objects and the products of women's labor.

Expanding the concept of body to encompass landscapes, films, and their makers, I follow Robertson, Mendieta, and McCullough's lead by calling into question a species-bound mono-humanistic definition of Man, described by Sylvia Wynter as invented for the advancement of white males living within a capitalist system dependent on their separation from and exploitation of others.[3] Robertson, Mendieta, and McCullough call for an eco-feminist and anti-colonial revision of what a body is.

Their own presence, behind and in front of the camera, along with the embodied works they leave us, constructs a definition of the body as a practice, not a product. Defining people and landscapes as bodies-in-process challenges ideas of fixed subjectivity and property relation, suggesting that individuals, communities, and ecosystems co-produce through ongoing relationships and contaminations.

Anna Tsing's application of contamination as a metaphor, which I introduced in Chapter 3, describes encounters that change us and open new paths for livable collaboration.[4] While extractive capitalism estranges places, communities, and species, contaminations as encounters invite responsivity and responsibility. With Tsing's metaphor in mind, I read Robertson's, Mendieta's, and McCullough's films for their presentation of multi-species encounters operating within what Tsing calls "third nature" (if first nature signifies ecological balance and second nature signifies an environment transformed by extraction). Growing from contaminating contexts of environmental degradation and social injustice, the films juxtapose ideas of illness and therapy, estrangement and reconnection, and contamination and purification to yield hope in wounded land. Third nature's contaminated spaces, the films suggest, can host unexpected encounters that put us in touch, in the words of So Mayer, with "the textures and scents of the so-much-larger-than-us-world," enabling more ecologically attuned ways of being.[5]

My primary focus here is Anne Charlotte Robertson, the Massachusetts filmmaker and gardener whose life and work are impossible to distinguish, so autobiographical was her artistic output and so politically attuned her personality.

Taking personal responsibility for her well-being during episodes of mental illness, Robertson gardened and filmed her garden as a form of diary. She worked alone, documenting both her aching loneliness and defiant independence. Robertson's combined filming and gardening practice culminated in her magnum opus, *Five Year Diary*, an autobiographical film that she began in 1981 and ended in 1997, far later than its title anticipated. "Making my diary has literally saved my life," she wrote.[6]

At over thirty-six hours spread across eighty-four Super-8 reels, the *Diary* documents sixteen years of life in a tremendous, unwieldy body of work that evolved in relation to Robertson's surroundings. The film chronicles her obsessions with her body, pathologized and medicated, haunted by ideals of thinness, beauty, and fertility, and in pain as she learned about other bodies—landscapes, ecosystems, and animals—wounded by pollution and climate change.

In the *Diary*, Robertson's experiences of pathologizing, poverty, and climate anxiety reflect societal changes occurring in the 1980s. Robertson witnessed health care becoming increasingly reliant on the pharmaceutical industry, welfare provision giving way to a market-driven logic of competition and individualism, highways and tech companies expanding across the Massachusetts landscape, and the news filling with reports of oil spills, air pollution, and species extinction. By placing her struggles within a framework of social and climate concern in the *Diary*, Robertson shows how the freedom of the market that neoliberalists celebrate turns out to bestow rights and freedoms to those already in positions of privilege while violating the rights of everyone and everything else.[7] Robertson displays both resilience and vulnerability in the face of such concerns.

Above all else, Robertson's body of work and her own body (which she films gardening, cooking garden produce, bingeing, dieting, and holding handfuls of Valium and handfuls of seeds) foreground ambivalence. Robertson's life and work reveal the presence of someone neither at home within a sociopolitical environment nor able to denounce or withdraw from it entirely. As Robertson becomes better known through the restoration and digitization of her work by Harvard Film Archive, it is vital that the full implications of her experience, performance, and representation of ambivalence are understood.[8] More than a personal or confessional filmmaker, Robertson is profoundly political—and *ecopolitical*—in her integrated understanding of personal well-being and environmental justice.

Robertson's complex self-representation invites consideration of contemporaneous bodies of work made by women in other landscapes across North America, which also foreground the presence of the female figure. In the latter part of this chapter, I therefore explore resonances between Robertson's work and films by Ana Mendieta and Barbara McCullough. Mendieta migrated to Iowa from Cuba as a child. In her teens she shuttled between orphanages and foster homes, experiencing xenophobia. McCullough came from a close-knit Black community in New Orleans. She relocated to Los Angeles with her family during childhood and found the city hostile and segregated.[9] In short experimental films made in the 1970s depicting a female body lying, sitting, or dancing in landscapes subjected to colonial or industrial damage, Mendieta and McCullough express healing and embodied joy within wounded space. Taking up space usually taken from women of color, they connect capitalism's biopolitical violence to its ecocidal methods of extraction, exposing the female body of color and bodies of land as sites of vulnerability and resistance.

Mendieta's and McCullough's approaches expand Robertson's ecofeminist concerns with what has become known since the 1980s as an intersectional understanding of gendered, classed, and raced oppression.[10] Through Mendieta's and McCullough's intersectional lenses, land is simultaneously a site of territorial oppression and anti-racist transformation. Senses of self and belonging are re-routed in the films from an interlocking system of oppression into re-rooted engagements with land as a shared space of multispecies sustainment. Planting references to ecocide and femicide alongside ideas of ritual honoring and regeneration, Mendieta and McCullough nurture complex engagements with land. Made to counter the white machismo of land art in Mendieta's case and Hollywood in McCullough's, these women's films juxtapose wounding and care, placing dereliction and deforestation alongside ritual cleansing, meditation, and dance.

This juxtaposition recalls a technique in organic gardening known as companion planting, which promotes natural habitats, growth, and pollination by cultivating different crops in proximity to one another. The technique would have been familiar to Robertson, who except for a dash of Miracle-Gro on her tomatoes, gardened organically. Companion planting creates symbiotic relationships. In order to thrive, roses are planted with garlic because garlic deters rose pests. Marigolds are planted with melons because marigolds control nematodes in the roots of melon. Tomatoes repel larvae that chew through cabbages. The companion-planted garden is neither a field of individuals nor a monoculture crop but instead is a complex cluster of species growing through productive contamination.

Robertson would no doubt have enjoyed the metaphor of companion planting for filmmaking. Her gardening-filmmaking juxtaposes the personal, political, and planetary in a set of common concerns and suggests that care for the close-at-hand co-produces wider forms of care (a little slug, filmed in close-up in Reel 22 of her *Diary*, after it has entered the kitchen on a lettuce causes her hours of deliberation over the safest place to put it and a wider worry concerning the responsibility of human beings in a so-much-larger-than-us world).

Robertson, Mendieta, and McCullough are companion planters in wounded land. They propose an intersectional and eco-feminist counternarrative to filmic and artistic representations of the American landscape rooted in fantasies of territorial conquest. Vivacious, nimble, and light of touch, their films dance alternative worlds into being.

GARDEN

Consisting of thirteen boxes of notes, drawings, letters, and diaries and eighty-four reels of film as well as hundreds of audio tapes, the Anne Charlotte Robertson Collection is massive and un-cataloged at the time of my writing. I watch the twenty-five-minute film reels, open boxes of seed packets and hospital discharge notes, and find pages of confessions, resolutions, poems, and a pair of life-size handprints made on a photocopier. This sprawling and devastatingly frank corpus of work is Robertson's life, infused with her vitality, biting political consciousness, wry humor, sadness, and desire.

Given that Robertson refused to separate accounts of life and work, I shall not do so here. She understood how arbitrary such oppositions could be and the political potential in refusing neat categories. In the context of such complexity, Robertson's archive invites a form of scholarship that Eve Kosofsky Sedgwick describes as "reparative reading."

Reparative reading requires engaging with several discourses in a nondualistic manner that respects differences and values moments of affinity.[11] Rather than drawing conclusions as a stable and knowing subject, the reparative reader engages with material to enrich understandings of where we are now and how we got here and to envision futures different from the present.[12] Sedgwick emphasizes the importance of allying thinking with feeling in this process, describing a reader who connects with her body, desires, and lived experiences and is open to being taken in unanticipated directions.[13] In other words, the reparative reader is an ambivalent reader who enjoys assembling disparate and sometimes contradictory fragments, welcoming surprise and multiple or divergent interpretations. Reparative reading is a kind of companion planting—a contamination of ideas.

Robertson herself was a reparative reader in the way she assembled and re-edited disparate images and discourses into a complex, never-finished corpus of material that reflects conflicting experiences. Thinking and feeling with Robertson through a reparative reading of her life and work, I become aware of my own emotional proximity to her. My archivist's gloves turn gray from weeks spent leafing through Robertson's papers. My throat prickles with dust that might be Robertson's skin cells, grains of soil from her garden, flecks of ash from her cigarettes. Here is a person exposed and unfolding before me in box after box and reel after reel of revelations, longing for emotional understanding, romantic love, professional recognition, and climate justice.

Robertson was often overwhelmed by her acute awareness of human-made climate change and was frequently hospitalized or confined by what she called the "drug chains" of prescribed anti-depressant and anti-psychotic medication.[14] Enrollment rates in disability support for mental illness escalated throughout the 1980s, and as Robertson discovered, the consumption of anti-psychotics is often required for continued receipt of security payments despite these medicines' risks.[15] Robertson struggled to hold down a job due to health issues and recorded her early films on cameras borrowed from the Massachusetts College of Art, where she studied 8mm filmmaking in the mid-1970s. Later she bought a secondhand Nizo camera, but its light meter and lens were unreliable, a fact she laments on the soundtracks of her films, also explaining that she cannot afford film processing or copies. Indeed, each time Robertson's originals were screened, they showed more scratches.[16] In between screenings and during hospital confinements, her films were crammed into her bedroom closet.

"I don't want the police to take my camera," Robertson pleads over footage documenting a manic episode in Reel 23. That same winter of 1982, retrieving her camera and filming again, Robertson explains in a voice-over that "frost had killed my garden while I was in the hospital." She later told Scott MacDonald that "I believe in film being necessary every day. Losing that camera, I lost my mind. Every time there's a breakdown, I try to take pictures of it."[17]

For Robertson, being well meant being in the garden, "watching the light fade, adjusting the camera iris," the camera going "click every eight seconds all day" and "calming me by the process."[18] Responding to changes in light, to flowers blossoming, melons ripening, and compost maturing, Robertson saw hope for social and environmental renewal. Hands-on cinephilia and love of plants (biophilia) became her ecotherapy. Robertson felt contaminated by traumatic encounters with institutional bodies—not least pharmaceutical, fossil fuel, and media industries peddling lifestyles of normative consumption. She was also contaminated, as in touched and transformed, by healing encounters with bodies of land as well as plants and animals.

Today, a reparative reading of Robertson's work sheds light on wider narratives of where we are now and how we got here, embroiled in the socially and ecologically harmful dependencies that characterize the Anthropocene's extractive present. Such a reading invites us to envision alternative futures (to dance other worlds into being), extending beyond Robertson's body of work and biography to considerations of the socio-political contexts in which she lived—many of which continue to condition ways we think about land and well-being today. Beyond self-identification or empathy for Robertson as I sit with her life's work comes a sense of urgency in telling her story.

Robertson considered *Five Year Diary* to be central to her story. She also saw her short films, written diaries, gardening, cooking, green protest letters to politicians, and cassette tape recordings for romantic crushes as part of this corpus. Like Somankidi Coura's filmmaking, photography, gardening, theater, and radio, the sheer variety of Robertson's output speaks to land cinema's expansive capacity, with each medium, distinct in form and historical significance, contributing to a visual culture of critical and creative expression.

Robertson's *Diary* and short films maintain a remarkable consistency of theme and formal tone, as she revisited and edited reels months and years after filming them. The *Diary*'s reels are labeled chronologically, with the first dated November 3 to December 13, 1981, and Reel 84 left undated but completed sometime after March 18, 1997. Alongside reels' numbers and dates, Robertson often added a descriptive title, such as *Another Breakdown: Will I Ever Mend?* and *The Definitions of Fat and Thin*. These titles announce Robertson's preoccupations with mental illness, social scripts of success and attractiveness, environmental pollution, and gardening's therapeutic value. Certain themes achieve additional prominence as Robertson devotes short films to them, such as *Melon Patches, Or Reasons to Go On Living* (1994), a half-hour film that centers the garden as a place of regeneration.

The *Diary* both excited and overwhelmed Robertson due to its unpredicted volume. Through incessant labor producing and editing this prodigious body of work on film and paper, in the garden, and on her own body image, Robertson is deliberately unclear about whether she is critiquing or succumbing to ideals of productivity. Documenting herself manically filming, writing, and producing fruit and vegetables (one summer, growing no fewer than thirty-one varieties of tomato), Robertson presents herself on the brink of exhaustion as she strives for recognition in a pervasive neoliberal ideal of productivity.

These harried portrayals of productivity place Robertson in a complicated relation to second wave feminism and present a challenge to historical periodization. Though she attended various feminist rallies throughout the 1970s and 1980s, some of which we see documented

FIGURE 16. Anne Charlotte Robertson's handful of seeds. Frame enlargement. Courtesy of the Anne Charlotte Robertson Collection, Harvard Film Archive, Harvard University.

FIGURE 17. Anne Charlotte Robertson's handful of pills. Frame enlargement. Courtesy of the Anne Charlotte Robertson Collection, Harvard Film Archive, Harvard University.

in the *Diary*, Robertson's desire to be a wife and mother could be seen as contradicting second wave goals for domestic liberation. Obsessive crushes on men and preoccupations with beauty also position Robertson ambiguously within feminist politics and filmmaking. The *Diary* amplifies this ambivalence. In Reel 80, stop-motion animates a menacing row of pill bottles advancing across a tabletop toward the camera. "I had no children," Robertson says in the voice-over. "All I had was a garden with seeds." Outside now, the camera roves over marigolds and roses. Combined allusions to the growth of flowers, children, and illness recall a scene in *Melon Patches* in which Valium transmutes into watermelon seeds in Robertson's outstretched hand as she associates seeds with psychopharmaceutical tablets and harvested melons with the pregnant abdomen (Figures 16 and 17).

The image of seedlike tablets fascinated Robertson. Medication did not always agree with her, lithium especially. Associated with modern science, the pharmaceutical industry, privatized health care, and diminishing welfare provision, tablets are Robertson's symbol for her era. They appear in the garden suddenly and uncannily resembling melon seeds, reminding her of her failure to succeed in the economic and reproductive terms prescribed by social convention. They arrive as a kind of machine in the garden, to borrow Leo Marx's term, interrupting Robertson's natural idyll.

Exploring technology's disruption of pastoral ideals in nineteenth-century American literature, Marx's *Machine in the Garden* (1964) references a common trope whereby industrial technology such as the steam locomotive disturbs rural scenery. Writers such as Henry David Thoreau, living not far from Robertson in Massachusetts a century earlier and observing a new train line running to Boston past his tranquil hut at Walden Pond, revealed society's contradictory commitments to rural ideals and modern progress.[19] The tablets and seeds in Robertson's films reveal contradictions too, placing modern (pharmaceutical) demands on behavioral conformity and productivity alongside social scripts requiring women to be naturally good at nurturing seeds into real or metaphorical babies. Robertson's cutting from tablets to seeds also wrests agency from such contradictory demands, planting ideas of kinship across species as an alternative to fraught human encounters. Despite and perhaps because of the machine in the garden, Robertson cultivates relations beyond the boundaries of social convention.

"You consider everything about me as weird and defective," Robertson told a psychiatrist, "when in fact I am a brilliant woman.... A lot of people are crazy out there in the nine-to-five world, but they lay into me and say I'm the crazy one."[20] The word "crazy" occurs throughout the *Diary* as Robertson draws attention to the gendered pathologies and social stigma she endures. She was reading R. D. Laing at the time, whose experimental approach to psychology helped foster a movement in the late 1960s and early 1970s that became known as antipsychiatry.

Partially drawing from Michel Foucault's concept of biopolitics, which explains how the modern state develops techniques to govern individuals' conduct via their bodily and psychological health, antipsychiatry held that madness was a sane reaction against insane socio-political conditions.[21] Following this proposition, the *Diary* presents neoliberal happiness as a kind of "cruel optimism" that promises individual success through the modification of the body and the consumption of products.²² If success is defined by an anti-social culture of capitalist competitivity, Robertson suggests, then she will never meet its insane demands.

Filming the moon in Reel 23, Robertson wonders whether she is "quite mad, quite crazy, quite insane."²³ She plants seeds in accordance with lunar cycles (a common practice in biodynamic gardening) and likens the moon to a clockface reminding her of ageing and changes in mood and circadian rhythm caused by anti-depressant medication. Robertson's lunar fixation also parodies an archaic yet pervasive set of ideas that links mental disorder to the biological and hormonal processes of menstruation, childbirth, and menopause. Nineteenth-century etiological accounts of women's nervous disorders frequently used an "ovarian" and "lunar" model to pathologize women and diagnose "lunacy."²⁴

Stealthily shifting social scripts from negative pathology to romantic hyperbole, Robertson continues: "I'm crazy, crazy, crazy, crazy in love."²⁵ She bifurcates any possible route to judgment by displaying signs of mental volatility and amorous zeal at once (in the process playing on the link between death and love that underpins so many historical representations of romance). The two meanings of crazy (to be labeled mad, to be madly in love) call each other into question, giving rise to an inquiry about the arbitration of sanity and the struggles of those judged to be failing at it.

Performances of failure characterize Robertson's written and filmed diaries, which bristle with redactions, score-throughs, and annotations. Robertson drew material for films from these written diaries, including her earliest, begun at age eleven with a resolution to lose weight. This early diary anticipates its author's later self-critical behaviors, enabling them in its format, with each page devoted to one day in the calendar year and covering a total of five years. Young Anne would have chronicled her day while reviewing her activities on that date in previous years. Translating this procedure into a three-minute film in 1985, *Talking to Myself*, Robertson appears on-screen and argues with another version of herself produced through double exposure. The voice-over is also doubled. This optical and aural effect suggests that one only becomes a subject (an individual in possession of rights and desires) through subjection to an order (social, legal, or symbolic). And when this order pathologizes "difference" as a disorder, as Robertson felt it did with her behavior, subjectivity splits into competing voices.

Beyond reflecting Robertson's lifelong experience of mental unwellness, such splitting also speaks to her time. As theorists of documentary's turn to a "cinema of the self" in the 1970s have argued, subjective or diaristic registers are inherently relational and therefore also portray the culture in which that self is formed.[26] Cinema's personal turn reflects what became known as the "Me Decade" for a widespread socio-cultural shift toward individualism and self-improvement (the 1970s earned this name partly from an article by Tom Wolfe, one of Robertson's long-running crushes). The Me Decade has been faulted for its privatization of stress as individual failing and its uncritically syncretic self-help methods (Robertson herself dabbled in pop psychologies, Zen Buddhism, Jung, Catholicism, astrology, Gestalt therapy, Goddess mythology, and various diets). The *Diary* grows from and in critical relation to this historical turn, parroting its vocabularies of self-improvement as a chorus of competing optimisms and reproaches (Figure 18).

Robertson's own body comes under attack within these internalized regimes. Pervasive ideals of a slim figure, perceived to be in control of her body and decisions, plagued her as she kept food diaries and dieted throughout her teens and adulthood. She had intended that the *Diary* document her weight loss, but the project changed ("instead—gained weight, took off costume"), the *Diary* continuing for sixteen more years. Compost bins and cooked meals appear again and again, often in sudden zooms that mimic the obsessive vigilance of weight watching. Reel 2 begins with scenes of Robertson in her kitchen reading aloud dictionary definitions of "fat" and "thin." She frantically shells peanuts, her voice growing hysterical in pitch and speed. She seems both amused and haunted by the definitions' references to success, failure, fecundity, poverty, wealth, excess. "Hunger is a metaphor," she wrote in her notebook, hinting at her sense of inadequacy within a world of normative (slim) beauty ideals.[27] But hunger, she also suggests, could express the

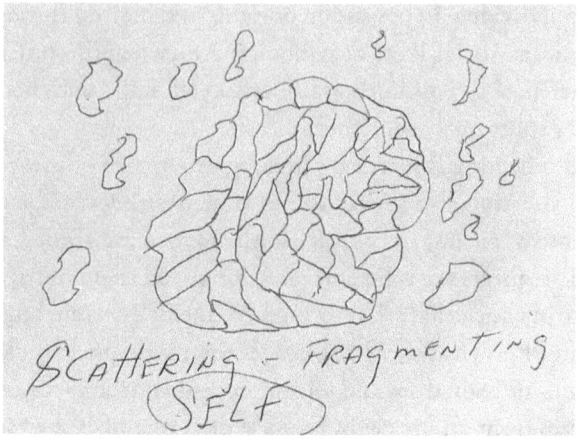

FIGURE 18. "Scattering—Fragmenting SELF." Drawing by Anne Charlotte Robertson. Courtesy of the Anne Charlotte Robertson Collection, Harvard Film Archive, Harvard University.

emaciated prospects of a world that lacks nourishing connections with nature.

In *Magazine Mouth* (1983), a seven-minute stop-motion film set to a marching band, oral consumption represents Robertson's sense of overwhelm by advertisements targeting women. A photograph of Robertson's face with a hole cut out for her mouth is superimposed over images of supermarkets, suburban homes, and manicured blond housewives, giving the effect that she is eating and vomiting a collaged American Dream. Humorous orality becomes Robertson's biting expression of socio-political frustration, the digestive system symbolizing her political revolt.

Awareness of landscapes damaged to make way for suburbia, supermarkets, and monocrops to supply the fast-food industry anguished Robertson. Reel 42 features scenes of industrial wastelands from Godfrey Reggio's 1982 environmental polemic *Koyaanisqatsi* (its title is a Hopi term for "life out of balance"). Composting her own food waste was Robertson's small-scale method for regaining balance.

Although drawing a straightforward causal relation between extractive capitalism and Robertson's preoccupation with food and compost risks simplified economic determinism, paying some consideration to the interests of capitalist forces and to processes of production and consumption reveals the eco-political nature of her work.[28] Capitalism structures experience in order that people satisfy its imperatives to produce and consume, regardless of planetary boundaries. In characteristically ambivalent self-awareness, Robertson parodies this experience, filming herself manically exercising in a yellow leotard and with a grimace, her camera in one hand and a dumbbell in the other while trying to restore balance in her metabolic system by burning calories. Reels 22 and 23 find her attempting to restore other balances, burying natural fiber brushes and a leather satchel she wants to "return to the earth." She also re-planted root vegetables for fear that unearthing had hurt them and buried reels of film to compost.

The material body of film was, to Robertson's mind, a natural substance, and filmmaking resembled gardening due to connections with plants, sunlight, and manual labor. Celluloid film is manufactured from plants (usually cotton plants) whose fibers are pulverized and mixed with a solvent to produce a translucent, flexible strip on which a crystalline layer of emulsion is overlaid. When exposed to light, celluloid film registers with a photographic negative. The analogy Robertson enjoyed is clear: plants react to light through photosynthesis and plant-based film stock reacts to light through photography (Figure 19). These similarities mean that photographs resemble, in André Bazin's words, "a phenomenon in nature, like a flower," and "the 'life' we see moving on the screen is a kind of re-animation" of plants.[29] As we saw in Chapter 2, Ogawa Pro's interest in documenting the sun's effects on rice plants by using film as a sensitive, botanical material relies on similar celluloid/cellulose associations. Other filmmakers, including Rose Lowder in France, also enjoy connections between no-waste practices in organic agriculture and filmmaking. Lowder uses every frame she shoots, having worked in television production and been appalled at the quantity of celluloid wasted on the cutting room floor.[30]

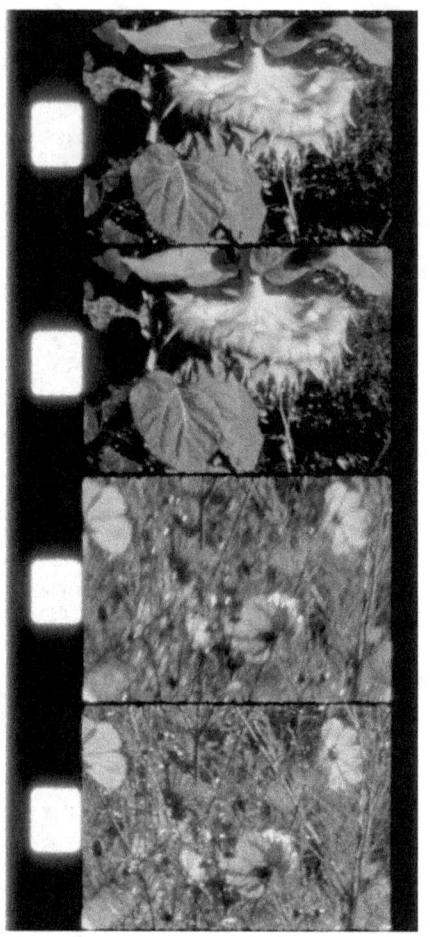

FIGURE 19. Botanical subject matter and ingredients. Film strip. Courtesy of the Anne Charlotte Robertson Collection, Harvard Film Archive, Harvard University.

If carried to a logical conclusion, however, an investigation of film's materiality ought to include the animal and mineral bodies involved in its manufacture. The light-sensitive emulsion that creates a visible image on film is suspended in a layer of gelatin, one of the chief ingredients of which is collagen. Collagen is produced by boiling animal bones and tissues. Robertson was an advocate of animal welfare and was vocal about her vegetarianism and participation in anti-hunting initiatives, but nowhere in her films does she mention the collagen constituent with which she worked. As for film's mineral components and compounds of organic and synthetic matter, complications continue. Greenwashed interpretations of celluloid as a plantlike body downplay film's industrial, hydro-carbonized, and military aspects.[31] Even when aimed at political resistance, films necessitate a certain transgression against ecological principles in order to be realized.

As if to compensate for such a contradiction, Robertson amplified the horticultural element of her practice by screening her films in the community gardens where she volunteered. Projecting film onto a tarpaulin where insects would gather, attracted by the light, Robertson performed live voice-overs for already multi-layered soundtracks and served homemade fruit cobblers and wines. In a weeklong show at New York's Museum of the Moving Image in 1988 (the most significant exhibition of Robertson's work during her lifetime), she installed herself and her bedroom in the gallery and invited audiences to sit with her and watch the *Diary*.[32] These garden and domestic installations drew audiences, materials, and environments together, merging private and public, life and work, and multiple living beings in a shared space of politicized reflection.

Robertson's sharing derives from a wider strategy of consciousness-raising popular in second wave feminism wherein the body became a gendered focus for political and performative reflection.[33] Robertson was certainly aware of this strategy, but her work complicates the feminist adage "the personal is political" by suggesting that the personal and political must also concern plants, animals, and ecosystems on whom humanity depends. The *Diary*'s soundtracks abound with voices, including Robertson's own, and birdsong, radios, sirens, and insects, vocalizing a kind of eco-feminism that sets the human female body among multiple others.[34]

Robertson's inclusive, multi-species approach partly stemmed from environmental discourses in the 1960s and 1970s that forwarded holistic understandings of nature as a symbiotic ecosystem of mutually constitutive and vulnerable elements. This approach contrasted earlier ecological theories that characterized nature as a field of competitive forces and humankind as separate and superior to them.[35] Anticipating Tsing's idea of third nature as a field of contaminating and collaborating encounters, the approach emphasizes connection across species.

Robertson used diary as a formal means of documenting these encounters, also drawing from more historical and spiritual forms of environmentalism associated with her locale in New England. She lived less than a hundred miles from Amherst, where the solitary writer and gardener Emily Dickinson wrote thousands of poems between the 1860s and 1880s about flowers, nature, and life spent within her garden and her bedroom. A century later, like Dickinson, Robertson used her garden as a salve.

Using gardening to improve physical and psychological health is a practice that has been known as eco-therapy since the 1990s, though its ideas are much older.[36] One of the first anthologies of English poetry, *Tottel's Miscellany* (1557), contains a recognition of the therapeutic benefits to "heavy hearts" of gardens that "chaseth" away "all doleful dumps." Many studies in eco-therapy emphasize that being outdoors in air and daylight helps maintain circadian rhythms, which in turn regulate sleep and reduce anxiety—symptoms that Robertson suffered.[37] Physical exercise from gardening improves circulation and cardiovascular health and produces endorphins that relieve pain.[38] Even soil helps due to its composition of natural bacteria that activate the immune system. Gardening also has a social function. From the nineteenth century, allotment or community gardening developed as a method of sustaining poor urban populations with fresh food.

If Robertson's volunteering in community gardens presents an alternative to competitive, extractive approaches to natural environments and social structures, however, it also risks obscuring the gaps left by cuts to welfare provision by providing vegetables and green space for those hit hardest by the state's scaling back of provisions and by keeping a green activist relatively quiet and distracted. And although gardens were places of refuge for Robertson, like the woods for Thoreau and the flowerbed for Dickinson, they are neither available nor accessible to everyone. Given Robertson's political orientations, these tensions would not have escaped her. "I pick blackberries, raspberries, and unemployment checks," she notes in a voice-over, juxtaposing sources of natural sustenance and socially manufactured stigma to contrast definitions of productivity and growth.[39]

Like many in her generation who had witnessed environmental catastrophes, including the 1969 Santa Barbara oil spill and Three Mile Island's nuclear explosion in 1979, Robertson decried pollution and its social damages. Her archive includes newspaper clippings of such calamities, pasted alongside handwritten poems and typed letters calling to action politicians, the pope, and "People of the World." Books including Rachel Carson's *Silent Spring*, which cataloged the adverse effects of chemical pesticides on humans and the environment, were widely read at the time and contributed to not only individual changes in lifestyle, such as Robertson's turn to organic horticulture and green campaigning, but also the foundation of America's Environmental Protection Agency, the Deep Ecology Movement, and Earth Day. It was in this spirit that residents of Jamaica Plain in Boston, where Robertson lived for several years, successfully halted the routing of an interstate highway in 1979 and founded an environmental festival, Wake Up the Earth. Had she lived longer, Robertson would surely have smiled to see the festival and Jamaica Plain's many community gardens still thriving today.

Leaving the archive late one afternoon, I visit one of the community gardens where Robertson worked. Snow settles on the sleeping ground, and I think of the global Slow Food movement, which formed in the late 1980s to nurture people's interest in the food they eat, where it comes from, and how it affects the planet. Robertson made her own Slow Food and slow film movements in this garden (Figure 20). As she worked to re-pair herself and her surroundings through slow circuits of growing, consuming, and composting, Marx's concept of metabolic rift would likely have appealed to her. Her gardening-filmmaking repaired the rift, regaining balance. Standing in the hushed dusk, I remember a moment in Reel 80 when Robertson turns to the camera: "We go to the garden;

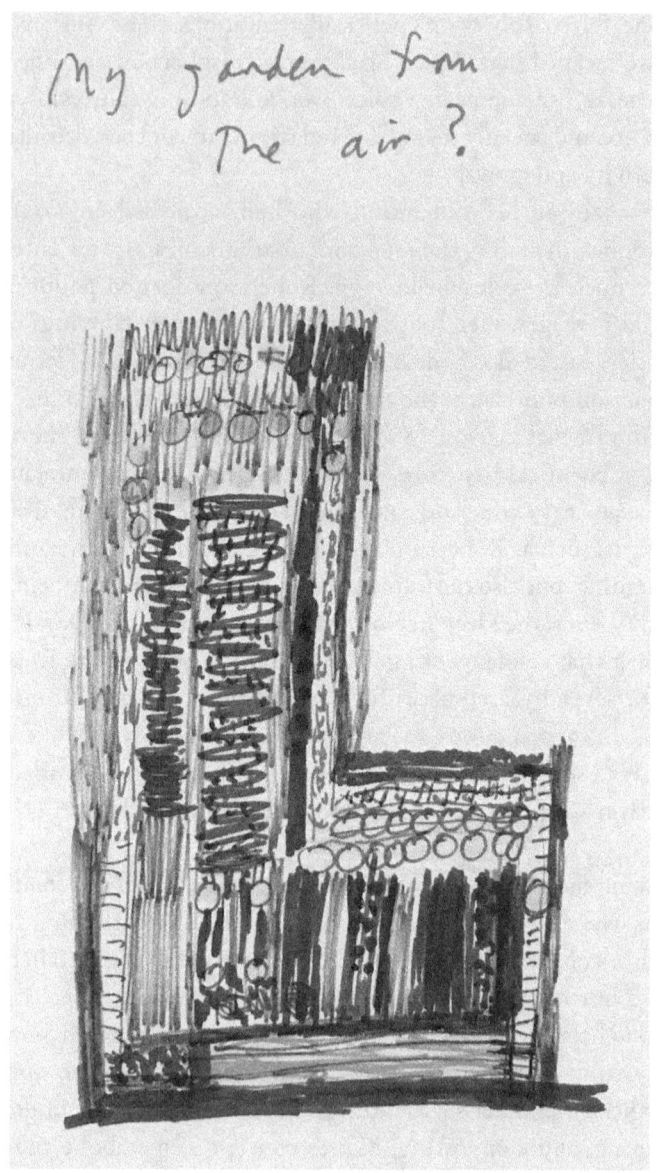

FIGURE 20. "My garden from the air?" Drawing by Anne Charlotte Robertson. Courtesy of the Anne Charlotte Robertson Collection, Harvard Film Archive, Harvard University.

we grow in the garden," she says. To grow one's garden and to grow oneself were, for her, the same thing.

FIELD

"I have been carrying on a dialogue between the landscape and the female body," wrote Ana Mendieta.[40] This dialogue became a series of works spanning performance, sculpture, photography, and film, known as the *Silueta Series*, made between 1973 and 1980. To make a piece for the series, Mendieta would lie submerged in soil, water (Figure 21), cut grass, and flowers or leave a trace of a female silhouette in the land by either piling small mounds of earth or ash in the shape of a woman or carving into the ground to leave a shallow depression. These ephemeral activities and markings were recorded as photographs or short films. Mendieta made siluetas in Iowa, where she had settled upon arrival from Cuba as a child and later studied painting and intermedia art, and in Mexico, where she often traveled as an adult. In works made concurrently with the *Silueta Series*, recorded on both super 8mm film and video, Mendieta pours animal blood over herself before rolling in chicken feathers (*Blood and Feathers*, 1974) and crawls on all fours wearing a fur skin (*Dog*, 1974). Becoming part animal and part earth in these works, Mendieta re-pairs herself and her surroundings. Lasting barely three minutes each, the filmed siluetas chronicle fleeting metamorphoses, translating Mendieta through media as well as species, from the live body to photographed and filmed documentation.

Surviving only in still and moving images, not in great monuments marking the earth, Mendieta's activities were ecologically light of touch. She worked within and against a male-dominated art market where minimalist land art and industrial materials and scales of sculptural production proliferated. "Men artists working with nature," she said in 1977, "have imposed themselves on it."[41] We might think of Robert Smithson's *Spiral Jetty* (1970), for example, a 1,500-foot-long basalt and earth formation constructed on the northeastern shore of the Great Salt Lake

FIGURE 21. Ana Mendieta. *Creek*, 1974. Super 8mm film, color, silent. © 2025 The Estate of Ana Mendieta Collection, LLC. Licensed by DACS, London. Courtesy Galerie Lelong, New York.

in Utah that required dump trucks, a tractor, and a front-end loader to haul over six thousand tons of material into place.[42]

Mendieta's works refuse a grammar in which an artist imposes materials and processes onto land in a subject-object relation that Marisol de la Cadena associates with anthropocentrism and extractive violence to the earth.[43] Instead, and in conversation with the same subjective turn that influenced Robertson, whereby the artist's body became the subject, object, and medium of the work, Mendieta situated herself in relation to the bodies of land and water where she lay. With this merging of substances, she expanded the feminist possibilities of focusing on self and body with an ecological decentering of the human. Although her works contrast the land art of her male peers precisely because they retain the figurative form, Mendieta planted the female body as always in affective and ecological relation with its surroundings. These site-specific and ephemeral actions were live landscape-portraits. Lying beneath cut grass, her breath causing the grass to rise and fall, Mendieta reminded audiences that humans and plants share and depend on the same ecosystem.

Neither pushing her weight around nor assuming privileged exteriority, Mendieta performed as an animal-plant-water-land-climate human being. Her works relate the environmental damage of heavy industry and agri-business she witnessed in the Midwest to violence inflicted on women when also objectified as resources. Mendieta made several performative works about rape and femicide. In these and the siluetas' prostrate mode, vulnerability is also strength gained as Mendieta developed an eco-feminist empathy with bodies of land, animals, plants, and water, prefaced on the shared trauma of patriarchal and extractive violence.

When Mendieta described her work as a "dialogue between the landscape and the female body," she added that it developed as "a direct result of my having been torn from my homeland during my adolescence. I am overwhelmed by the feeling of having been cast from the womb. My art is the way I re-establish the bonds that tie me to the universe."[44] Mendieta came to the United States as an exile from post-revolutionary communist Cuba in 1961.[45] Knowledge of this experience of displacement amplifies the siluetas' grounded impact. Though Mendieta arrived as a foreign body on US soil, her filming of physical immersion in its landscape signals a sense of reunion. Planted in the earth, her form suggests a process of burial and regrowth in a pre-colonized context more ancient and ecologically rooted than any national border or geopolitical strategy for containment and assimilation. Mendieta's reference to land as a "womb," along with her filmed siluetas' fleeting duration and the biodegradable constituents of their staging, establish a relation with colonized and agro-industrialized land—wounded land—that does not impose and order but instead conjoins Mendieta's body with that of the troubled North American landscape.

Describing land as a body carries risks of which Mendieta was well aware. Landscapes are often personified as female in colonial accounts of discovery, conquest, and cultivation.[46] The word "rape" originally described a violent seizure of property—a land grab. Early legal definitions of territory established ownership through the clearance of land (along with any Indigenous people dwelling upon it), followed by its cultivation. As Irit Rogoff has written, Mendieta subverts this territorial law of the land, converting it into an idiosyncratic form of land stewardship.[47] Barely leaving a trace, Mendieta's supine body resembles an offering. Less morbid than organic, her posture resonates with Robertson's repeated filming of compost heaps (and several pumpkins she painted with ladies' faces and filmed in time lapse as they rotted). Robertson's pumpkin ladies and Mendieta's reclined siluetas made in earth or ash perform cyclical reunions with land, returning to the ground (the womb) from which they grew.

Mendieta's association of childhood exile with post-partum longing for earth was one of many personal statements included in the catalog of her first retrospective, held at New York's New Museum in 1987. Drawing on statements such as these, biographical interpretations of Mendieta's work abound. Certainly, Mendieta's itinerance and interest in rooting herself in land recalls her experiences of displacement. But imposed causalities also suffocate her work, drawing on worn associations between personal trauma and public art practice that provided effective means, as Jane Blocker has written, to feminize and depoliticize her.[48] Mendieta regularly contended with racist and sexist receptions of her work that exoticized her immigrant Latina identity and interest in nature and Indigenous religions and marginalized her within the New York art world (defined by a predominantly male, Eurocentric, urban and commodity-oriented elite as a center). After her untimely death, matters only worsened.[49]

Like Robertson, however, Mendieta refused to play victim during her lifetime. Looking with a kind of "third eye" that Fatimah Tobing Rony describes in her account of anti-colonial feminist filmmaking, Mendieta surveyed herself as a Cuban woman through the eyes of others to critically examine their racialized and gendered gaze. Subverting what she saw, she generated lush images of sensual engagement, her body cooled by spring water and blanketed by fresh-cut grass.[50]

Exuberant and often humorous (especially when rolling in chicken feathers) as well as poignant (when resembling a burial), Mendieta's earthworks and bodyworks re-route visual pleasure from a system in which, as Claire Johnson put it at the time, "woman is presented as what she represents for man."[51] Mendieta presents herself becoming wondrously transformed through earthy enjoinment and enjoyment. This is resistant filmmaking, to borrow Rony's term. It undoes visual biopolitics' damaging effects yet insists on its own form of visual pleasure.[52]

Mendieta looks happy. She lies unclothed so that her skin feels the cool damp of the loam or the tickle of wildflowers. In transitive form, in subject position, she looks carefully, responsibly, and with all her senses at the world around her. Mendieta's position practices Rony's definition of an anti-colonial, feminist way of looking: she is the object of our looking and a subject looking back.

In the siluetas that Mendieta made in Iowa, a state known as America's breadbasket and characterized by massive monoculture crops of corn and wheat, Mendieta planted her body as a visceral reminder of humanity's dependence on nature and capitalism's damaging control of it. Her diminutive yet defiant silhouette (she was 4'11" and weighed ninety-three pounds) sensually engaged with land in a non-financialized gesture of vulnerability and embrace. Her siluetas offer a reminder that corporate farms in a state named Iowa are part of the Americas plural, a landmass encompassing the totality of North and South America and far pre-dating corporate, state, and national claims.

The siluetas that Mendieta made in Mexico continue this work of reparation across expanded time frames and regions. Mendieta first visited Mexico in 1971. The Mexican siluetas she made from 1973 onward drew inspiration from various Indigenous cultures she encountered there. Pre-Colombian cultures' reverence for nature suggested to Mendieta a vital antidote to the modern agri-business treatment of crops and labor forces occurring north of the US-Mexican border. Drawn to ritual and ceremonial aspects of these traditions as well as Indigenous Caribbean cultures such as Taíno, which she knew from Cuba, Mendieta scratched marks into stone to imitate rock carvings and lit gunpowder poured on the ground in the outline of goddesses to make fleeting, fiery effigies.

Mendieta's use of animal blood and feathers in the *Silueta Series* and adjacent works also derived from an interest in Cuba's Santería religion, which combines Yoruba traditions of sacrifice and purification brought to Cuba by enslaved people from West Africa and Catholic elements introduced by Spanish colonizers. Mendieta's syncretic approach and interest in Santería itself as a syncretic religion reached across estranged regions in an extension to her framework of art practice, eco-feminism, and anti-colonial politics.

Mendieta's refusal of a single authoritative source of inspiration in favor of many influences could be criticized for its lack of specificity and associated with a wider (and predominantly white, middle-class, and Euro American) trend for goddesses in second wave spiritualist feminism.[53] But such a response would insufficiently differentiate her emplaced fascination with Cuban and Mexican cultures from contemporaneous women artists who appropriated diverse manifestations of feminine divinity in projects for empowerment that often overlooked considerations of race (we might think of Robertson here, describing herself as a "goddess" and shuttling between New Age religions and self-help mantras of empowerment). Mendieta distanced herself from this kind of "white feminism," as she called it.[54]

Mendieta's power lies precisely in this positioning. Embodying Trinh T. Minh-ha's insider/outsider figure of an anti-colonial filmmaker, poised between cultures and occupying multiple perspectives, Mendieta navigated proximity and distance from not only currents in second wave feminism but also Cuban and US identities and trends in body, performance, and land art.[55] Processing alienation from and affinity with multiple cultures and landscapes and the trauma that this exilic positionality entailed, her performed and filmed communions with earth tapped an energy "which runs," she wrote, "from insect to man, from man to specter, from specter to plant, from plant to galaxy."[56]

PLOT

"Striving to tap the spirit and richness" of her community "by exposing its magic, touching its textures, trampling old stereotypes," Barbara McCullough's Los Angeles–based film and video work also draws on ritual's potential for temporal and geographic reparation.[57] "I do not intend this to be stuff for a broad audience," she warned an interviewer. McCullough made experimental films about diasporic African identity in Black artist communities and for those communities themselves. She had taken her work to PBS television, "but they weren't interested."[58] Her formal experimentation and critical engagement with transatlantic histories and ritual struck many as insufficiently mainstream and excessively political. Like Mendieta and Robertson, McCullough was marginalized. "I don't have any illusions," she said, about "how white critics deal with Black artists [and] about who does or does not like my work."[59]

McCullough's 1979 film *Water Ritual #1: An Urban Rite of Purification* explores historic displacement and connection in an enigmatic choreography. Lasting just eight minutes and shot on black-and-white 16mm film, it follows a young Black woman exploring a ruined lot in the desecrated landscape of Watts, Los Angeles. The area, an intersection at 118th Street and Main Street, had been home to a predominantly Black community until Los Angeles city authorities razed the area to make way for the construction of a highway. Houses were bulldozed, and gardens were ruined. Land and community became terra nullius available for "development." Collaborating with her friend the dancer Yolanda Vidato, who performs under the name Milanda in the film, McCullough choreographed a ritual for camera inspired by Yoruba traditions of purification that mourns and blesses this landscape of violent dispossession (Figure 22). Milanda gathers soil from the parched ground, stirring it in a calabash; arranges shells, cornmeal, bits of glass, a fish head, and a little palm branch; and removes her clothes, dances, crouches, and urinates.

In a very sensual way, like Mendieta lying in a stream or a bed of grass, McCullough's Milanda uses her body as a tool for political and aesthetic work. Embodying Trinh's insider/outsider figure, McCullough steps outside of the cultures of which she is a part, turning her camera toward them in a kind of double consciousness that foregrounds performance to complicate any attempt to frame her as an authentic insider to either Los Angeles's Black/women/artist communities or to the Yoruba culture of her enslaved ancestors.[60] Milanda's danced performance draws from these communities and traditions but stages them in the ruins of the contemporary, mediating between regions and histories to

FIGURE 22. Mourning and blessing a place in *Water Ritual #1: An Urban Rite of Purification*. Frame enlargement. Thanks to Barbara McCullough. Courtesy of Third World Newsreel.

emphasize their shared trauma within narratives of transatlantic slavery. McCullough's mise-en-scène on the razed lot and with ritual objects is at once local and cross-cultural in its expression of "personal and political freedom struggles."[61]

Water Ritual featured in a video McCullough made two years later, *Shopping Bag Spirits and Freeway Fetishes: Reflections on Ritual Space*. In that video, McCullough places the earlier film in relation to nine artist peers in the Los Angeles community "whose work . . . shows an affinity for symbolic things related to an African past."[62] Interested in her peers and keen on collaboration, McCullough belonged to the Opened Eye, "an organization primarily of third-world people, whose main interest is to see that under-exposed artists have an avenue of showing their work." She was also part of the L.A. Rebellion.

A loose grouping of Black American filmmakers, the L.A. Rebellion film movement gathered after an uprising against racism in Watts in 1965. Many were young film students at the University of California, Los Angeles (McCullough attended from 1972, majoring in communication studies and taking film classes with the Third Cinema scholar Teshome Gabriel, alongside workshops in video, photography, and dance).[63] Collaborating on each other's films, McCullough and other students including Charles Burnett and Julie Dash shared a sense of Black pride and, as McCullough put it, a desire to generate "another image" besides those produced by Hollywood and within blaxploitation and New Hollywood films popular at the time.[64] Understanding race, class, and gender as intersectional oppressions shaping everyday life, they drew inspiration from Third Cinema's critiques of neocolonialism and Hollywood.

Ritual enactment was one method by which L.A. Rebellion filmmakers such as McCullough, Zeinabu irene Davies, and Ben Caldwell (McCullough's cinematographer on *Water Ritual*) connected contemporary struggles with histories of dispossession and resistance throughout the United States and in Atlantic passages between Africa, Europe, and the Americas. "We've lost a link," McCullough said, "with our cultural past. But we have ... fragments. To be motivated as a Black person, to have my spiritual sense intact, I have to ... reach out to my past."[65] As Allyson Field notes in her edited volume on the L.A. Rebellion, in films such as McCullough's, meaning lies with the maker and her interpretation of Black spiritual and cultural traditions and "not within the gaze of some idealized White observer, either inside or outside the text."[66] Exploring this process of signification as what she calls "visitation," Jennifer DeClue describes McCullough and other Black feminist filmmakers' experimental journeys into their ancestral pasts as means to conjure new narratives and reckon with historical violence. This kind of "conjure-work," DeClue adds, entails "a methodology of tenderness" and mourning.[67]

Taking up new narrative meaning as well as physical room in the surrounding social and spatial context of racial capitalism, McCullough's Milanda sits on the ground with her legs in a wide V shape and sets to work with her calabash, shells, and cornmeal. How much space the female body occupies is a recurrent motif across many L.A. Rebellion films, including Julie Dash's *Four Women* (1975), where a dancer progresses through multiple personas and gestures to carve out space and subjectivity, and Alile Sharon Larkin's *A Different Image* (1982), whose protagonist sits with her legs apart like Milanda. "We're in this environment," McCullough explained, "and we make it our own.... But we're still not... of this environment.... I don't care how many hundreds of years go by[,] ... there's still a link with something else."[68] In the environment but not of it, because also connected to an environment across the Atlantic and "hundreds of years" before, Milanda extends her limbs to reach beyond the present.

Milanda arranges "bits of... a deteriorating urban environment," McCullough explained, "that, when reassembled with other objects... have a beauty of their own, joined together in this circle."[69] On the soundtrack, Don Cherry's improvisatory trumpet emphasizes the camerawork's restless dancing (McCullough loved music from the time of her childhood in New Orleans, where her father was a musician and played for Mardi Gras). Anticipating Cherry's freewheeling notes, the camera brushes up against the gritty rust and crumbling wood of Milanda's surroundings, refusing to delineate and define as it explores shadowy recesses.

In an interview, McCullough recalled wanting to have Milanda sit on the ground at "that particular spot" on 118th and Main "because it looked like... a blighted situation[,] ... a desolate area," and at the same time "had the sense of being in the country, the backcountry."[70] Her reference to "the backcountry" introduces a contrast between spaces of urban spoil and rural subsistence that the film mediates through Milanda's ritual acts of purification. Modernity's so-called progress (epitomized by highway construction) collides with "backcountry" references that transport us back in time. "My ancestors... weren't necessarily urban people," McCullough said.

While Los Angeles's highway expansion concretizes a Capitalocene fixation on space-time compression in 1970s America, McCullough's "backcountry" invites associations with capitalism's Plantationocene past of biopolitical and agricultural violence, which imported her ancestors, as Katherine McKittrick puts it, "not as members of society, but as commodities that would bolster crop economies."[71] Contributing "to the racial contours of uneven geographies" in contemporary Los Angeles, plantation and highway logics converge on 118th and Main in burned wood and smashed glass.[72]

McCullough and Vidato's collaborative work in that "blighted situation" brings an ancestral past of ritual and solidarity into contact (contamination) with a future of Black women artists' creativity. As Trinh puts it, in a suitably dance-like metaphor, "the step backward is constantly also a step forward" for women of color working between cultures.[73] This was also a step forward for filmmaking, which had not often been accessible to women and people of color before this and whose histories so often focus on a canon that is distinctly white.[74]

On the unruly edges of plantation logic, in homes razed to enable the development of transportation infrastructures for individual car owners, McCullough fosters an aesthetics and politics that resist racial capitalism.[75] The film develops a narrative of connection between Milanda and the earth that challenges social and species hierarchies. Tending her ritual circle, Milanda recalls the practices of enslaved people in plots of land on the edges of plantations. As Wynter explains, the purpose of such plots was to reduce overhead costs by placing responsibility for food provision on the enslaved rather than on their owners. But these plots yielded much more than sustenance, enabling people to cultivate what would have been considered impossible under slavery: cultural practices that materialized deep connections with the earth and fostered definitions of growth antithetical to the murderous, ecocidal values of the Plantationocene.[76]

Like Mendieta tracing her body's imprints on the earth without proprietary intentions, Milanda's urinating is not territorial because the land she inhabits is not terra nullius (despite the efforts of the California Department of Transportation). The film's title gestures at its interest in stewardship—we are witnessing the careful purification of wounded land as Milanda releases toxins from her body as well as a moment of anger in which—as Virginia Bonner has suggested—McCullough and Milanda are "quite literally pissing on the capitalistic destruction of this Watts neighborhood."[77] Anger and beauty, mourning and blessing, coincide in the gesture and the place.

In the end, 118th and Main were destroyed for nothing: Los Angeles's Interstate 105 was rerouted a few blocks north. Abandoned by the urban authorities, the land lay in trauma. But as if watering the ground to regenerate it (cleansing "the putrefaction of society," McCullough explained), Milanda's actions one afternoon in 1979 planted hope for McCullough and Vidato, their community, and the land.[78]

DANCING THE WORLD INTO BEING

In distinct and interconnected ways, Robertson, Mendieta, and McCullough faced and filmed systemic oppression on their lives, bodies, and surroundings as a climate of related conditions. The public health researcher Arline Geronimus calls the effect of such conditions "weathering." Weathering, Geronimus writes, "is about hopeful, hardworking, responsible, skilled, and resilient people dying from the physical toll of constant stress on their bodies, paying with their health because they live in a rigged, degrading, and exploitative system."[79] But weathering, Geronimus continues, "is a contronym, that is, a word with opposite meanings. Weathering can describe deterioration and erosion, as in "that rock has been weathered by geological processes over millions of years," but it can also signal strength and endurance, as in "the family weathered the recession very well."[80]

Robertson's, Mendieta's, and McCullough's films chronicle this simultaneous process of erosion and resistance, their socially manufactured struggles planted alongside their nature-based sources of remedy and pleasure. By creatively cultivating despoiled lands and attending to other-than-human beings within them, the filmmakers challenged a visual eco-politics shored up by iconographies of inert nature and all-powerful man—iconographies allied with a visual biopolitics of race- and gender-based discrimination.[81] Cultivating anti-colonial and eco-feminist relations of care for land and all its inhabitants, Robertson, Mendieta, and McCullough filmed to dance the contaminated, complex, so-much-larger-than-us world back into being. Their films wrest the notion of cultivation from Plantationocene histories and figures of women from images of pastoral passivity. In Chapter 5, we meet more women fighting for these rights.

FIVE

On the Picket Line, on the Television

REPRESENTATION, EMPATHY, AND DISTANCE

"TO BE IN THE SHOES of an Other still leaves you with your own feet," writes Jade E. Davis.[1] In a recent critique of what she calls "empathy culture," Davis identifies a problematic gaze at work in photojournalism, documentary, and television that portray marginalized and at-risk people as passive victims with the aim of fostering audiences' empathy.[2] Such a gaze "reduces a person to an object, denying them their full humanity" by transforming and consuming their "suffering as an aesthetic experience," Davis writes. Deriving "from a position of power and dominance" on the part of the spectator, she continues, this empathetic gaze developed in tandem with television, which injected "a new sense of proximity across people and places."[3]

What should we make of land cinema created with an eco-political agenda that broadcasts cases of land dispossession and labor exploitation in one part of the world for television audiences in another? Does it serve the kind of voyeurism Davis describes? Or can it help repair an estranged relation by connecting people, places, and shared but differential relations to extractive capitalism? With this question in mind and drawing on arguments by Trinh T. Minh-ha and Pooja Rangan introduced in Chapter 1 about the presumptively white, male, and privileged gaze of social documentary, this chapter explores the potentials and risks of land cinema that is made to raise consciousness across difference and distance.

My focus is on two land cinema films, both screened on British television's newly launched Channel Four in the 1980s. Made collectively by filmmaking groups in Britain and Colombia and in collaboration with laboring and agricultural subjects, most of whom are women, the films attempt to give voice to working-class and Indigenous perspectives, reaching new audiences through television broadcast.

My aim is neither to celebrate these films wholesale, nor to criticize their shortcomings but instead to discover in their forms and methods of production and broadcast ideas for how land cinema might help sustain eco-political work now and in the future. The films offer what Caroline Levine has recently called "workable blueprints" for organizing eco-political action geared toward climate justice.[4] Chapter 6 traces some of these forms and methods in land cinema today.

Written while on strike with Britain's University and College Union and in support of nurses, doctors, teachers, and postal and transport workers also striking in 2023 and in awareness of growing picket lines in other countries—not least in the United States, where the Writers Guild of America called for better protections in the film and television industry—this chapter's study of two historical films involving unionization has an eye on present possibilities for collective action.

WALES

The women turn their collars against the drizzle and rub mittened hands. They've set some wooden pallets alight to warm the picket line. Shirley Butts, the union leader, tells an off-camera interviewer that women are paid less than their male counterparts at this electronics factory. "We feel that this is a fight, and we'll fight it 'til the end." She speaks in English, but her lilt is Welsh.

Shot over five years and screened on Channel Four in 1982, the documentary *So That You Can Live* follows Shirley Butts in her everyday life in and out of work, on strike, and struggling to make ends meet by living off the land; she sells birds' eggs "so that you can live" (Figure 23). With opening credits announcing an intention to portray "what it means to live in South Wales," *So That You Can Live* uses Shirley's experiences to encapsulate a wider problem of deindustrialization and

FIGURE 23. Selling poultry eggs "so that you can live." Frame enlargement.

economic decline. Also following Shirley's teenage daughter Diane, the film emphasizes the intergenerational trauma of prolonged extractive onslaughts on lands and livelihoods and the systemic sexism that tasks women with reproductive labor as well as menial day jobs.

During the course of the film, which condenses five years into eighty-five minutes, we see Shirley and her husband Roy move from waged work in town to subsistence farming in the countryside. Diane prepares for school exams and searches for work in London. Her brother Royston also leaves home. The camera wanders to the employment center where advertisements are few and list overseas addresses. So-called economic development devastated life for people such as the Buttses in the 1970s. As an increasingly neoliberal agenda reorganized Britain's economy and instigated a move toward just-in-time production, low-, semi-skilled, and manual labor jobs were casualized, automated, or sent abroad.[5]

Tracking shots explore this landscape of loss, which also bears scars of earlier industrial development (Figure 24). Rows of terraced houses abut collieries, now closed. Windows are boarded up. New forestry cannot

FIGURE 24. Industrialized South Wales in *So That You Can Live*. Frame enlargement.

hide abandoned railway tracks, pitheads, and coal tips. A forlorn and uncertain energy lingers in the cold mist blanketing the land. In Swansea Miners' Library, the camera finds a worn copy of Karl Marx's *Capital*, lying open on a chapter about "surplus value." Combining these melancholic vignettes, the film constructs a diagram of extractive capitalism and its material and emotional fallout.

Raymond Williams discusses capitalism's effects on landscapes such as this in his 1973 book *The Country and the City*. Williams grew up close to where *So That You Can Live* was filmed. A well-known figure in leftist politics and public intellectualism, Williams co-founded the *New Left Review* in 1960, publishing critiques of Britain's classism and reports about socialism abroad.[6] *So That You Can Live* contains direct voice-over quotations from Williams's books—Diane is tasked with reading from *The Country and the City* as well as *The Fight for Manod* (1979) and *Politics and Letters* (1979). Williams also wrote texts for the film that describe landscape as a sedimentation of social history and unresolved class tension.

A historian of the working-class and village who valued the anecdotal and everyday in countering history's grand narratives, Williams has been described as a "counter-historian."⁷ He suspected the elitist pretensions of a vanguard enlightening "common people" and believed in ordinary people's ability to know their own situations.⁸ Oral testimony was central to Williams's counter-historicism because it allowed people to articulate their experiences and opinions in their own dialect-rich and accented ways. *So That You Can Live* subscribes to this faith in direct speech. Deriving from Shirley, the film's title establishes testimony and life experience as central concerns. Williams's perspective on South East Wales and Diane's Welsh-accented delivery of his words attracted the film's makers as further notes of authenticity. The filmmakers, by contrast, were strangers to the region.

So That You Can Live was made by the London-based filmmaking collective Cinema Action. The group formed in 1968, when British filmmaker Ann Guedes (b. 1933) was in France with her partner Gustav Lamche and their children. Upon being deported for political agitation during the May uprisings, they established Cinema Action. Other leftist filmmakers and activists including Eduardo Guedes (whom Ann later married), Richard Mordaunt, Marc Karlin, Humphry Trevelyan, and Steve Sprung also joined Cinema Action, though Mordaunt, Karlin, and Trevelyan would soon form their own group, the Berwick Street Film Collective.⁹

Cinema Action and the Berwick Street Film Collective were among a growing number of film cooperatives and workshops in the 1970s. Others included Amber, the Sheffield Filmmakers Co-op, the Leeds Animation Workshop, and, in the early 1980s, the Black Audio Film Collective, Ceddo, and Sankofa.¹⁰ Like the Newsreel groups in the United States, Ogawa Pro in Japan, and Chris Marker's SLON and Jean-Luc Godard's Dziga Vertov Group in France, these collectives eschewed auteurist individualism, developing essayistic registers and collective modes of production that Morgan Adamson has described as generating a "politics of the common."¹¹ This leftist cinema wanted to raise consciousness of working-class, feminist, and anti-colonial struggles—Cinema Action's name announced as much. Filmmaking was activism.

Cinema Action's films were funded by small grants from the British Film Institute, donations from trade unions, and meager screening fees. "You were independent," recalled Trevelyan, "of the hegemonies of broadcast[,] ... the ideologies of people who control the media," and agendas associated with political parties.[12] Owning the means of production was also crucial.

Cinema Action's cameras, tape recorders, and cutting machines were donated by other filmmakers. Members occupied squatted and subsidized premises in North London, some also living together. They loaned their premises and equipment to other filmmakers for free while away visiting "canteens, branches, sites, and public meetings" to show films and facilitate discussions. "The concept of a collective," Ann Guedes explained, "meant that everything could be shared."[13]

Influenced by Godard and Marker, with whom members had worked while living in France, Cinema Action labeled its early films "*ciné-tracts*," "campaign films," and "peoples films."[14] These short, tract-like documentaries chronicled workers' strikes across Britain: *Fighting the Bill* (1970) was made to assist the campaign against Britain's Industrial Relations Act, *Film from the Clyde* (1971) documents the work-in of shipbuilders in England's Northeast, and *The Miners' Film* (1975) witnesses strikes that helped bring down the Conservative government (if only temporarily). According to member Steve Sprung, Cinema Action brought its camera "to the factory gate where people were picketing" to function "as a catalyst" in raising consciousness among workers about their current struggle and its relation to the "history of their industries" and "the world in general."[15] This is what brought Ann Guedes to Wales in 1976.

Carrying a van loaded with films along with a projector and a list of unions to visit, Guedes headed to a factory in Treforest where women were striking for equal pay. Approaching Shirley Butts at the picket line outside the General Electric Company, Guedes invited her to collaborate on a film project about industrial change. She also asked whether she could try something new: Could she follow Shirley home from the picket line, into her domestic life?

This move, from one place of work to another (often overlooked) one, signaled a shift in Cinema Action's methods, from making *ciné-tracts* to experimenting with a slower, more exploratory mode of filmmaking attuned to aspects of gender sometimes overlooked in class struggle. Cinema Action was not unique in its increasing focus on gender; after leaving Cinema Action, Trevelyan collaboratively made *The Nightcleaners* (1975), which documents the struggles of women cleaners in London, and *Women of the Rhondda* (1973), which gathers testimonies of Welsh miners' wives involved in industrial disputes in the 1920s.[16] *So That You Can Live* follows these films in its careful attention to oral testimonies that recount women's political situations in relation to working-class men.

Made not only for Shirley, her family, and the local community, *So That You Can Live* was also intended for a wider audience. One of the group's founding principles had been "letting people speak in their own voice." In keeping with this, the film listened to women whose perspectives had hitherto been marginalized. Another early principle had been never to show work on television ("we wanted to show the work ourselves").[17] When Channel Four television launched with a promise to broadcast diverse voices far and wide, however, Cinema Action switched tack.

COLOMBIA

In 1989 a Colombian documentary called *Amor, mujeres y flores* (*Love, Women, and Flowers*, 1988) screened on Channel Four in Britain, as *So That You Can Live* had done seven years earlier. Shot over five years by the documentarian Marta Rodríguez (b. 1933) and her professional and life partner Jorge Silva (1941–1987), *Amor* exposes exploitative conditions on cut flower plantations in the Bogotá savanna and champions workers as they unionize and strike for better protections and pay. Most of the workers are women, and many are Indigenous. Their strike recalls the picket line sequence in *So That You Can Live*. "Finishing this film

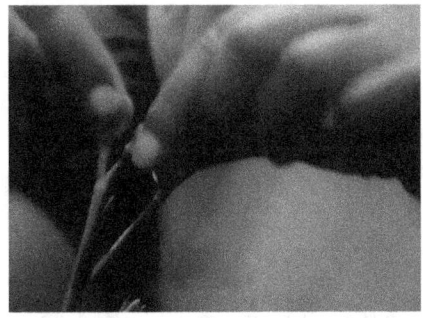

FIGURE 25. Manual labor on the flower plantation in *Amor, mujeres y flores*. Frame enlargement.

required a lot of love," reads an on-screen epigraph. A play on the title *Amor*, the statement also foreshadows the film's tragic production.

"Flowers, flowers, joy / a world of color / tenderness, poetry, beauty, love." As the film opens, a woman's voice softly reads this poem of Silva's in Spanish, with English subtitles. Written in 1985 while making *Amor*, the poem associates flowers with "nature, color, sunshine, light, sensuality," and "utopia." The camera grazes over carnations, flooding the screen with crimson and pink. Silva's reference to utopia—a word derived from the Greek "no place" and similar in pronunciation to "good place"—is telling. To believe that these flowers stem from a place of natural goodness is a fantasy. In one of the film's many talking-head testimonies, a farmer describes herself as "a withered flower." While flowers have color, another sighs, "we lose our color because of them." Far from lovely, these flowers come from poisoned soil and hands.

Throughout *Amor*, close-ups catalog hands performing tasks that the women tell us destroy eyesight, skin, and nerves. Hands twine wire around stems, weed, bind, and pull leaves (Figure 25). Close-ups feel intimate, testifying to the trust Rodríguez and Silva gained during the extended production. But the close-ups are also alarming. Burnt, blinded, poisoned, and continuing to work, the bodies on-screen are intended to jolt audiences into a visual realization of suffering, activating the type of response that David MacDougall describes as a "prehensile vision" of sensory contact and Jane Gaines describes as an empathetic mirroring process that might stir us politically.[18]

Filming inside the plantation, the camera's shallow depth of field is claustrophobic. There is no sky, only a cloudy plastic roof. Sequences of workers spraying, cutting, binding, and packaging carnations seem sped up, but they are not. "We work at the speed of light," one employee explains. Just as the fungicide fumigator is programmed, so are the workers. "Even toilet breaks are timed."

Such frank testimonies, like the trusting close-ups, offer clues about Rodríguez and Silva's methods. Their approach was collaborative—not only in working together but also with those filmed. *Amor*, like Rodríguez and Silva's earlier projects, took years to complete because it invested in long-term relationships as an ethics of listening. This relational approach reflects a larger turn in documentary and experimental filmmaking in the late 1970s and 1980s, which questioned middle-class, paternalistic, and presumptively white perspectives in cinematic representation and saw subjects take up cameras themselves to create and disseminate their own narratives.[19] Although Rodríguez and Silva, like Cinema Action, retained directorial credit on films, their methods of developing scenarios and editing footage with subjects shift toward this co-creative questioning of authority and opening of authorial perspective.

Amor also questions authority on the plantation. Women tell Rodríguez (out of frame beside Silva, who operates the camera) that they have no authority, dignity, or rights. Many are in debt from taking sick leave or medication to treat illnesses caused by organophosphate. This fungicide burns them. They suffer sinusitis, rheumatism, bronchitis, asthma, epilepsy, and leukemia. Masks and gloves are few. Company doctors and insurance personnel hush concerns, and plantation managers fire anyone whose complaints continue.

One man speaks on behalf of management in the film. He is a white businessman whose Spanish accent is North American. He extols the virtues of the Bogotá Plains in providing excellent conditions for his cash crop and says nothing of the labor conditions. His sole reference to manual labor is an objectifying cliché: every flower flown to Europe, he smiles, "has been touched by a Colombian girl."

Girls and women comprise most of the film's testimonies, their concerns voiced in a working environment that affords little room for local and predominantly female epistemologies and in which modern technologies silence Indigenous expertise in floriculture. In a film made between 1974 and 1981, *Nuestra voz de tierra, memoria y futuro (Our Voice of Land, Memory and Future)*, Rodríguez and Silva make this same point. An Indigenous woman discusses mugwort's healing properties, her appearance followed by shots of a bottle of Parathion, a highly toxic insecticide produced by IG Farben, the German chemical conglomerate notorious for its role in the Holocaust.[20] Parathion is banned in most countries but not in Colombia. Global capitalism, the filmmakers imply, does not treat everybody equally. Some people are kept safer than others, and while some knowledge is valued as expertise in chemistry, other epistemes are dismissed as botanical folklore.

Amor's emphasis on women's testimonies also highlights the fact that environmental problems disproportionately harm women in less developed economies where labor and environmental protections are few and that poor and Indigenous women frequently bookend day jobs with unpaid labor at home.[21] Rodríguez never subscribed to a particular type of feminism. Evoking Ana Mendieta's skepticism in Chapter 4, Rodríguez associated feminism with North American variants that she found too white and middle class in their desire to liberate housewives.[22] Indigenous women in Colombia had long since had to work outside their own homes as maids. Nevertheless, *Amor*'s focus on Indigenous women reflects what T. J. Demos calls an "eco-intersectional" form of thinking by presenting extractivism, in this case floriculture, as simultaneously violating women, people of color, poor people, and the lands and ecosystems they inhabit.[23] Recalling *So That You Can Live* in this respect, *Amor*'s attention to women's labor in a damaged ecosystem tracks extractivism from the workplace and the landscape into the home.

Extractive violence also reaches women's bodies and wombs. *Amor* abounds with close-ups of pregnant abdomens. By foregrounding pregnancy, the film presents violations of land and labor rights by multinationals as a colonial past that is not past.[24] History repeats with each girl who becomes a woman and a mother. Mariela is sixteen when we first meet her. She tells us that she developed leukemia after joining the plantation. The camera attends her wedding, hovering behind bouquets that seem monstrous now that we know their chemical composition. "Behind every beautiful flower is death," Mariela says. She also tells us that she is pregnant.

Such testimonies implore European television audiences to consider the human cost of imported flowers. "No one was showing the stories of people who had no voice, and no power, in mainstream society," Rodríguez explained.[25] "We were very interested in the process of political awakening that often accompanied the filmmaking process," whereby people suffering "inequality, violence, and poverty" could "speak, on their terms, about what affected them."[26] *Amor* invites this "political awakening" in its audience by visiting the markets where Colombian flowers are bought (Figure 26). Tracking shots glide over frilly carnations, cutting to generic views of the Eiffel Tower and signage for a Van Gogh exhibition. Soft saxophone plays in the background. In a Dutch auction house, traders clutch phones to their ears and point at trolleys of flowers processing before them. Earlier we have seen these flowers planted, weeded, picked, trimmed, and bundled; packaged in boxes with layers of newspaper; loaded onto trucks; and boarded onto planes. If only the flowers' newspaper wrappings reported their terrible origin, we might think, now that we have witnessed it.

Exposing Colombia's flower trade was dangerous. Corporate and state authorities vested in maintaining the industry intimidated Rodríguez, Silva, and the workers they filmed. Toward the end of the film, unionized workers carry placards demanding change. After fifty-five days on strike, during which the camera glides through an empty plantation, workers win control of the company. Smiling through tears, women gather flowers into bundles. Birdsong enters the soundtrack as if nature has permeated the plantation. But the reprieve is temporary.

FIGURE 26. Flowers for the European market in *Amor, mujeres y flores*. Frame enlargement.

Intertitles report that the plantation's owners refused to recognize the union and summoned the army. "This is only the beginning," one worker announces. For Silva, however, it was the end.

Due to health issues incurred by dangerous working conditions and stress, Silva died in January 1987 at age forty-six. *Amor* closes with a dedication to him. Alone and in grief, Rodríguez completed post-production, editing the film to a fifty-two-minute broadcast slot for Channel Four. Television, she hoped, could give voice to previously silenced communities and function as a kind of empathy machine, inviting European audiences to step inside Colombian women's shoes and make connections across the world.[27]

THE PROMISE

With an "emphasis on marginalized and voiceless communities," Channel Four launched in November 1982 with a promise to represent "a more diverse set of perspectives" than British television had previously seen.[28] Until then, three channels were available. The British Broadcasting Corporation (BBC) owned two of them, and Independent Television (ITV) owned the other. Established in 1922, the BBC aimed at public utility and education of the variety pioneered by John Grierson, discussed in Chapter 1. ITV launched in 1955 with a more commercial outlook. By the 1970s there were calls for a fourth channel to cater to changing tastes and demographics, which included Britain's Windrush generation and various youth cultures formed in the 1960s. Accordingly, the British government commissioned an inquiry into the future of broadcasting. Published in 1977, the Annan Report recommended establishing a fourth channel.[29] The British Broadcasting Act of 1980 made this recommendation law.

As plans for Channel Four materialized, a group of filmmakers that included former Cinema Action members Karlin and Trevelyan, who had initiated the Independent Filmmakers Association (IFA) in 1974, met to discuss possibilities for film on the small screen. The IFA aimed to represent the interests of its members in the face of public funding cuts and in opposition to the BBC's orthodoxy. The IFA called for class-conscious, feminist and anti-racist programming, and emphasized the importance of showing material deemed too formally experimental by existing channels. When Channel Four finalized its staff, IFA members Alan Fountain and Rod Stoneman formed its Independent Film and Video Department. They were keen to program films that prioritized "direct speech," with less mediation "from 'television professionals'" and more "participatory access."[30]

So That You Can Live embodied this ambition. The documentary addressed British industrial history from a feminist perspective and diversified representations of Britain with voices from Wales. During Channel Four's first week on air, the film premiered to launch *The*

Eleventh Hour, one of the channel's most politically and formally experimental strands, airing each Monday at 11 p.m. with films commissioned by the channel or purchased from independent producers. Over the coming years *The Eleventh Hour* would also host Margaret Tait's films, which again represented an "Other" Britain, not even Scottish but instead Orcadian. Irish films were also broadcast in Gaelic with subtitles. The Black Audio Film Collective meanwhile contributed essay films offering postcolonial and diasporic perspectives. Alongside British independent film and video work, Channel Four programmed avant-garde and political cinema from overseas. Chris Marker, Terayama Shūji, Patricio Guzman, and Ousmane Sembène were among those featured. *Amor* was an ideal project for Channel Four to fund and broadcast, chiming with these films and forwarding a social agenda for diversifying television with educational and humanitarian perspectives.

Promises to give voice to marginalized perspectives with the aim of fostering diversity, empathy, and humanitarian aid can sound hollow today, as ubiquitous as they have become in promotional texts for socially engaged film and art.[31] Beyond their cliché, the problem of such promises, as Trinh cautioned in the early 1990s, is their assumption of a colonial and paternalistic position of privilege and an autonomy or immunity from the conditions they purport to critique or solve. Allowing subjects of documentary "to speak for themselves," Trinh explains, and "completing their speech with the insertion of a commentary that will objectively describe/interpret the images according to a scientific-humanistic rationale" entails objectification.[32] Davis takes a similar position, arguing that "empathy is the embodiment of a colonial sentimentality based on missionary thinking" and perpetuates a gaze whereby disenfranchised people are reduced "to their circumstances and oppression."[33] Leveling similar criticism at Grierson's documentaries of the 1930s, which aimed at social reform and national cohesion, Brian Winston argues that "a tradition of the victim" forecloses the possibility of subjects appearing as active, self-determining agents of change.[34] "Change and action stop being necessary in empathy culture," Davis continues, "because the feeling and sense of understanding are action enough."[35]

Feeling moved does not shut down a plantation or win a strike. And yet Rodríguez and Silva and Cinema Action were not alone in their belief that exposition could drive change—labor documentaries in the United States by Harvey Richards and Barbara Kopple present important evidence that films made by and about racialized, gendered, and classed people on strike have indeed helped their causes.[36] Gaines's belief in film's "political mimesis" resonates with this promise.[37] Many humanitarian agencies also emphasize the power of images in mobilizing public shame.[38] But critics working at the intersection of trauma studies and visual culture see in this logic an anachronistic faith in public actions and institutions and caution against "compassion fatigue," explaining that "a pseudo-familiarity with the horrible reinforces alienation, making one less able to react in real life."[39]

Even if to be seen and heard was empowering for subjects and did motivate action in audiences, who determines what forms visual and audible representation take? In *Immediations: The Humanitarian Impulse in Documentary* (2017), Rangan situates social-purpose filmmaking, ranging from Grierson's to television documentaries about "slum children," within a problematic matrix that reinforces relations of dependency and relies on photojournalistic tropes. Rangan locates the problems and potentials of humanitarian ethics in the domain of representation, warning that any attempt to humanize the other "by 'capturing' their humanity in some representable trait (e.g., the face, the eyes)" forces humanity into culturally and politically coded confines.[40]

As scholars have pointed out, the assumption of the category of human as transparent and unproblematic belongs to a modern and especially, but not only, Western understanding of selfhood as pertaining to individual rights and visibility.[41] Such an understanding erases "kinship, religion, nationality, and other webs of identity and relationship," explains Craig Calhoun, and prioritizes thinking in terms of administrative control, the state, and populations.[42] When images of distant suffering inundate the media, "the story seems to be: Moral white people come from the rich world to care for those in backward, remote places."[43]

Dating to the late twentieth century, the idea of humanitarian intervention as an act of witnessing requires suffering to be seen and heard, but as Michel Foucault has written, promises of visibility are a trap that forces vulnerable others into a predetermined framework of biopolitical relations.[44] Those who produce and broadcast images mediate them, encoding some places, in Calhoun's words, as "backward, remote" and some people as always and only dispossessed.

In *Immediations,* Rangan warns that insufficient decoding of representational tropes leads to an uncritical celebration of "the dispossessed as paradigmatic figures of resistance." Taking images as evidence of truth and resistance "is both seductive and dangerous," she continues, "because it subscribes to a rhetoric of immediacy" and underplays the forms that mediate representation.[45] Rangan's term "immediation" collides "immediacy" with "mediation" to indicate how humanitarian intervention both depends on an idea of directness and hides its hand when shaping public perception through the media.

Associating itself with immediacy, humanitarian intervention also sets itself against political deliberation; the preservation of life becomes a first-order principle, with "saving human lives" the moral justification for suspending the rule of law.[46] As Elaine Scarry cautions, such "emergency" temporality has no time for reasoned critical thinking: icons of humanitarian disasters appeal to emotion, appearing as distressing symptoms whose causes are left unexplored.[47] Such icons feed a lucrative psychodrama of trauma. Images created by advertisers working for Western aid agencies and charities ("merchants of misery" according to one critic) often represent distant suffering in an almost pornographic way.[48] This fetishization of suffering bodies is often racist, perpetuating a visual biopolitics that Fatimah Tobing Rony identifies as being at work in images of poor women of color.[49] Far from benefiting the people it exposes, visual representation can further disadvantage them by invading their privacy and aestheticizing the lack thereof.[50] Suffering bodies are often presented as just that—not suffering persons but rather bodies, rendered "anonymous, speechless, ahistorical or generic."[51]

Accompanying the celebrated "eyewitness" image, the testimonial voice must perform a social script compatible with humanitarian expectations. Organizations offering such voices a platform (television broadcasters and filmmakers included) often assume a self-effacing silence, selecting individuals as mouthpieces to speak for the suffering masses. The fact that speakers are often identified as having an accent indicates the continued assumption that they are exceptions to a constructed norm. As Rangan puts it, "what accent tells 'us' is actually 'us.'"[52] To perceive an accent is to experience difference between the speaking subject and the discriminating ear, the vulnerable other and the beneficent audience.

Amid such seeming deadlocks of marginalizing and mediating control, what are some alternatives for filmmaking? Surely the answer is not an iconoclasm that effaces and mutes the potential for marginalized subjects to express themselves and thereby transform the social parameters of who is seen and heard. *So That You Can Live* and *Amor* are instructive in this inquiry.

Both films witness their subjects and makers defending the importance of listening and ceding authoritative and authorial control while also decoding tropes of representation by foregrounding them. Developed throughout the filmmakers' careers, this critical experimentation embodies a compromise that Rangan describes as simultaneously holding space for "the subversive potential" of marginalized subjects and inquiring how, why, and with what effects these subjects are mediated through aesthetic form.[53] This experimentation speaks to a feminist corrective seen in much documentary filmmaking in the 1970s whereby works by racialized, classed, and gendered makers question categories of self and other and examine power differentials at play in processes of production and dissemination.[54] Tracing the paths that Cinema Action and Rodríguez and Silva took in this experimentation, from grassroots denunciation films to television broadcast, sheds light on possibilities for aesthetic and political forms of representation today.

FROM TRACT TO TELEVISION

Unlike the Navajo farmer in Chapter 1 who asked the social scientists visiting his reservation whether their film would help his sheep and was answered only with bemusement, a farmer, miner, or dockworker might count on Cinema Action and Rodríguez and Silva's early films to help them unionize, campaign, or strike. Their activist approach to land cinema brought farmer, Indigenous, and union struggles into filmmaking contexts in ways that resonate with the engaged practices of Third Cinema.

Third Cinema is associated with Latin America, where in the 1960s and 1970s countries including Chile, Argentina, and Brazil fostered vibrant underground filmmaking cultures committed to representing working-class perspectives and denouncing US and European support of right-wing dictatorships in the name of neoliberal "development."[55] Many looked toward Cuba as a leader in leftist filmmaking, as Cuba had established a culture of cinema as it transitioned to communism in the 1950s. The term "Third Cinema" was coined by two of the movement's best-known filmmakers from Argentina, Fernando Solanas and Octavio Getino.

Solanas and Getino wanted to describe a mode of filmmaking that rejected both First Cinema, the Hollywood model that made film as profitable entertainment, and the Second Cinema of the auteurist and often European avant-garde.[56] Third Cinema plays with the term "Third World," but from the outset Third Cinema contained examples from beyond the Third World, with filmmakers looking to marginalized sites and subjects in economically developed countries—as did Cinema Action in Britain. Though they did not know Rodríguez and Silva, Cinema Action members admired Third Cinema. Karlin later moved to Nicaragua, and Trevelyan worked in Argentina alongside Solanas and Getino as well as Fernando Birri, Margaret Tait's former collaborator.[57]

Third Cinema emphasized interactive modes of reception. Solanas and Getino's epic documentary *The Hour of the Furnaces* (1968), which was filmed and screened clandestinely during Argentina's dictatorship, included strategically placed intertitles indicating where the projectionist should pause and invite the audience to debate what they'd just seen.[58] Similarly, Cinema Action saw its films as akin to pamphlets or posters (Sprung was also a member of a poster collective, printing campaigns about colonialism, women's labor rights, Amílcar Cabral, Palestine, Chile, and trade unionism). "The people decide for themselves what the films should contain and put their message over in their own way," Cinema Action announced in an information sheet accompanying screenings in 1975.[59] "If you are doing the showing yourselves," Cinema Action instructed, we "hope you have a good discussion after the film," and when returning the print, "please slip a note in the film-can telling us how many attended your showing, if you had a discussion and your ideas for the next working class film."[60]

Another aspect of Third Cinema that Cinema Action and Rodríguez and Silva's land cinema shares is formal imperfection. In his manifesto "For an Imperfect Cinema," Julio Garcia Espinosa called for a mode of working that eschewed spectacle and technical finesse in favor of a roughness that galvanized action.[61] Films could seem unfinished aesthetically because the political formations to which they contributed were also still in progress. Urgency, however, is not the same as haste.

Rodríguez and Silva began making films together in the 1960s, describing them as "denunciation films" aimed at social change.[62] From the outset, their approach was paced and patient. Influenced by Paulo Freire's idea of "conscientization" through working-class pedagogy, the couple believed that film could help laboring and farming communities become aware of their oppression in order to challenge it.[63] They researched, planned, shot, and edited films over months and years. *Chircales* (*The Brickmakers*, 1967–1972), for example, was shot over five years. The film followed a family of brickmakers in a barrio where Rodríguez taught literacy. The filmmakers introduced a tape recorder and a stills camera first until "we had become part of their lives, [so] it was possible for them to assume a very casual, unaffected stance in front of the camera."⁶⁴ It helped that Rodríguez and Silva came from poor backgrounds themselves.

Rodríguez's mother was a peasant, and her father was a coffee exporter. Her mother raised her on a small farm outside Bogotá, surrounded by wealthy ranches and poor farmers—a formative experience of socioeconomic inequality. During her twenties Rodríguez lived in Spain and France, working in a women's prison and assisting Spanish migrant workers in Paris. Returning to Bogotá, she taught poor children and studied sociology with the Marxist priest Camilo Torres, who called for the political liberation of oppressed people. Interested in Colombia's many Indigenous nations, Rodríguez switched her major to anthropology and traveled to Paris to study ethnographic filmmaking with Jean Rouch. Returning to Colombia in 1965, Rodríguez found little by way of film culture and so started a cinema club of her own. Silva soon became a member.

Silva was an autodidact with a tireless work ethic and a commitment to political struggle. His mother was an Indigenous worker who migrated to Bogotá as a domestic maid. His father was absent. Silva spent some of his childhood in an orphanage and never graduated from high school. As a teen he worked as a bricklayer, later turning to journalistic photography and film.

These itinerant and challenging backgrounds placed the couple in a unique position to make films with poor and Indigenous Colombians and in dialogue with international contexts of Marxist organizing, political journalism, anthropology, and Third Cinema. Rodríguez and Silva were not humanitarian visitors, philanthropists, or colonial anthropologists; they were insiders/outsiders to the places and communities they filmed, sharing a differential relation to overarching conditions of extractive capitalism and (neo)colonial violence.

Cinema Action's differential relation with subjects was more marked than Rodríguez and Silva's. With members from France, Germany, England, and Portugal, Cinema Action was a cosmopolitan group more mobile than its working-class subjects. Several members came from middle-class backgrounds (a thorny topic was whether members had attended fee-paying schools—many had and concealed this. Sprung was an exception, entering film to avoid "going to work in a car factory").[65]

Promoting "working class films" about "contemporary life in Britain" from "an emancipative and historically correct perspective," Cinema Action troubled some contemporaries and critics.[66] Certainly, Cinema Action's early campaign films rejected Griersonian commentary—Guedes wanted to let subjects speak "in their own way."[67] But some critics identified an "effacement of any markings of the speaking source of the discourse."[68] Whose discourse was it? Whose "correct perspective"? Such criticisms reflect an uneasiness, growing in the 1970s into a rift within the New Left about the appointment of a political vanguard and aesthetic avant-garde to educate "the masses" about their own situations.[69] Although Cinema Action engaged workers in the making and viewing of films, its members' desire to "set themselves against a possible passivity of their audience" also implies a lingering didacticism.[70]

Critical reviews of Cinema Action's early campaign films reflect these concerns. Critics worried that self-effacing tendencies in the films assumed an "ideology of transparency" and disavowed "the selection and organization of images and sound according to political principles."[71] Cinema Action's "*verité* forms," one review complained, "purport to capture the world as it really is" and assume the "innocence of the image" further "legitimized by synchronous speech."[72] Cinema Action's *Fighting the Bill* (1970) illustrates these tensions. The film uses intertitles ("smash capitalism") and montage, with shots of campaign meetings abutting stock footage of Indochinese and Palestinian guerrillas and liberation protests in Vietnam. Such devices advance the film's internationalist anti-capitalist discourse, but Cinema Action avoids identifying itself explicitly as the source and mediator of the argument. *People of Ireland* (1973) also constructs arguments through intertitles ("the people should own the means of production," "the cause: crisis of capitalism") without identifying Cinema Action as the author. Through intertitles, Cinema Action attempts to weave the Troubles into its existing corpus of films, simplifying specifically Irish and anti-colonial contexts into a broader anti-capitalist argument.[73]

Despite such criticisms, Cinema Action's drive to relate local struggles to global ones is powerful for the way it recognizes shared class interests. This international perspective reflects Cinema Action's 1968 origins in France, where factory and student demonstrations against local injustices erupted alongside Vietnam antiwar protests, anti-colonial independence movements, and a surge of interest in socialist and communist projects in Cuba and China. Godard had released *La Chinoise*, about a group of young Maoist activists in Paris, just months earlier and had joined Marker, Agnès Varda, and others to make *Far From Vietnam*, a collective documentary protesting American imperialism. "Paris," recalled Ann Guedes, "informed my thinking tremendously."[74] Like much land cinema, not least that of Bouba Touré working between France and Mali, international awareness mapped local struggles onto global and planetary ones, seeking cross-cultural solidarity.

Solidarity was one thing, but effacing differences in perspective was another, and some Cinema Action members grew uneasy. The films were "represented as if the workers had made them," Sprung noted, which "was a misrepresentation."[75] From the outset of production in 1976, *So That You Can Live* confronted this issue through self-reflexivity.

Combining Shirley's and Diane's voices with those from Williams's texts and interviews with a farmer, an archaeologist, and a Welsh socialist historian, *So That You Can Live* multiplies voices to problematize authority and pluralize perspectives. As Claire Johnston wrote in a 1982 review, the film's "fragmented narrative structure" performs an important tension "between speaking a history and being spoken by a history" that renders the world in "deceptive simplicity."[76] In one scene, Diane tells a local historian that she's learned more about history from her grandmother ("my gran") than at school. History, Cinema Action implies, is not a stable set of facts but rather a shifting landscape of perspectives.

So That You Can Live also includes moments when subjects address the filmmakers (Diane, for example, speaks about first meeting Guedes: "I didn't know you then.... I was really shy"). This self-reflexivity characterizes a phase in documentary in the 1970s that Bill Nichols has described wherein filmmakers increasingly vocalized the mediating structures of their films, revealing that "documentaries always were forms of re-presentation, never clear windows onto 'reality.'"[77] The plurality of voices in *So That You Can Live* also reflects a feminist project to amplify women's perspectives so long silenced and interrupted.[78] The film listens to Diane as carefully as it does the professional industrial archaeologist.

But what should we make of Williams's words, transposed into Diane's Welsh accented voice-over? Are Williams's summaries of Wales, class, and landscape presented as active fabrications of meaning, to echo Nichols, or as deriving from an authoritative perspective to which Cinema Action still clung? Some critics (Welsh critics included) welcomed the device: "Read by Diane," one review argued, Williams's texts "are removed from the world of academe, inflected with the accents of ordinary speech, and put to work in the service of the people for whom they were written."[79] Whereas earlier films about industrial life in South Wales had been made by documentarians separated by geographical and social distance, Williams's Welsh identity gave the film directness. But, as Williams was by then ensconced in London and Cambridge leftist intellectualism and with Cinema Action visiting South Wales only intermittently for filming, such a conclusion seems generous.

Cinema Action leans on Williams to compensate for its distance from Wales. *So That You Can Live* speaks little of the particular condition of Wales and the Welsh language and culture in relation to English colonialism. The film's haunting synth soundtrack and panning landscape shots create, as some critics pointed out, an elegiac mood conjuring images of "the obscure countryman dwelling in rural simplicity."[80] Such mediation does not help explicate what was happening in Welsh politics at the time.

Deindustrialization was not confined to Wales in the 1970s, but Wales has a particularly painful history regarding industrialization and its social and economic aftermath. Invaded by English colonizers from the eleventh century, Wales was brought under English rule in the thirteenth century and incorporated into England in the sixteenth century and into Great Britain and the United Kingdom in the eighteenth and nineteenth centuries. As the British Empire grew, South East Wales—in particular the Valleys area where the Buttses live—saw rapid industrialization and a population surge as English and Irish workers joined the region's coal and iron industries. These annexations and demographic changes eroded the Welsh culture and language in South East Wales. The fact that the Buttses speak in accented English rather than Welsh signals this effect (by contrast, North West Wales resisted English infiltration longer, and because its slate quarry industrialization tended to attract only short-distance migrants, monolingualism in Welsh continued well into the twentieth century).[81] In the 1960s, a Welsh nationalist campaign increased visibility for Wales as an independent nation, and Plaid Cymru (Party of Wales) won its first seat in the UK Parliament in 1966. During the making of *So That You Can Live*, Plaid Cymru was campaigning for the creation of a Welsh Assembly government. Though an initial referendum failed in 1979, the following decade saw increasing support, leading to success in 1997. Mentioning these contexts in the film would advance important anti-colonial arguments. But perhaps, as with *People of Ireland*, such contexts seemed too regionally specific for Cinema Action's "working class films."

Despite its lack of Welsh specificity, *So That You Can Live* is an important film for Wales. Not only did it launch Channel Four's *Eleventh Hour*, but it also launched another channel. One week before its broadcast on Channel Four, *So That You Can Live* screened on a brand-new Welsh-language channel called S4C (Sianel Pedwar Cymru, or Channel Four Wales). The establishment of S4C was a major step for Wales, foregrounding voices hitherto marginalized on television and following decades of campaigning for linguistic and cultural recognition. *So That You Can Live* was S4C's first film.

Though some Cinema Action members resented the competition involved in obtaining broadcast slots and commissions, Guedes recognized that Channel Four's and S4C's interest in diversity chimed with her own.[82] Moreover, television's reach might help alleviate concerns voiced by Williams that by the end of the 1970s leftism was far from where most of the people who were the objects of its concern were living and thinking.[83] In 1974, Williams wrote a study of television as a cultural form in which he delineated both its danger, when programmed and controlled by social authorities, and its exciting potential, when appropriated by a "young radical underground" with "an eager sense of experiment and practice."[84] Though no longer a member of Cinema Action by 1981, Karlin expressed similar motivations: "independent filmmakers," he explained, "can intervene with and in the culture of television."[85]

Rodríguez and Silva's path to television was not straightforward either. Back in 1971 in an effort to formalize their engagement with subjects as collaborators, the filmmakers established La Fundación Cine Documental as a center where Indigenous groups could develop non-fiction films about land dispossession, labor exploitation, and pollution. They encouraged collaborators to draw from their own visual and narrative traditions rather than replicate those of film, television, and radio imported from the United States (filming for television was not yet on Rodríguez and Silva's agenda). Central to the collaborative process was the discussion of films. Rodríguez and Silva's film *Campesinos* (*Peasants*, 1974–1976), however, sparked more discussion than predicted when screened for people in Cauca, the valleyed area of southwestern Colombia where they shot this and several other films.

Campesinos employs a filmic vocabulary informed by Marxism to denounce exploitation at a coffee plantation. Cuts between shots of rural landscapes, peasants, and property owners diagram relations of economic exploitation through land dispossession. Since the 1960s, industrial tycoons, many of whom were European or North American, dominated Colombia's coffee trade, purchasing swaths of Indigenous land for monoculture plantations pumped with chemical pesticides and fertilizers. As a result, Colombia's economy became characterized by a concentration of land and wealth in the upper centile of the population. Conflict between the government, crime syndicates, and far-left guerrillas (and, more recently, far-right paramilitaries) exacerbated structural inequality and led to the displacement of millions, including many Indigenous people. The Cauca area contains more than 20 indigenous nations, including the Coconuco, Nasa, and Guambiano communities. *Campesinos* promised to tell their story.

But Cauca audiences didn't recognize themselves in the film. Where was their culture? Viewing a scene in which a non-Indigenous farmer gives a speech and Indigenous people listen, the audience complained: Did Indigenous people have no voice of their own? To Rodríguez, *Campesinos*'s montaged close-ups of peasants' faces, ragged clothing, and bare feet recalled Luis Buñuel's experimental 1933 film *Las Hurdes*, which she admired for its avant-garde editing and searing parody of European humanitarianism and documentary.[86] To audiences in Cauca, *Campesinos*'s narrative was jarring. "We showed them the close-up of an Indigena whose face was covered with sweat, but you couldn't see his tool or the work he was performing. They asked us, 'What's with him? What is that supposed to mean?,'"[87] Rodríguez explained. "When they saw someone speak by themselves uninterrupted, like a traditional talking-head interview, they thought that person was crazy. They wanted to see who the person was talking to. They made it very clear that *Campesinos*'s narrative viewpoint did not reflect their view of reality."[88] Rodríguez and Silva realized that they needed to learn their subjects' "different feeling for time and space—a rhythm" and decided to live in the Cauca Valley "on and off for five years." "We came to understand that imagination and myth," Rodríguez summarized, were as central to "their reality" as documenting facts about land dispossession and exploitative labor conditions.[89] Whereas in earlier films such as *Chircales*, Rodríguez and Silva had followed a Marxist line by portraying religion in the community as a form of false consciousness, they now began to see the importance of localizing Marxist ideas within Latin American, Colombian, and Cauca perspectives.

Rodríguez and Silva's next film, *Nuestra voz de tierra, memoria y futuro*, was the fruit of those years of immersion. The plural first-person "our" (*nuestra*) in the film's title signifies its makers' hope for better understanding with Cauca communities. Refusing a "master narrative" like those Trinh identifies in paternalistic documentary, *Nuestra voz*'s eponymous voice (of "land, memory, and the future") expresses concerns for representing the many multi-species and multi-generational perspectives in the region. The film's titular juxtaposition of voices emphasizes the land's repositories of lived experience and unborn potential. Refusing extractive capitalism's short-termism (with its protagonists who arrive, according to Rob Nixon's description, with "official landscape maps ... to extract, despoil, and depart"), *Nuestra voz* is made with and about those who live with extractivism's slow violence.[90]

Nuestra voz is a feature-length film whose narrative refuses conventional arcs of action and resolution. We see Indigenous people struggle to reclaim land confiscated by Spanish colonizers (conquistadores), the Catholic Church, and Euro Colombian elites operating within Colombia's capitalist-military system. The once-sustaining land has been gutted of its life-giving capacity, as an instrumental logic of extraction has transformed it into monoculture plantations for export and inert territory for land banking. Members of the Regional Council of Indigenous People reclaim this land through legal and guerrilla tactics, fighting police with hoes and machetes, entering landowners' haciendas, and tilling the earth as an act of protest.

In addition to documenting eco-political upheavals, *Nuestra voz* contains re-enactments of a devil myth central to the Cauca region. Members of Cauca's Indigenous Council were present during the film's editing to advise. Rodríguez described this collaborative, iterative method and the merging of actual and acted scenes as creating *ficción documental* (documentary fiction).[91] Her phrase signals an important destabilization of knowledge production that invites audiences to question the authoritative claims of documentary—including creative treatments of actuality by documentary auteurs such as Grierson—and look instead toward possibilities in collective production led by those portrayed in the film.

Nuestra voz's re-enacted myth tells a story of capitalist expansion from the time of Spanish invasion to the present. In the myth, the devil is portrayed on horseback, with spurs like a conquistador. He sometimes also resembles a modern-day policeman—he is a composite of all those who have exploited Indigenous people. The devil makes pacts with landowners against peasants. Silva interpreted the myth as an Indigenous representation of surplus value and its exploitation of human labor power, and was keen to include it in the film as a magical, symbolic challenge to capitalist modernity's systems of representation and value.[92]

Calling the devil myth a "myth" betrays the pervasive effects of epistemological imperialism. As Elizabeth Povinelli writes, Indigenous systems of knowledge are often typologized as animistic beliefs, traditions, or myths but are rarely called sciences.[93] Colonialism has long depended on such categorization for its framing of Indigenous people as more primitive and therefore moribund.[94] In *Nuestra voz*, like mugwort's contrast with Parathion, Cauca epistemologies stand as vital alternatives to the murderous and ecocidal ideologies of extractive capitalism.

Alongside devil re-enactments, *Nuestra voz* pays tribute to regional heroes, several of whom appear in the film but were killed by local militias before its release. In honoring the dead and endowing reenactments with equal importance to documentary sequences, the film holds space for pre-colonial worlds and worldviews that operate alongside and against the extraction-assimilation world of (neo)colonial and industrial capitalism.

This world (which scholars have called a "one-world world" presided over by a white male individual, or "Homo Economicus") forces many worlds into one.[95] Retaining many worlds in a differential relation to dispossession (Marisol de la Cadena calls this the making of an "uncommons," a coming together of heterogeneous worlds that cannot form without others), *Nuestra voz* destabilizes any individual authority to speak about the situation as a view from nowhere.[96] In its very title, the film suggests that it speaks as a chorus of uncommon voices, pertaining to multiple constituents of land, echoes of memory, and possibilities for the future, which come together to refuse a grammar of subject and object relation. Speaking as a hybrid of land-memory-future (or land-memory-future-people-animals-plants-soil-water-climate), *Nuestra voz* maps relations of ecological entanglement and responsibility.[97]

In contrast, *Amor* avoids flashbacks, reenactments, and dream sequences. Unlike rural Cauca, where Indigenous groups maintained a strong sense of identity in the face of marginalization, in Bogotá's industrial periphery, years of displacement and migration and losses of land, language, and culture had complicated Indigenous identities. *Amor* responded to this situation through directness, delivering a message of condemnation from Bogotá's plantations to audiences in Europe. By the time she made *Amor*, Rodríguez said, she felt that the "militant film language of the 1960s and 1970s had become exhausted."[98] By contrast, television's aesthetic of immediacy promised to target the consumers of cut flowers on the other side of the world.

Amor is edited to suit television, replete with establishing shots and saxophone interludes. Some critics and filmmakers felt uneasy about such tropes. Rodríguez was not alone in approaching European television for production assistance and a platform; her friend in Bolivia, Jorge Sanjinés, also worked with Channel Four and Italy's RAI (Radiotelevisione italiana), experiencing pressure to editorialize. *Amor* originally lasted 210 minutes, the next cut was 90 minutes, and producers in London pushed for 52 minutes (sometimes imposing "cultural and narrative models that are not ours," Rodríguez said). But she also said, "Channel Four is great!"[99] As Michael Chanan puts it, although Latin American filmmakers risked having their work absorbed or even shaped by European broadcasting, they could also benefit from funding and exposure.[100]

Amor's televisual language reveals Rodríguez's canny strategy for speaking to European audiences in a recognizable idiom. Mapping economic ties between Colombia and Europe in easily digestible testimonies, cutaways, and musical interludes, the film re-connects estranged regions while calling attention to its own visual and sonic mediations. Importantly, the film's self-conscious aesthetic refuses the objectification of which Trinh, Rangan, and others warn. *Amor* does not objectify a voiceless mass. Its images are not the aerial perspectives and wide-angle apocalyptic landscapes often associated with environmental film and photography.

Environmentalism and photography share a long history, including the Sierra Club's images of national parks and NASA's Earthrise photograph. Although these distanced perspectives illustrate important planetary angles, they speak little to lived issues of environmental justice, sometimes even abstracting specific harms through formalism. As

Nixon writes, capitalism has a "tendency to abstract in order to extract, intensifying the distancing mechanisms that make the sources of environmental violence harder to track and multinational environmental answerability harder to impose."[101] Max Liboiron has recently drawn the relation between pollution and obfuscation even more starkly, describing pollution as colonialism.[102] *Amor*'s attention to the close-at-hand effects of pollution on the plantation refuses abstraction and foregrounds colonialism's violence.

At the same time, suffering bodies are not reduced to pornography. Women interviewed in *Amor* speak not as homogenous victims but instead as individuals who are also members of an organized union. And their testimonies, it turned out, had an impact.

Over eight hundred thousand people watched *Amor* the night it was broadcast.[103] Upon seeing the film, the Colombian embassy in London reprimanded Rodríguez for representing Colombia in an unfavorable light, and the Inter-American Foundation, which had partially funded *Amor*, demanded that its name be removed from the credits.[104] One of the two flower plantations where *Amor* was filmed was shut down.[105] Rodríguez continues as the director of La Fundación Cine Documental to this day. *Amor* was restored and rereleased in 2023.

Such results suggest that *Amor* was successful in converting empathetic images into action. By foregrounding its interviews with women on strike, *Amor* also asked audiences to recognize in aesthetic representation the potential of political representation. Words spoken on the picket line and on the television could affect real change. And in shifting a traditional focus in labor struggles from male workers in urban factories to women's experiences on plantations, Rodríguez forwarded an eco-feminist politics central to land cinema.

WORKABLE BLUEPRINTS

In *The Activist Humanist: Form and Method in the Climate Crisis* (2023), Levine criticizes the environmental humanities for continually identifying repressive norms and calling for their undoing "without proposing what should be built in their place" to combat environmental and social degradation.[106] Taking their cameras to the picket lines and their films to union meetings and Indigenous councils, Rodríguez and Silva and Cinema Action are exemplary in pushing gestural appeals into action. Later they pushed again, experimenting with the burgeoning promise of television. Viewing something at a distance (*tele-* + *-vision*), they implied, should not serve voyeuristic empathy culture but instead should foster common planetary concern.

Rodríguez and Silva and Cinema Action's experiments were simultaneously political and aesthetic forms for rearranging what, how, and whose stories are told and seen. The fact that the filmmakers' earliest works look so unlike their latest illustrates the tirelessness of their experiments in redistribution.[107] Questioning the potentials and liabilities of filmmaking, they understood representation as operating simultaneously in the realm of pragmatic demands and their aesthetic prefiguration. Long-term collaborative methods were key, as was bridging between local action and calls for systemic, global change. Made "not only about people engaged in these struggles but also with and by them as well," the films extend a committed kind of filmmaking exemplified by Third Cinema in uniquely ecological directions.[108] Seen today, imperfect and charged with eco-political urgency, the films offer workable blueprints for the future.

SIX

*Extraction Is Stealing,
Relationships Give Meaning*

EVERY IMAGE IS A PERSPECTIVE, a narrative, a politics, a demand. Today as divisive representations of social and ecological crises crowd our screens and imaginations, visual literacy is paramount. *What does this image want from me?*[1] *Why? Why now?* In the previous chapters I have offered both a history of images of land and a tool kit for decoding them. Asking questions about perspective and about the land relations being represented or obscured in a film or photograph empowers viewers as active participants in conversations about climate justice.

As I wrote this book, I was teaching in the art department of a university where I began noticing a range of reactions to conventional images of climate crisis (think forest fires, famines, floods—the kinds of scene T. J. Demos calls "burning images").[2] Students' reactions often included anxiety, anguish, fatigue, and pessimistic resignation. In response, I devised a seminar that went in search of images that challenge rehearsed ways of representing climate breakdown. The seminar gathered historical and contemporary examples of artists and filmmakers whose work intervenes in the social script with alternative ways of seeing, feeling, and acting in the face of crisis.

The word "crisis" was important. I did not use it to evoke a state of paralysis, alarm, or deadlock but instead used it to access its original medical usage in describing a turning point in an illness, after which the afflicted may die or recover. In other words, crisis is about a decisive moment, a change of course. In our seminar, we discussed climate crisis as also a potential turning point and searched for images that have moved people, affectively and politically, to change individual, collective, and systemic behaviors. Land cinema became a key source of inspiration.

Throughout this book, I have presented a history of land cinema in the 1970s and 1980s as a collection of turning points, activated and documented by images that address crisis in oppositional and propositional ways to denounce extractivism and focus on relations of justice. The films, photographs, farms, gardens, communities, screenings, and strikes I have discussed activate spaces in crisis as spaces of mediation between pragmatic demands for eco-political formations and their experimental aesthetic prefiguration. Political and aesthetic forms converge there, on the land and on film. Land cinema cultivates eco-political concerns within its text, contexts, and material construction, understanding these parts as interrelated. Put another way, land cinema is eco-political in the way it looks and in the ways in which it is made.

Land cinema's eco-political agency also lies in its reparative capacity, dismantling a common presumption that climate crisis is new or in any way unforeseen rather than an expansion of what the world's poorest have endured over five centuries of colonial predation. Land cinema's longer view also opens space for acknowledging historical instances of strength and solidarity, not just suffering.[3] Working against an insistence that there is no alternative to capitalism, land cinema cultivates images, imagination, and grounded evidence that other ways can and have existed—flourished even.[4] As scholars of 1960s and 1970s radicalism have noted, a neoliberal consensus has downplayed the change-making events and initiatives of those decades.[5] This book revisits that era and its aftermath, finding land cinema as proof of important shifts in eco-political consciousness and action in the 1970s and 1980s—many of which endure to this day as continued projects, such as those of Marta Rodríguez and Somankidi Coura, and in new iterations and experiments, such as those I discuss in the pages that follow.

Employing what Saidiya Hartman calls the subjunctive tense of history,[6] land cinema enables us to ask *what if*? What if "growth" and "progress" meant multispecies abundance, as they did for Somankidi Coura, rejuvenating an exhausted plantation in a former colony? What if "development" signified a social movement toward solidarity as it did for Rodríguez, Jorge Silva, and the Colombian farmers they supported in confronting exploitative agri-business? Our current understanding of such terms is conditioned by extractivism. Other economies would support these other expanded definitions. Land cinema offers glimpses of an outside to historical order, a counternarrative, "another arrangement of the possible," as Hartman puts it.[7]

In advancing alternative perspectives and values, land cinema also invites a comparative form of critical study that looks beyond and beside the canon. Most histories of documentary's political potential, for example, open with Robert Flaherty and John Grierson. Though these men's contributions were profound, if we shift our lens toward ecological matters, we must adjust our focus for myriad other filmmakers and interventions.[8] Similarly, in art historical frameworks, though land artists such as Richard Long and Robert Smithson are important figures in the field, stories of other approaches need telling. "Canon building is empire building," wrote Toni Morrison.[9] "We need a different history," argued Lis Rhodes.[10] Land cinema teaches that multiple histories of eco-political struggle have grown over the past half century, often in the hinterlands of better-known narratives.

Working in the margins of extractive capitalism, filmmakers discussed in this book approached landscapes as both sites of rupture where the rift driven between (some) humans and the rest of nature is laid bare and sites of repair. Their films remember past episodes of land despoliation and renew a common membership of that land as a reparative project. As Leanne Betasamosake Simpson writes, "extraction is stealing" and "relationships give meaning."[11] Through its cultural (and sometimes agricultural) consideration of land as an integrated web of lifeworlds, land cinema repairs meaningful relations estranged by extractive plunder.

I now turn to three sites of rupture and repair in which contemporary artists and filmmakers are working. Taking up key characteristics of land cinema in the 1970s and 1980s, these artists and filmmakers approach the plantation, the zoo, and the village as critical landscapes of concern. Epitomizing extractive projects of imperial and urban expansion, the metropolitan zoo has long been recognized as a symbol of colonial control.[12] The plantation and rural village meanwhile feed and fuel urban expansion and yet rarely feature in conventional tales of modernity, which privilege factories and technological infrastructures (a focus also characteristic of early cinema).[13] Situated on a sugar plantation island in the Philippines, around a zoo in Brazil, and in a small village in central China, the examples below encapsulate land cinema's enduring characteristics and indicate the genre's powerful potential as a framework today.

A PLOT ON THE EDGE OF A PLANTATION, NEGROS ISLAND

There are two words for hunger in Hiligaynon. *Gutom* describes regular hunger. *Tigkiriwi* describes a hunger that immobilizes the body and mind when a person has not eaten for days. In *Langit Lupa* (*Heaven and Earth*), a fifty-six-minute non-fiction film made in 2023 by the Filipinx and Taiwanese American artists Enzo Camacho (b. 1985) and Ami Lien (b.1987), a Negros farmer describes how *tigkiriwi* gnaws at the stomach. "That is what sugar farmers endure," he says, "for three to four months each year." Because the island's plantations are monoculture cash crops, exported by hacendados (landowners), its land lies barren after harvest and before planting. If stormy weather coincides with this fallow period, fishing boats cannot sail, so farmers and fisher folk go without income and food. They call these grueling months *tiempo muerto*, or dead season.

Negrense people resist this deadly situation, however. Practicing a form of survival and resistance ("survivance," we could call it, borrowing an Anishinaabe coinage),[14] the island's communities reestablish land relations by growing their own food on it. Much like the enslaved African communities whom Sylvia Wynter describes in Caribbean contexts, cultivating small plots on the edges of plantations, Negrense people grow eggplant, okra, sweet potatoes, water spinach, and peas to feed themselves. Although, as Wynter points out, self-sufficiency reduced maintenance costs for plantation owners, it was also a source of cultural sustenance, rejuvenating land through the mixed planting of meaningful culinary, spiritual, and medicinal plants.[15] Wynter is a key reference for Camacho and Lien. In the Philippines, the practice of growing a plot beside a plantation is known as *bungkalan* (from the Tagalog *bungkal*, meaning to till soil). *Bungkalan*, agrarian self-help and a form of eco-political activism, wrests the idea of tilling from terra nullius associations with colonial land expropriation and reroutes it toward stewardship and commoning. Parallels between *bungkalan* and depictions of radical agrarian resistance in land cinema films discussed in earlier chapters by Ogawa Pro, Somankidi Coura, and Rodríguez and Silva, could not be clearer.

Bungkalan has been described as a praxis of action and reflection that connects environmentalism with social justice.[16] *Bungkalan*'s cooperative cultivation of organic polycultures through sustainable agro-ecology counteracts the semi-feudal, profit-driven model of the hacienda system as well as the exhaustion of land and biodiversity through plantation monocultures. Mixed crops grown on *bungkalan* plots include many types of fruit, vegetable, and rice as well as nitrogen-fixing legumes that also function as windbreakers. Focusing on sustaining respectful human-nature relations through cooperative labor, *bungkalan* facilitates intergenerational learning and prioritizes food crops over cash crops. Practicing organic and collective agriculture, *bungkalan* exercises multiple forms of social cooperation, including emergency aid among farmers, the exchange of working shifts between families or teams, and the planting of vegetables and herbal medicines for the community.[17] *Bungkalan*'s progressive vocabulary draws on the rich agricultural terminology of Tagalog farmers, in which ideas of organic and social care are co-constitutive, and political organization stems from land-based cultivation in the face of extractive violence.

Steeped in this vocabulary, Camacho and Lien describe *bungkalan* as "both protest and cultivation, outrage and care."[18] This complex combination of affect is gradually introduced in *Langit Lupa* through interviews with elderly farmers and in collaboration with Negrense children, with whom Camacho and Lien devised re-enactments of peasant campaigns and memorials. The Philippines is one of the deadliest countries in the world for environmental and land activists.[19] Many peasant campaigns have ended in tragedy, one of which—the Escalante massacre of 1985, when paramilitary forces murdered twenty civilians and injured many more—is commemorated in and by this film. Such commemoration is more important than ever today, as Ferdinand Marcos Jr.'s regime suppresses testimonies of structural violence and continues to surveil and intimidate *bungkalan* initiatives.

The children with whom Camacho and Lien re-enact a procession to remember Escalante serve as reminders throughout the film of inheritance and futurity in terms of both intergenerational trauma and *bungkalan*'s future-oriented practices for cultural and agricultural repair. During the re-enactment, the children process toward the camera in a subtle implication of the audience, carrying farming tools in their arms. The camera is positioned at their head height, a formal decision that refuses to look down on, or dismiss, these inheritors of the future. A haunting composition combining voice and synthesis plays on the soundtrack, devised by the Filipino artist Alyana Cabral, who collects traditional folk songs from peasant communities, working with local choirs to keep the songs and their messages alive.

Camacho's own mother is from Negros. He is a child of the island in this sense and, at the same time, another of this book's many insider/outsiders, filming an ongoing history of land-based trauma from a distance opened by living in Berlin and New York City and exhibiting work in biennials and galleries across the world. Despite this distance, Camacho and Lien spend several months of the year on Negros, making work "first and foremost for communities on the island."[20] Grassroots screenings held on *bungkalan* plots connect local and international perspectives much as they did in Third Cinema's participatory model, which Camacho and Lien cite as an influence. Recalling Bouba Touré's travels between Parisian migrant hostels and Somankidi Coura's cooperative farm in Mali, the artists' itinerance practices a form of what Kuan-Hsing Chen calls "internationalist localism."[21] This mobility is a central methodology for land cinema because it rejects both the universalizing approaches of globalization and a rhetoric of localism that disguises parochial oppression.²² Communicating a shared but differential relation to extractivism, land cinema filmmakers foster cross-cultural solidarity as they mediate between localized action and wider campaigns for change.

The Escalante massacre is important in this local/planetary mediation, marking both "a rupture and [an] inflection point."²³ Describing the massacre as such, the artists invite audiences to think back and forward through time. The massacre, they suggest, is a crisis that is also a turning point. Likening their approach to what Douglas Crimp calls "mourning and militancy," Camacho and Lien understand activism as arising from rather than being prevented by anguish and loss.²⁴ *Langit Lupa* learns from the past to face the future.

In its mourning and militancy, the film again recalls earlier land cinema projects combining tales of historical land dispossession with documentation from present-day despoliation, including those by Barbara McCullough, and Rodríguez and Silva. Discussing their work with communities on Negros, Camacho and Lien emphasize the colonial déjà vu of exploitation on the island, which began when Spanish colonizers arrived in 1565, continued in Negros's annexation to the United States in 1901 and subsequent exploitation as a cash crop for sugarcane, and reached nightmarish levels of violence in the mid-1980s as the Marcos dictatorship's monopolization of the sugar trade led to famine. It was in protest against this social and ecological devastation that farmers in Escalante marched in 1985. Throughout *Langit Lupa* are static landscape shots that frame the island as a place haunted with these memories—memories that resist erasure and infuse the future with anger and energy (Figure 27).

Citing *fūkeiron* as an influence, Camacho and Lien linger on the plantation's monoculture topography as an index of violence. Although all we can see in many shots is a field of sugarcane, when viewed through an eco-political lens, we find ourselves occupying a site of murderous and ecocidal extraction. In this sense, *Langit Lupa*'s landscape shots also recall those of the Vietnamese film and photographic artist Nguyễn

FIGURE 27. Sugarcane plantation on Negros Island, in *Langit Lupa* (*Heaven and Earth*). Frame enlargement. Thanks to Enzo Camacho and Ami Lien.

Trinh Thi, whose *Landscape Series #1* (2013) portrays everyday sites across Vietnam as quiet witnesses of history. The work is a slide show comprising hundreds of images sourced from newspaper photographs in which citizens point toward something beyond the frame, implicating suppressed histories of colonialism, conflict, and government-sponsored nuclear testing.

As well as being indictments, Camacho and Lien's landscape images are also offerings for remembrance and repair. The artists title the installation version of the film, which they exhibit beside images made with handmade paper containing pulped plants, *Offerings for Escalante*. Alongside footage shot on a digital camera and with 16mm color film, *Langit Lupa* also contains images created using phytography, a technique whereby chemicals found within plants act as a natural developer for celluloid film.[25] Like pulped paper, the film is a material trace of land (Figure 28).

Phytograms resemble materialist films of the 1970s, with the outlines and imprints of plants used to develop the film dancing across its surface. The effect recalls the cellulose basis of film itself in a material

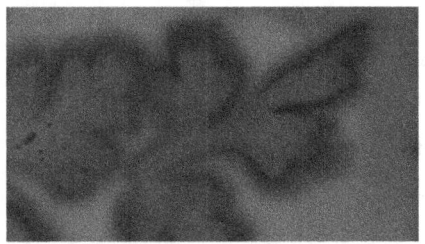

FIGURE 28. Phytogram in *Langit Lupa* (*Heaven and Earth*). Frame enlargement. Thanks to Enzo Camacho and Ami Lien.

nod to cinema's land-based origins. But rather than invite audiences to consider film's reliance on industrially produced cotton, livestock, and mined silver, Camacho and Lien re-root cinema in the plot on the edge of the plantation. We are looking at shapes of plants grown outside and in resistance to the plantation, imprinted and developed on film that is made with those same botanical ingredients. The film's material basis becomes a form of *bungkalan*.

The phytograms also make an eco-critical intervention in the history of photography and film by inviting us to consider the botanical, filmic material as an index for histories of labor and land use. Phytography's botanical alternative to photography offers an earthy analog for making political change, offering evidence that other ways of relating to land and its constituents do exist.[26] Extending filmmakers such as Rose Lowder's materialist interest in celluloid film since the 1970s and resonating with a more recent materialist turn in film studies and photographic history seen in Nadia Bozak, Siobhan Angus, Alice Lovejoy, and Kirsty Sinclair Dootson's investigations into the chemical composition of film stock, phytography addresses cinema's extractive material legacy by experimenting with sustainable alternatives.[27] Anne Charlotte Robertson would surely delight in this organic relocation of cinema.

The phytograms are not entirely pastoral, however. They recall the plot's strained relation with the plantation and soil's simultaneous vibrancy and vulnerability. Another artist filmmaker who has explored this sense of vulnerability is Tomonari Nishikawa. In his two-minute film *sound of a million insects, light of a thousand stars* (2014), Nishikawa represents pollution by projecting 35mm color negative film that he previously buried under fallen leaves near the Fukushima Daiichi Nuclear Power Plant. Flickers and scratches on the film are material indexes of the radioactive disaster that the Japanese state has tried to bury. Like Camacho and Lien's phytograms, Nishikawa's film visualizes earthly and botanical traces of life, establishing environmental relations with wounded lands.

For Camacho and Lien, these relations are also social. Facilitating papermaking and phytography workshops, the artists source plants "with the help of the grandmothers" who know about botanical chemistry. This emphasis on local land-based epistemes speaks to the artists' wider belief in dismantling hierarchies of thought, their expanded cinematic and artistic practice celebrating what Usha Iyer has recently described as "polycentric, dialogic, connected, reciprocal knowledges."[28] Like the women peasants in Rodríguez and Silva's *Nuestra voz de tierra, memoria y futuro*, who describe mugwort's healing properties, Negrense grandmothers are celebrated for their land-based expertise in selecting banana stalks, cilantro, coconut husks, papaya seeds, and garlic and onion skins to pulp into thick, colorful surfaces and phytographic developer. Rejecting the blankness of bleached white paper as being akin to terra nullius thinking, Lien sees paper ("the ground of the image") as always and already a site of contact and relation between different substances.[29] A similar approach guides their filmmaking, with phytograms emerging from direct material encounters with plants and people's land-based labor and expertise.

Learning on and from the land also cultivates political solidarities. On Negros, Camacho and Lien explain, political pedagogy is common, with "seasoned peasant activists" traveling from plantation to plantation teaching other farmers "how to build legal claims" or "replace chemical fertilizer with a mixture of fermented fish guts, rice, and molasses."[30] Citing Paulo Freire's grassroots approach to education as political consciousness, the artists see themselves as relocating culture "to the domain of collective survival and struggle." We want to learn, they explain, "from the innovative practices of the Filipino peasantry in order to fundamentally rethink what it means to be both an artist and a citizen." Expanding their filmmaking practice to include teach-ins and workshops held at *bungkalan* sites—that is, on the plot at the edge of the plantation—the artists' collaborative productions and screenings cultivate a pedagogy of resistance against the plantation's political and ecological hold.

Maintaining relations across estranged and asymmetrical rifts opened by extractivism, be they between Negros and Metro Manila or the Philippines and the United States, Camacho and Lien's work returns the plantation to the metropolis's purview, projecting it into biennials and galleries as a trace of capitalism's forgotten other as well as fuel and food. When Achille Mbembe writes that "democracy, the plantation, and the colonial empire are objectively all part of the same historical matrix," he could almost be describing the message of *Langit Lupa*. So-called liberal democracy, Mbembe explains, exteriorizes its violence to "the colonies and other third places" and registers peasant killings "as an aberration, located squarely outside the walls of the civil society we believe we inhabit."[31] *Langit Lupa* dismantles those walls. "The colonial plantation laid the foundations for the whole world order we have inherited," write Camacho and Lien. "We can trace its legacy not only in the plantations that still exist today in the Philippines and elsewhere, but also in our urban slums and our gated communities, in our war zones and our stock markets, in our prisons and our art museums. This is to say that, in many ways, we have never left the plantation."[32] The film itself, strewn with leaves and produced through botanical reaction, develops the plantation as a situation of prolonged crisis into a site of mediation through material contact between Indigenous, colonial, and industrial worlds.

Camacho and Lien's work also reveals a set of truths about photography and film. In their links to vision, photography and film can help us see differently. In their historical development alongside imperial means to shape narratives of supremacy, including in colonial representations of plantations as exotic conquests and industrial triumphs, photography and film can call attention to their perspectival power. And in their imbrication with extracted fossil fuels, plant fibers, and animal products, photography and film can identify their own materiality as entangled with extractivism and as potential plant- and land-based media for rupture and reparation. On the edges of the plantation, other ways of seeing and making can develop: oppositional and propositional, critical and creative.

IN AND AROUND BRASÍLIA ZOO

The Brazilian artist-filmmaker Ana Vaz (b. 1986) describes her 2022 film *É Noite na América* (*It Is Night in America*) as an eco-terror tale. This feature-length film, which also exists as a three-channel video installation of the same name, is terrifying, sorrowful, and hypnotic. It opens with a four-minute continuous take, shot with a tripod that revolves to survey Brasília's dense cityscape. Accelerating as it un-scrolls this giddy image of high-rise offices, electricity cables, and rooftops, the film is washed in a deep blue tint. The soundtrack is a maelstrom of construction and traffic noise mixed with whirring, whooshing, indistinct roars that might be wind, the howls of animals, or sound played backward so that it swallows itself.

Vaz shoots the next sequence inside a car driving in darkness within a constellation of red taillights. Using a composition by Vaz's father the sound artist Guilherme Vaz, she layers long notes played on a horn with clashes of cymbals and gulfs of silence. The unnerving effect is not unlike that of the bass clarinet and tenor saxophone squawks in *A.K.A Serial Killer*. Interrupting and irregular noises set the landscape on edge. Dawn breaks in orange and purple streaks above the road. And then the animals start appearing.

A giant otter comes first. Brought from Germany "to repopulate the land of its ancestors," Ana Vaz explains, the otter is filmed circling inside a water tank.[33] It is hard not to hear its screeches as screams. Later, a fox infected with distemper ("from living too close to humans," the vet says, as she injects a paw) looks back at the camera, and again it is hard not to read sorrow in its eyes. Are we anthropomorphizing wild animals if we look and listen to them in such ways? And yet a refusal of recognition would surely disregard their rights. These and other animals we meet in the city's plumbing systems, caught on its roads, or held in its zoo gradually introduce the film's central preoccupation with relationships between humans and animals. Building on an "animal turn" in recent cinema studies, Vaz's film focuses on settler colonialism's disregard of the rights of nature and Indigenous rights within the modern city.[34]

It Is Night in America presents land—specifically Brasília's many highways and the cages of its zoo—as a site of displaced, disregarded, and discarded lives. Vaz describes the numerous animals she follows with her camera as refugees without a refuge.[35] Much footage is shot at night and at dawn, when "the creatures return to the city," Vaz explains, and "nest in the parking lots. They glorify the inhabitants' garbage in a nocturnal feast that escapes ... the monuments, the roads, the edifications."[36] We see monkeys, wolves, owls, capybaras, anteaters, boas, and other wonderous creatures of the Cerrado upon which Brasília was built still occupying the asphalted land and yet injured, sickened, or restricted by it.

Brasília was officially opened in 1960. Oscar Niemeyer planned the city not as a grid but instead in the shape of an airplane. One could hardly imagine a more modern and technological emblem than that. One of the first buildings planned was a zoo. Inaugurated even before the city itself, Brasília Zoo stands as evidence that modernity prioritizes the containment and display of wildness. The zoo, John Berger argues, is a colonial project for establishing the dominance of some humans (a category Wynter describes as *homo economicus*) over the rest of the world, including other people, animals, lands, and seas.[37] Vaz includes archival photographs of the zoo in the film as a reminder of Brasília's colonial, modernist claim to mono-humanistic mastery.

On the soundtrack we hear calls to Brasília's police helpline. Someone phones from near the city's "north wing," not far from the zoo, the National Park, and the industrial sector, the caller explains, with words mapping this functionalist city. The caller has found a snake and doesn't know what to do. Someone else calls about a skunk, or perhaps it is an opossum, "I'm not sure. I'm from the backcountry, but I've forgotten all I knew about wildlife."

Vaz layers these recordings over sequences shot inside the zoo, a veterinary surgery, and on highways built across animal tracks, composing a portrait of Brasília as a land of strained, pained relations. If this city is a collective unit for living and working, she suggests, then the presumptive "we" it houses is an anthropocentric and mono-humanistic category of exclusion.

Vaz's background in ethnography informs this critical stance, speaking to several land cinema filmmakers and theorists including Rodríguez and Trinh, whose work intersects ethnography, documentary, and feminism to explore and resist power dynamics between filmmakers and subjects, selves and others.[38] Vaz's film produces myriad perspectives in a way that evokes what contemporary Anthropocene thinkers including Marisol de la Cadena and Arturo Escobar have described as an "uncommons" or a "pluriverse"—that is, a negotiated gathering of heterogeneous worlds.[39]

Vaz represents the city as a habitat of heterogeneous co-existence to develop an alternate political ecology that recognizes both people and animals within a complex history of extraction, dispossession, and erasure. As Maan Barua writes, we urgently need manifold and situated histories such as these because they offer "starting points for imagining landscapes and inhabitation in other ways" and propose "a politics of living alongside."[40] Barua's words recall Trinh's formulation of "speaking nearby" rather than about filmed subjects.[41] Nearby and alongside the multiple others she films, Vaz creates a space of multispecies gathering that holds room for difference. In so doing, her approach evokes the constituent parts of the Spanish word for "we," *nosotros*, which thinkers including Gloria Anzaldúa have used to explore insider/outsider, self/other identifications, with "*nos*" meaning "us" and "*otros*" meaning "others."[42] "We" can only exist when "I" or "you" come together with multiple "others": we (*nosotros*), because of others (*otros*), within us, alongside, and nearby.

The film's formal devices help forward this collective and differential configuration. The camera is often positioned low, as if meeting animals

FIGURE 29. A nocturnal inhabitant of Brasília, from *It Is Night in America*. Frame enlargement. Thanks to Ana Vaz.

at their height. In the film's installation version, projected onto screens two meters high, an owl's face in close-up becomes taller than a man (Figure 29). As in the way Robertson filmed flowers and cats in her garden in zooms, this re-scaling of the other-than-human wrests visuality from an anthropocentric frame (the film's final credits also include all the animals Vaz has represented). Exercising an eco-ethical capacity to respond that Donna Haraway's calls "response-ability,"[43] the film invites us into encounters where our species differences are no longer antagonistic divisions but rather opportunities to respond to "others" among and within us (*nosotros*). Whereas, as many scholars have observed, cameras resemble guns when photographing becomes an act of stalking prey for a picture, Vaz refuses the scopic clarity and elevated position associated with shooting dynamics.[44] "I take cinema as a perspectivist medium," she writes, "a medium able to produce partial realities, building ... world-forms made from myriad perspectives[,] ... a medium able to transform and dehumanize human perception, untaming our knowing bodies from the tyranny of mastery, reason and linear time."[45]

The film's unusual spoken and subtitled language also defamiliarizes perspectives. The voice on the soundtrack slips from Brazilian Portuguese into a syllabic scramble. "It's ightn na merica," reads an English subtitle written to approximate the effect, "eythr allcornerd, but being with eth animals ni the ooz we learn a tol fo things." ("It is night in America[;] ... they're all cornered, but being with the animals in the zoo we learn a lot of things"). This scramble-language is a dialect spoken in one of Brasília's satellite towns where workers who constructed the city were housed, having been displaced from their own land. Many were Indigenous and very poor. They created this dialect, which Vaz describes as a "fugitive" or underground language, and called it Gwalin, itself a scramble of *língwa*, the Portuguese word for "language."[46]

The experience of estrangement Vaz creates through language invites questions pertaining to the colonial imposition of a European language in Brazil, the continued use of English as a lingua franca in film exhibition contexts, and the expectation that the world be visible and legible to human eyes, ears, and minds. Listening to and reading a language that resists full comprehension, audiences are presented with an experience of familiarity and distance. Importantly, this experience is akin to that described by Haraway upon exchanging a look with an animal and sensing both recognition and difference.[47] Vaz decenters a human and European perspective to commemorate those who were displaced from the city and endure its continued violence. Like Camacho and Lien's reinsertion of the plantation into modernity's urban-centric narrative, *It Is Night in America* disrupts Brasília's colonial fantasy of function and control. The film's title forwards this intervention, prompting questions of whose night it is and whose America.

Such questions also emerge from another formal device that defamiliarizes. Though not all scenes are filmed at night, a nocturnal tone bathes the entire film due to the expired 16mm film stock used. Vaz also underexposed as she shot, darkened footage during post-production, and added a blue tint to some scenes. Such techniques are known as day for night shooting or American night shooting and were often used in low-budget Hollywood westerns to simulate a night scene while filming in daylight. Vaz's formal decision is also conceptual, evoking the western genre's celebratory depictions of settler colonial landscapes in North America and the ongoing trauma of colonial-capital expansion across South America, including in Brazil's Cerrado.

Switching day for night, scrambling words, and alternating perspectives between human and animal, the film critiques exclusionary systems and reconfigures a pluriversal "we." *Sentipensar con la tierra* (feeling-thinking with the earth) is the phrase Escobar uses, following Orlando Fals Borda, to describe the sensual, embodied experience entailed by such reconfigurations.[48] The film's final scene is fittingly sensual. Held for three minutes, the camera fixates on a gigantic waterfall. Draping itself in white billows of spray and tumbling into cavernous undertows, the waterfall defies scaling. It fills the frame, there is no landmark nearby, and there is neither edge nor end to it. Nature is more powerful than us. Or rather, within "us" as an "other," nature calls us back to our senses, un-taming us with its pull, its roar.

VILLAGE LOCATED FORTY-SEVEN KILOMETERS FROM THE CITY, HUBEI PROVINCE

Zhang Mengqi (b. 1987) also wants to bring audiences from the limits of the city back to the land—precisely forty-seven kilometers from Suizhou city to her father's village of Diaoyutai. Zhang began filming the village in 2010 and has made ten films there to date, all with *Self-Portrait* and *47km* in their titles. Diaoyutai "has had two or three other names in the past," Zhang explains, "when Mao [Zedong's] land reforms reshuffled rural districts and governance."[49] She calls Diaoyutai village "47km" because this is the instruction given to bus drivers: stop forty-seven kilometers from Suizhou—though in truth the distance is shrinking as the city grows.

This naming indicates a distance from urban life. One might think, then, that the village is a peripheral backwater, out in the sticks, a margin to the center. But Zhang's attentive, patient documentaries portray the village as a center unto itself. Time is slower here. Memories seem deeper.

"I ate tree bark and soil to survive," an old woman tells Zhang. She is recounting experiences of the Great Famine, which was incurred by economic and social policies of Mao's Great Leap Forward and led to the deaths of over thirty million people between 1959 and 1961. China's Great Famine is absent from school history textbooks and is censored in the media, but here its shadows linger. And as the nation races on, pronouncing economic and technical advancements, Zhang films days, seasons, and farmers in their own rhythms. Though nothing like the famine years, life in this village is still hard. Like the plots and plantations on Negros and the wild habitats displaced from Brasília, the village represents urban modernity's rural other.

Today the village is home mainly to old people and their grandchildren, while parents have migrated to the city for work. Zhang has made the opposite move, returning to live in the village. "I'm an unusual kind of auntie here," she explains, "carrying my camera everywhere." Resonating with many of the landscape-portrait films discussed in this book, Zhang's *Self-Portrait* series is at once a document of her surroundings and a personal reflection on them. "The village existed from the start," she explains, "as a kind of marker of relation to me. 47km marks the start of my journey, my self-portrait."[50] Zhang's words recall those of Margaret Tait, returning to Orkney as a commitment to rural life and a means to explore her own politics. Like Tait, Zhang wrests perspectives from the city's centrifuge. And also like Tait, Zhang is an insider/outsider, having grown up in urban Suizhou away from her village relatives and moved to Beijing as a young adult to train in contemporary and folk dance. As so often is the case with land cinema, it was distance that afforded Zhang perspective and access. In Beijing, far from the village, Zhang met Wu Wenguang.

A leading figure in Chinese independent documentary, Wu founded an initiative in 2010 called the Folk Memory Project. He invited dozens of filmmakers across China to travel to its rural provinces and interview survivors of the Great Famine. Zhang was one of Wu's first recruits. She soon set off to Diaoyutai with a small digital camera.

The rawness of the narratives Zhang collected in the village and at such a vast scale by now, fifteen years into her project, invite comparison with the filmmaker Wang Bing's devastating oral histories of modern China. The Folk Memory Project has also grown, with over 150 filmmakers now visiting 246 villages to interview more than 1,100 elderly people.[51] While some Chinese directors such as Zhang Yimou have depicted the hardship of life under Mao (and have been censored in China for doing so), Zhang feels that cinema often forgets "the ordinary people who were hungry, like the farmers."[52] From her first self-portrait in the series, she focused on remembering.

Self-Portrait with Three Women (2010) places the filmmaker in conversation with her mother and grandmother as they recall experiences of birth, parenting, and work. Establishing her project with this matrilineal grounding, Zhang introduced herself to the village, where her presence operating a camera or dancing was initially considered strange. Gradually she made friends with "all the children and all the older ladies. . . . I helped to build the library in the village, and I taught them dance and filmmaking. It is very much a different relationship from [as] if I was just a filmmaker and they are the subject of my film."[53]

Self-reflexivity contributes to this intimacy, with villagers addressing Zhang behind the camera and Zhang sometimes stepping before the lens. Zhang's relational approach and curiosity in exploring differences between her own urban upbringing and the rural backgrounds of her elders recall Tait's focus on her elderly neighbor in *Land Makar*. *Self-Portrait: Window in 47km* (2019) also focuses on relationships between generations in the village. As Zhang interviews an eighty-five-year-old survivor of the famine, a young girl sits nearby drawing his portrait. Time circles and pools as the old man reaches back in his mind and the afternoon's light advances. The film opens in a static shot of an exterior wall painted with a slogan, faded so that all we can see is ". . . ism." Zhang asks her young companion what "-ism" she aspires to if not Maoism. "People-ism," the girl replies, her answer encapsulating Zhang's wider approach as well as that of the Folk Memory

FIGURE 30. Faded slogans, 47 km from the city. Frame enlargement. Thanks to Zhang Mengqi.

Project, with its non-extractive commitment to filming subjects (Figure 30). This is a "People-ism" approach to cinema. Appearing in several of Zhang's *Self-Portrait* films, more grown up in each, the girl is now in her twenties and documents life in the village with a camera Zhang gave her in a shift toward community co-creation that Rodríguez would surely applaud. Zhang's long-term commitment to the village and its citizens speaks to not only Rodríguez's work in Cauca but also that of Ogawa Shinsuke.

Ogawa's move to rural Yamagata in the 1970s and his collective work with Ogawa Pro in rooting political concerns about ecology, farmers' livelihoods, and globalization in the landscape are important sources of inspiration to both Zhang and Wu. Wu was the first recipient of the Ogawa Shinsuke Prize at the Yamagata International Documentary Film Festival, which Ogawa helped launch, and Zhang's films are frequent favorites there. Echoing Ogawa, Zhang describes the slow pace with which she films at Diaoyutai as "village time": "they relate to time differently in the village," she explains, following solar and lunar cycles rather than clocks.[54]

Zhang's interest in time is also influenced by her background in dance. She often accompanies screenings with live performances using a flashlight, negotiating the darkness between audience and screen. Responding to excerpts of interviews playing behind her, she crouches, her mouth agape in a silent howl, her hands scrabbling. "The histories of famine I'm being told are often very heavy," she says. "Dancing awakens, and filming awakens."[55] Recalling McCullough's filmed choreography with Milanda in the demolished Los Angeles neighborhood, Zhang's performances both mourn and bless the village. And like Camacho and Lien's commitment to keeping memories of peasant radicalism alive, Zhang's performances, screenings, and workshops engage villagers in ongoing conversations. "I like performing in the village because it feels direct," she explains. "Villagers come right up to me and say, 'no, your movement here is not right, it should be more like this.' I often use gestures taken from farming activities, and they recognize them."[56] Similar phrases have appeared throughout this book; such responsivity is a hallmark of land cinema. Gestures taken from farming activities and farming tools held up in acts of commemoration or protest root people in histories of agrarian radicalism. Land cinema contributes to this history as a record of what has been and a tool for activating what is yet to come.

What came in late 2019 was a surprise to everyone. Diaoyutai is barely a two-hour drive from Wuhan. When the COVID-19 virus spread from that city, the Chinese government imposed a strict lockdown. Zhang spent the pandemic months in the village and was struck by differences between narratives presented by the government, restrictions enforced in town, and village life where people were in "possession of their own time." *Self-Portrait in 47km: 2020* (2023) is structured into twenty-four parts as it follows villagers who "preserved their own concept of time" in accordance with sunlight and weather.[57]

Just before the pandemic, Zhang built a community house so she could live in the village year-round and host screenings, workshops, and discussions. *Self-Portrait: Fairy Tale in 47km* (2021) documents the construction of the house and includes sequences in which village children participate in its design. Because Zhang's films cannot be shown in public cinemas due to censorship, the house is a crucial venue (as are online streaming platforms and underground cinemas).[58] Painted blue and decorated not with a Maoist slogan but instead with a line from Derek Jarman ("blue, an open door to the soul"), the house encapsulates Zhang's expanded practice for remembering, awakening, and regenerating in community. Facilitating acts of witnessing, collective identification, and political agency, the house is home, to borrow a phrase from Angela Aguayo, to an emerging "documentary commons."[59]

Zhang's pedagogical workshops, like those organized on plots at the edge of the plantation by Camacho and Lien, are integral to land cinema's creation of a specifically eco-political documentary commons. The workshops teach that viewing is not passive consumption but instead is an act of resistance and that films made at distances deemed marginal from metropolitan perspectives are central to challenging structures of power. The workshops help filmmakers and audiences shift perspectives and ask questions—not least *in whose interest is an image made.*[60] They also extend a definition of cinema beyond that of being a filmic product into a wider social framework for debate and organizing. As Aguayo notes, "it is not enough for a documentary to 'be' activist"; it must also "create a public space for social change."[61] Zhang's house is one such space. Most days, it is filled with children. In an echo of Rodríguez and Silva's film title *Nuestra voz de tierra, memoria y futuro*, Zhang's films and the social and spatial architecture she has built to house them speak of the land and its troubled past and of the future, arriving in patters of little feet and bursts of laughter.

It is no coincidence that Zhang, Camacho and Lien, and so many of the earlier filmmakers considered in this book pay attention to very old and very young people. These generations carry wisdom from the past into the future. Some filmmakers, including Rodríguez (and more recently the Aboriginal Australian group the Karrabing Film Collective) also include the teachings of ancestors as central components of their films. Extraction, in all the forms I have presented it, is stealing from these past and future generations, damaging their intricate structures of accumulated cultural meaning. Relationships maintained across these generations and embedded in landscapes meanwhile repair and give meaning.

Like all those discussed in this book, the filmmakers considered here commit long-term to communities in a refusal of a common extractive practice whereby filmmakers enter communities to record injustice and then exit "with images that only benefit the maker's professional goals."[62] Land cinema stays with the trouble and the joy and everything in between as a commitment to intergenerational change-making and teaches us to see the repetitive and the mundane as crucial elements in the labor of cultivating communities and landscapes with care. Revaluing such values, especially as the feminist filmmakers in this book did in their long-term commitments to maintaining community gardens and collective filmmaking workshops, avoids an emphasis on revolutionary rupture that characterizes many histories of avant-garde art and film. Instead, through processes of continuous cultivation, land cinema nurtures ecological, political, cultural, and economic conditions that enable multiple lifeworlds to flourish over time. Land cinema is filled with figures such as those Rob Nixon describes as "long-termers"—people who measure value according to sustainable metrics and timescales, unlike the prospectors who land, extract, despoil, and depart.[63] And as Vaz's film makes clear, generational responsibility also pertains to the care of animals, plants, and soil—in other words, to land as an integrated system. Every filmmaker in this book shares this understanding of land, whereby land is both "geos" and "bios" with past, present, and future contained in its sediment.[64]

Today, some nations are beginning to emphasize generational responsibility to climate justice through formal policymaking, though much remains recommendation rather than law. In 2015, Wales passed the Well-being of Future Generations Act that drew inspiration from Seventh Generation planning, a concept long used by the Iroquois Nation to make decisions based on their impact seven generations on. In Japan, a movement called "future design" has popularized citizen's assemblies in which local residents contribute to planning their communities, with half of those gathered representing people in the present day and the other half tasked with imagining themselves in four decades' time. These kinds of practices refuse to let the slow violence of climate injustice be pushed to the Global South and future generations.[65] Land cinema does something similar, as it invites audiences to recognize regional entanglements between the Global North and the Global South and connect episodes from the past to present and future challenges. But unlike a policy document or a citizen's assembly, land cinema is also deeply sensuous.

Understanding the power of sights and sounds to reconnect us with land through embodied, aesthetic experience, land cinema refuses spectacle in a Debordian sense, whereby images serve passive consumers (recently, for example, proffering images of climate catastrophes that replicate disaster movie aesthetics). Instead, land cinema embraces the visual as visionary, producing images as imaginative interventions. This is not to say that its images are ungrounded, however, or stuck in what Caroline Levine describes as a "preparatory moment" of "nebulous" hopes so common in the aesthetic humanities.[66] Documentation of Somankidi Coura's flourishing organic farm is surely proof that land cinema's work moves beyond gestural appeal into practical action that spans economic, ecological, political, and aesthetic fields.

Somankidi Coura's farming, Camacho and Lien's *bungkalan*, and Robertson's community garden screenings are hardly filmmaking projects that culminate in packageable film products. Instead, these practices demonstrate that land cinema is a social and spatial commitment encompassing film, filmmaking, film screening, and film culture and extending off the edge of the screen, out of the projection room, and into discussions and barricades and vegetable plots.

Although—and perhaps especially because—moving images are available to so many of us today, in our pockets and at the swipe of a finger, the experience that land cinema offers of gathering as collective makers and audiences achieves heightened significance. Cinema's promise of a social architecture has never been more important. Watching together, land cinema can carry us out of ourselves to experience other perspectives and other landscapes at the same time that it situates our own within a bigger picture.

I remember when film first moved me like this.

A CINEMA BETWEEN THE SEA AND THE MOUNTAIN: WALES

I'm back in the landscape with which I opened this book's prologue. Mynydd Graig Goch, Red Rock Mountain, is a black silhouette outside the car window. I am lying on the back seat, heavy with sleep. Outside, the spring air is cool but already scented, and lambing season has begun. I'm coming home from Film Club.

In those years, once a month volunteers would present a film in the cinema that nestled against the mountains. Below the cinema lay sand dunes and a silky bay. I would eat a chocolate cornetto as the volunteers read their introduction. Wong Kar Wai, Andrei Tarkovsky, Ozu Yasujirō—the names meant nothing to me then. I had no idea what a director was, let alone where to locate directors' works on a map or timeline. Above us in the projection booth the reels would thump and crackle, their opening credits in foreign scripts racking in and out of focus. And then the first scenes. Their sights and sounds, scents and temperatures, paces and moods were intoxicating. They transported me far from my Welsh mountains and, at the same time, made me look at my surroundings differently.

Those nights, driving home from Film Club around the final bend in the track, with Graig Goch's broad shoulders filling the window frame, my world—now more dream than clarity—became a moving image over which I played others. I saw steam billowing from a noodle stand and a woman in a high-collared silk dress, impossibly glamorous. I could almost smell her. On other nights, there were dreadful scenes of a leaking city, acrid machine oil fog, stray dogs, and men, or sunlight, a kimono hung to dry on bamboo canes, a cheerful train, and a red teapot.

Carried in the darkness of the sea and the mountain, I watch my first and most intimately known landscape overlaid by these others, catching bars of music, and the intonation of a language I don't yet understand.

Land cinema is about being somewhere and also being somewhere else and seeing how these places are connected.

SELECTED FILMOGRAPHY

Adachi Masao (Japan)
    1969 *A.K.A. Serial Killer* (*Ryakushō: Renzoku shasatsuma*), made with Matsuda Masao
    1971 *Red Army–PFLP Declaration of World War*, made with Wakamatsu Kōji

Ana Mendieta (Cuba/US/Mexico)
    1973–1980 *Silueta Series*
    1974 *Blood and Feathers*
    1974 *Dog*
    1974 *Grass Breathing*

Ana Vaz (Brazil)
    2022 *It Is Night in America* (*É Noite na América*)

Anne Charlotte Robertson (US)
    1981–1997 *Five Year Diary*
    1985 *Talking to Myself*
    1983 *Magazine Mouth*
    1994 *Melon Patches, or Reasons to Go On Living*

Arlene Bowman (US)
    1986 *Navajo Talking Picture*

Barbara McCullough (US)
    1979 *Water Ritual #1: An Urban Rite of Purification*
    1981 *Shopping Bag Spirits and Freeway Fetishes: Reflections on Ritual Space*

Bouba Touré (Mali/France)
    2008 *Bouba Touré, 58 rue Trousseau, Paris, France*
    2022 *Xaraasi Xanne (Crossing Voices)*, made with Raphaël Grisey

Cinema Action (UK)
    1982 *So That You Can Live*

Enzo Camacho and Ami Lien (Philippines)
    2023 *Heaven and Earth (Langit Lupa)*

Margaret Tait (UK)
    1952 *A Portrait of Ga*
    1956 *The Drift Back*
    1966 *Caora Mor Big Sheep*
    1974 *Colour Poems*
    1976 *Place of Work*
    1981 *Land Makar*

Marta Rodríguez and Jorge Silva (Colombia)
    1976 *Peasants (Campesinos)*
    1981 *Our Voice of Land, Memory and Future (Nuestra voz de tierra, memoria y futuro)*
    1988 *Love, Women, and Flowers (Amor, mujeres y flores)*

Ogawa Productions (Japan)
    1982 *Nippon Country: Furuyashiki Village (Nippon-koku: Furuyashiki-mura)*
    1986 *The Sundial Carved with a Thousand Years of Notches: Magino Village Story (Sennen Kizami no Hidokei: Magino-mura Monogatari)*
    2001 *Red Persimmons (Manzan Benigaki)*, completed posthumously by Peng Xiaolian

Zhang Mengqi (China)
    2010 *Self-Portrait with Three Women*
    2019 *Self-Portrait: Window in 47km*
    2021 *Self-Portrait: Fairy Tale in 47km*
    2022 *Blue House*
    2023 *Self-Portrait in 47km: 2020*

NOTES

PROLOGUE

1. Nixon, *Slow Violence and the Environmentalism of the Poor*.
2. Demos, "The Agency of Fire."
3. Levine, *The Activist Humanist*, 11.
4. Ghosh, *The Great Derangement*.

INTRODUCTION

1. Donna Haraway argues that environmental responsibility necessitates being "response-able': having "the capacity to respond." Haraway, *Staying with the Trouble*, 78.
2. Waugh, *Show Us Life*; Dickinson, *Rogue Reels*; Eshun and Gray, "The Militant Image"; Grant, *Cinéma Militant*; Adamson, *Enduring Images*; and Aguayo, *Documentary Resistance*, 228.
3. See Harvey, *A Brief History of Neoliberalism*; Mirowski, *The Road from Mont Pelerin*; and Slobodian, *Globalists*.
4. Tomii, *Radicalism in the Wilderness*.
5. Gordon, *A Modern History of Japan*, 260.
6. Martínez-Alier, Baud, and Sejenovich, "Origins and Perspectives of Latin American Environmentalism," 38–41.
7. For more on Indigenous epistemologies and governance, including those recently formalized in the constitutions of Bolivia and Ecuador, see Escobar, *Designs for the Pluriverse*; and Cadena and Blaser, *A World of Many Worlds*.
8. Martínez-Alier, Baud, and Sejenovich, "Origins and Perspectives of Latin American Environmentalism."

9. Freire, *Pedagogy of the Oppressed*.
10. I follow Maan Barua here in my preference for "other-than-human" over "non-human," because while the former can encapsulate plants, animals, and spirits in possession of different capabilities and differentiated capacities, the latter implies a lack. Barua, *Plantation Worlds*, 222.
11. Diawara, *African Cinema*, 23.
12. Cabral, *Return to the Source*, 39; and César, "Meteorisations."
13. Parrott and Lawrence, *The Tricontinental Revolution*.
14. Klein, "Dancing the World into Being."
15. Angus, *Camera Geologica*, 14.
16. Yusoff, *A Billion Black Anthropocenes or None*.
17. Lowe, *The Intimacies of Four Continents*, 11.
18. For comparisons between extraction as a physical practice and an ideology, see Szeman and Wenzel, "What do we talk about when we talk about extractivism?"
19. Whyte, "Is It Colonial Déjà Vu?"
20. Oberle et al., "Global Resources Outlook," 27.
21. McKittrick, "Plantation Futures," 7. See also Davis et al., "Anthropocene, Capitalocene, . . . Plantationocene?"
22. Williams, *Problems in Materialism and Culture*, 70–71.
23. Mitchell, *Landscape and Power*, 5.
24. Casid, *Sowing Empire*, 7.
25. Jackson, *Discovering the Vernacular Landscape*, 5–7.
26. Wells, *Land Matters*, 2.
27. Berger, *Ways of Seeing*; Cosgrove, "Prospect, Perspective and the Evolution of the Landscape Idea"; and Casey, *Getting Back into Place*.
28. See Barrell, *The Dark Side of the Landscape*; and Bermingham, *Landscape and Ideology*.
29. This problem is exemplified in Michael Heizer's *City*, a concrete construction measuring 1.5 miles in length that took fifty years to complete and opened in 2022. This "land art" occupies the ancestral territories of the Nuwu (Southern Paiute) and Newe (Western Shoshoni) peoples. Heizer has spoken of his blood ties to the land, seemingly oblivious to the painful irony in such a phrase. His grandfather operated a tungsten mine on the land less than a decade after it was seized from Paiute hands.
30. Mirzoeff, "Visualizing the Anthropocene," 217, 220.
31. Kagawa-Fox, "The Crucial Role of Culture in Japanese Environmental Philosophy."
32. Casid, *Sowing Empire*, 46–47.

33. Winther-Tamaki, *Tsuchi*, 14, 64.
34. Merchant, *The Death of Nature*; Plumwood, *Feminism and the Mastery of Nature*; and Gaard, *Critical Ecofeminism*.
35. d'Eaubonne, *Le féminisme ou la mort*.
36. See Acosta, "Extractivism and Neoextractivism: Two Sides of the Same Curse"; Arboleda, *Planetary Mine*; and Gudynas, *Extractivisms*.
37. Shiva, *Staying Alive*.
38. Marx, *Capital*, 1:637–38; and Marx, *Capital*, 3:949.
39. Marx, *Economic and Philosophic Manuscripts of 1844*, 74.
40. Plumwood, *Environmental Culture*, 4.
41. Ghosh, *The Great Derangement*, 9.
42. Foster, *Marx's Ecology*; and Saito, *Marx in the Anthropocene*.
43. For studies of more recent artistic projects for climate justice, see Gómez-Barris, *The Extractive Zone*; Simpson, *As We Have Always Done*; Escobar, *Designs for the Pluriverse*; and León, *Another Aesthetics Is Possible*.
44. Yusoff, *A Billion Black Anthropocenes or None*; Tsing, "Unruly Edges"; Tsing, *The Mushroom at the End of the World*; and Cadena, "Uncommoning Nature."
45. Tsing, "Unruly Edges."
46. Cadena, "Uncommoning Nature."
47. Trinh, *When the Moon Waxes Red*, 60.
48. Rangan, *Immediations*, 56.
49. Rangan, "Audibilities," 281; and Rangan et al., *Thinking with an Accent*.
50. Kahana, *Documentary Film Reader*, 724–25.
51. Winston, "The Tradition of the Victim in Griersonian Documentary."
52. Waugh, "Acting to Play Oneself"; and Rouch, *Ciné-Ethnography*.
53. Mekas, "The Diary Film"; Renov, *The Subject of Documentary*; and Lebow, *The Cinema of Me*.
54. Gaines, "Political Mimesis."
55. Angus, *Camera Geologica*, 17.
56. Sontag, *On Photography*, 14.
57. Angus, *Camera Geologica*, 15–17. My thinking on the materialities of film is also indebted to Bozak, *The Cinematic Footprint*; Lovejoy, "From Forests to Film"; and conversations with Kirsty Sinclair Dootson.
58. See Gabriel, *Third Cinema in the Third World*; Chanan, *Twenty-Five Years of the New Latin American Cinema*; Willemen, *Questions of Third Cinema*; Dissanayake and Guneratne, *Rethinking Third Cinema*; Ekotto and Koh, *Rethinking Third Cinema*; and Mazierska and Kristensen, *Third Cinema, World Cinema and Marxism*.

59. Solanas and Getino, "Towards a Third Cinema."
60. Espinosa, "For an Imperfect Cinema," 24–26.
61. Barclay, "Celebrating Fourth Cinema."
62. Schneider and Till, "Beyond Discourse."
63. Liboiron, *Pollution Is Colonialism*.
64. Balsom and Peleg, *Feminist Worldmaking and the Moving Image*; and Iyer, "A Pedagogy of Reparations."
65. Mohanty, *Feminism without Borders*.
66. Juhasz, *Women of Vision*, 2; and Warren, *Subject to Reality*, 11–12.
67. Rhodes, "Whose History?"
68. There are exceptions, of course, including Hikari Hori's work illuminating the contribution of women to Japanese cinema, Angela Aguayo's foregrounding of filmmakers of color in US political documentary, and Jennifer DeClue's work on Black feminist avant-garde filmmakers in the United States. Hori, *Promiscuous Media*; Aguayo, *Documentary Resistance*; and DeClue, *Visitation*.
69. Gallagher and Greenblatt, *Practicing New Historicism*, 54–56.
70. Sedgwick, *Touching Feeling*, 1.
71. Sedgwick, 130.
72. Foster, "The Artist as Ethnographer?"; and Boetzkes, *The Ethics of Earth Art*, 4–5.
73. Luca and Jorge, *Slow Cinema*; and Çağlayan, *Poetics of Slow Cinema*.
74. Mayer, "Centre."
75. Levine, *The Activist Humanist*, 23–24.
76. Nixon, *Slow Violence and the Environmentalism of the Poor*, 14–16.
77. Haraway, *Staying with the Trouble*.
78. My exploration of plants, animals, and atmospheres here may sound aligned to recent trends in new materialism and a "vegetal turn" in the humanities, but the agency of other-than-human matter is not my focus. In studying filmmakers who respected and represented lands, plants, animals, and weathers, I am interested in understanding a shift in worldview that critiques anthropocentric approaches to land. As such, my arguments pertain less to discourses about the vibrancy or agency of materials themselves than to historical-materialist approaches that examine the representational strategies, labor relations, and material basis of visual media. See, for example, Tsing, *The Mushroom at the End of the World*; Arabindan-Kesson, *Black Bodies, White Gold*; Barua, *Plantation Worlds*; and Angus, *Camera Geologica*.
79. Povinelli, "Elizabeth Povinelli in Conversation with Kathryn Yusoff."
80. Davis, *The Other Side of Empathy*.
81. Levine, *The Activist Humanist*, 11

CHAPTER 1. POETS OF THE LAND

1. Tait, "A Poem for a Morning," in *Margaret Tait*, 67–68.
2. Script for *Heartlandscape*, Margaret Tait Collection, Orkney Archive, D97/11/9. Reprinted in Neely, *Between Categories*, 88.
3. Tait, "A Poem for a Morning," 67–68.
4. Tait, "Storms," Untitled poem, "Now," "Air," "The Unbreakable-up," and "Sprung Sonnet," in *Origins and Elements*, 11, 5, 25, 28, 35, 49.
5. Tait, "Storms," 11.
6. Tait, *Margaret Tait*, 166.
7. Tait, "Description of Land Makar."
8. Trinh, *When the Moon Waxes Red*, 74–75.
9. Tait, "The Scale of Things," in *The Hen and the Bees*.
10. Tait, *Origins and Elements*, 50.
11. Poem 1263 in Dickinson, *The Poems of Emily Dickinson*; and Tsing, *The Mushroom at the End of the World*.
12. Rabinovitz, "The Future of Feminism and Film History," 42.
13. Tait, "The Trow O' Windhoose," in *Origins and Elements*, 4.
14. Tait discusses this cinematographic experiment in her poem "Now," 22–25.
15. Thanks to So Mayer for this phrase and numerous conversations about Tait over the years.
16. Neely, *Between Categories*, 87–88.
17. Neely, 23.
18. Sitney, "Poetry and the Film"; and Tait, *Margaret Tait*, 166.
19. Tait, *Margaret Tait*, 77.
20. Tait, 150–52.
21. MacDonald, *A Critical Cinema 5*, 87; and Dorsky, *Devotional Cinema*, 41.
22. Tait, "Light," in *Margaret Tait*, 88.
23. Neely, *Between Categories*, 4, 27.
24. We might think of Marie Menken, Maya Deren, and Chick Strand here as influencing Jonas Mekas, Stan Brakhage, and Bruce Baillie. See Blaetz, "Rescuing the Fragmentary Evidence of Women's Experimental Film."
25. Tait hoped that profiles on BBC Scotland and Channel Four television would increase interest in her work. *Blue Black Permanent* is her only feature film. Neely, *Between Categories*, 27.
26. Tait, *Personae*, 63; and Neely, *Between Categories*, 27.
27. Rangan, *Immediations*.

28. Eric Barnouw praises Grierson's attention to working-class life in *Documentary*, 88, as does Angela Aguayo in *Documentary Resistance*, 35, but Brian Winston is more critical in "The Tradition of the Victim in Griersonian Documentary."

29. Tait, "To Anybody At All," in *Origins and Elements*, 17.

30. Renov, *The Subject of Documentary*, xxiv (my emphasis).

31. Green, *That's What She Said*, 310; and Ritts Benally, "Thinking Good," 25–27.

32. Schulz, "Navajo Women and the Politics of Identity."

33. Voyles, *Wastelanding*, 40; and Iverson, *The Navajo*, 62.

34. Smith and Kauanui, "Native Feminisms Engage American Studies."

35. Voyles, *Wastelanding*, 7–8.

36. See Estes et al., *Red Nation Rising*, chap. 2.

37. Williams, *Problems in Materialism and Culture*, 70–71.

38. Million, "Felt Theory."

39. Singer, *Wiping the War Paint Off the Lens*, 10. After making *Navajo Talking Picture*, Bowman programmed some Native American film festivals in Los Angeles and taught film production in Californian state colleges and reservation schools. She continued to make films about Indigenous identity and discrimination, though these projects lacked the critical bite of her first film (Bowman described them regretfully as "safer"). One was a television documentary about women's struggles to join the traditionally male powwow circuit, and another was a fragmentary narrative drama about a marginalized Native artist.

40. Since the late 1990s, the Navajo Nation's Film Office has offered guidelines for image making on its reservations. For more on matrilineal traditions, see Schweitzer, *American Indian Grandmothers*. For a discussion of problems in importing "full-scale ethical systems" into documentary practice, see Winston, *Lies, Damn Lies and Documentaries*, 148; and Ruby, *Picturing Culture*. For more on Indigenous behavioral expectations on- and off-screen, see Leuthold, *Indigenous Aesthetics*, 197; and Singer, *Wiping the War Paint off the Lens*, 76.

41. The film was labeled thus by the anthropologist Les Field, quoted in Lewis, *Navajo Talking Picture*, xviii.

42. Lewis, *Navajo Talking Picture*.

43. Angus, *Camera Geologica*, 17.

44. Rangan, *Immediations*; Rony, *The Third Eye*; and Rony, *How Do We Look?*

45. Raygorodetsky, "Indigenous Peoples Defend Earth's Biodiversity—but They're in Danger."

46. For critiques of resilience, see Borie et al., "Mapping Narratives of Urban Resilience in the Global South"; and Chandler and Reid, *Becoming Indigenous*.

47. Tait, "To Anybody At All," 17.

48. Whyte, "Is It Colonial Déjà Vu?"

49. Bozak, *The Cinematic Footprint*; Lovejoy, "From Forests to Film"; and Angus, *Camera Geologica*.

50. West Aith is a nineteenth-century stone croft on the southeast banks of the Loch of Skaill. By 2008 West Aith was derelict and listed on *Scotland's Buildings at Risk Register*. Inspection showed that the house was being used to store hay.

51. MacKinnon, "'Decommonising the Mind.'"

52. Mackinnon, "Colonialism and the Highland Clearances."

53. These are the words of the landowner Sir John Sinclair and the land surveyor John Blackadder, quoted in MacKinnon, "'Decommonising the Mind.'" See also Makdisi, *Romantic Imperialism*, 76–80.

54. Federici, *Re-Enchanting the World: Feminism and the Politics of the Commons*, 15–24.

55. Linebaugh, *Stop, Thief!*, 1.

56. MacKillop, *More Fruitful Than the Soil*; and Jonsson, *Enlightenment's Frontier*.

57. Tait, "Journalism," in *Origins and Elements*, 18.

58. Curtis, "Britain's Oldest Experimentalist . . . Margaret Tait" 62–63.

59. Notebook from May 1997 in Neely, *Between Categories*, 81 (my emphasis).

60. Tait, "Letter to David Curtis."

61. Tait, *Personae*, 63.

62. Much scholarship focuses on these trends, including Bill Nichols's explorations of power, class, and the ethics of representation; Catherine Russell and Alisa Lebow's work on auto-ethnographic and first-person perspectives in non-fiction film; and Scott MacDonald's studies of the sensory turn in experimental and ethnographic filmmaking.

63. Trinh, *When the Moon Waxes Red*; Rony, *The Third Eye*; and Rony, *How Do We Look?*; Rangan, *Immediations*.

64. Trinh, *When the Moon Waxes Red*; and Rangan, *Immediations*.

65. Bermingham, *Landscape and Ideology*; and Casid, *Sowing Empire*.

66. Mitchell, *Landscape and Power*.

67. For more on painters who presented or problematized this aesthetics, see Barrell, *The Dark Side of the Landscape*.

68. Tait, "Letter to Alan Fountain."

69. Neely, *Between Categories*; Krikorian, "'On the Mountain' and 'Land Makar,'" 103–5, 191; and Smith, "Margaret Tait."
70. Tait, "To Anybody At All," 17.
71. Tait, *Lane Furniture*, 8.
72. Nichols, "The Voice of Documentary," 53–65.
73. Trinh, *When the Moon Waxes Red*, 59.
74. Aguayo, *Documentary Resistance*, 37.
75. Rangan, "Audibilities," 281. Rangan borrows the phrase "organ of discrimination" from Stoever, *The Sonic Color Line*, 12–14.
76. Lesage, "The Political Aesthetics of the Feminist Documentary Film."
77. Trinh, *When the Moon Waxes Red*, 59.
78. Lebow, *The Cinema of Me*, 1.
79. Faris, *Navajo and Photography*, 19.
80. Russell, "Playing Primitive."
81. Silko, *Yellow Woman and a Beauty of the Spirit*, 184.
82. Rony, *The Third Eye*, 7–8.
83. Rony, 90–92, 195.
84. Lippard, *Partial Recall*, 30.
85. Lippard, 21.
86. John Ford in Eyman, *Print the Legend*, 351.
87. Fanon, *Black Skin, White Masks*, 112, 118 n15.
88. Du Bois, *The Souls of Black Folk*, 3; and Rony, *The Third Eye*, 5–6.
89. Rony, *The Third Eye*, 95–96.
90. Worth and Adair, *Through Navajo Eyes*, 138.
91. Rony, *The Third Eye*, 211; Rangan, *Immediations*, 56; and Trinh, *When the Moon Waxes Red*, 72.
92. Lewis, *Navajo Talking Picture*, 130.
93. Bowman in Norrell, "Diary of an Invisible Navajo Filmmaker."
94. Ginsburg, "Indigenous Media," 95–96. The anecdote is also discussed in Worth and Adair, *Through Navajo Eyes*, 290; and Rangan, *Immediations*, 57.
95. Allen, "Celebrate Sheep—Symbols of the Good Life for Navajos."
96. Pack, "Indigenous Media Then and Now."
97. Trinh, *When the Moon Waxes Red*, 60.
98. Plumwood, *Feminism and the Mastery of Nature*.
99. Denetdale, "Representing Changing Woman."
100. Bruzzi, *New Documentary*, 47.
101. Balsom, "'There Is No Such Thing as Documentary.'"

CHAPTER 2. FARMER-FILMMAKERS,
FIELDWORK, AND GROWTH

1. Ladji Niangané in Grisey, *Sowing Somankidi Coura*, 109.
2. For example, Rony, *How Do We Look?*; Campt, *Listening to Images*; and Sharpe, *In the Wake*.
3. When not otherwise indicated, Touré's words derive from the voice-overs of *Bouba Touré, 58 Rue Trousseau, Paris, France* and *Xaraasi Xanne—Crossing Voices*.
4. Kimura, *Yamagata no mura ni akai tori ga tonde kita*.
5. Photography's use in land reform campaigns after World War II surely contributed to Ogawa Pro's belief that its images could bolster rural Yamagata. Winther-Tamaki, *Tsuchi*, 60–67.
6. Fujii, "Yanagita Kunio and the Culture Film."
7. Nornes, *Forest of Pressure*, xviii.
8. Toshio Iizuka, "Email to Becca Voelcker," October 25, 2019; and Grierson, "The Documentary Producer," 8.
9. Nornes, *Forest of Pressure*, 44.
10. The thorny issue of loans is explored in *Devotion: A Film about Ogawa Productions*.
11. Ogawa, "Cinema giapponese degli anni '60," 29.
12. Diawara, *African Cinema*, 23.
13. Grisey, *Sowing Somankidi Coura*, 22, 197.
14. Grisey and Touré, "Happiness Against the Grain," 26.
15. Parrott and Lawrence, *The Tricontinental Revolution*.
16. Bakhoré Bathily in Grisey, *Sowing Somankidi Coura*, 139–40, 151; and Ladji Niangané in Grisey, 103.
17. For a critique of the Green Revolution, see Shiva, *The Violence of the Green Revolution*.
18. Jonsson and Wennerlind, *Scarcity*.
19. Waring, *Counting for Nothing*; and Voelcker et al., "Positions."
20. Gibson-Graham, *The End of Capitalism (as We Knew It)*; Raworth, *Doughnut Economics*; Shiva, "How Economic Growth Has Become Anti-Life."
21. Hickel, *Less Is More*; and Saito, *Marx in the Anthropocene*.
22. Tsing, *The Mushroom at the End of the World*, 65.
23. Sekula, "Photography between Labor and Capital"; and Krauss, "Photography's Discursive Spaces."
24. Yusoff, *A Billion Black Anthropocenes or None*, 16.

25. Marx, *Capital*, 1:926.
26. Yusoff, *A Billion Black Anthropocenes or None*, 40.
27. Moore, *Anthropocene or Capitalocene?*; Davis et al., "Anthropocene, Capitalocene, ... Plantationocene?"; Haraway and Tsing, *Reflections on the Plantationocene*; and Barua, *Plantation Worlds*.
28. Tsing, "Unruly Edges"; Yusoff, *A Billion Black Anthropocenes or None*, 36–37; and McKittrick, *Sylvia Wynter*.
29. Tsing, "Unruly Edges," 141.
30. Nornes, *Forest of Pressure*, 15–18.
31. Fujii, "Yanagita Kunio and the Culture Film."
32. Centeno-Martín and Raine, "Tracing Tendencies in the Japanese Documentary Mode."
33. Barua, *Plantation Worlds*, 17.
34. Apter and Sawa, *Against the State*, 181–85. Ogawa Pro member Fukuda Katsuhiko left the collective in 1977 and made *A Grasscutter's Tale* (1985) with his partner, Hatano Yukie, portraying an indomitable Sanrizuka grandmother farmer, Katsu Someya.
35. For more on militant filmmaking and the Third Cinema movement, see Chapter 5.
36. *A Visit to Ogawa Productions*, directed by Ōshige Junichiro and Ōshima Nagisa, 1981/1999.
37. Kimura, *Yamagata no mura ni akai tori ga tonde kita*, 15–20.
38. Jesty, "Image Pragmatics and Film as a Lived Practice in the Documentary Work of Hani Susumu and Tsuchimoto Noriaki."
39. Konig, "Interview with Ogawa Shinsuke, Tokyo."
40. Iizuka, "Email to Becca Voelcker."
41. This gender imbalance persisted despite the prominence of female documentarians such as Atsugi Taka in imperial and wartime Japan and Haneda Sumiko at Iwanami. See Hori, *Promiscuous Media*, 114–55; and Centeno-Martín and Raine, "Tracing Tendencies in the Japanese Documentary Mode," 5. For more on Ogawa Pro's uneven attribution of credit, see Yasui and Tanaka, *The Legendary Filmmaking Collective NDU and Nunokawa Tetsuro*.
42. Iizuka, "Email to Becca Voelcker."
43. *Devotion: A Film about Ogawa Productions*.
44. Ladji Niangané in Grisey, *Sowing Somankidi Coura*, 107.
45. Grisey, 261–63, 292.
46. Ousmane Sinaré in Grisey, 47.
47. Mann, *From Empires to NGOs in the West African Sahel*.

48. Ousmane Sinaré in Grisey, *Sowing Somankidi Coura*, 47–51.
49. Marx, *Capital*, 1:637–38; and Marx, *Capital*, 3:949. See also Justus von Liebig, "Letters on Modern Agriculture (1859)" in Foster, *Marx's Ecology*, 153.
50. Sokhona in Grisey, *Sowing Somankidi Coura: A Generative Archive*, 160–61.
51. Grisey and Touré, "Happiness Against the Grain," 27.
52. Other Ogawa Pro films made in Yamagata include *Magino Village Story: Raising Silkworms* (1977) and *Red Persimmons* (completed posthumously by Peng Xiaolian in 2001).
53. More recently, films produced at Harvard's Sensory Ethnography Lab have experimented with immersive techniques and other-than-human perspectives. Extreme duration meanwhile characterized an eight-hour film about Japanese farming in 2020, *The Works and Days (of Tayoko Shiojiri in the Shiotani Basin)* (dir. Winter and Edstrom).
54. Ohnuki-Tierney, *Rice as Self*; Robertson, *Native and Newcomery*, 89; Totman, *Japan*, 55, 207; and Kagawa-Fox, "The Crucial Role of Culture in Japanese Environmental Philosophy."
55. Ohnuki-Tierney, *Rice as Self*, 82.
56. Cwiertka, *Modern Japanese Cuisine*; and Cwiertka and Miho, *Branding Japanese Food*.
57. Grierson, "The Documentary Producer," 8.
58. Ohnuki-Tierney, "Rice as Self," 4–5.
59. Scheiner, "The Japanese Village."
60. Andrews, *Dissenting Japan*, 4, 164, 260.
61. Ogawa Pro's excavation recalls Takayama Noboru, who excavated archaeological material to present as sculptural objects and in photographs throughout the 1970s. See Winther-Tamaki, *Tsuchi*, 133–37.
62. Doane, "The Indexical and the Concept of Medium Specificity"; and Angus, *Camera Geologica*.
63. Markus Nornes attempts the same effect by rendering "Japan" in quotation marks.
64. Robertson, "It Takes a Village."
65. Ivy, *Discourses of the Vanishing*.
66. Robertson, "It Takes a Village," 116.
67. Mao sent many to the countryside or factories to undergo "re-education" through manual labor during the 1960s and 1970s. Ogawa Pro's methods were very different in their emphasis on preserving tradition.
68. Daney, "When Serge Daney Met Ogawa Shinsuke."
69. Nornes, *Forest of Pressure*, 158–59.

70. Matos Cabo, *Of Sea and Soil*, 61.
71. Konig, "Interview with Ogawa Shinsuke, Tokyo."
72. Iizuka, "Email to Becca Voelcker,"
73. Ogawa, "Documentary's Sense of Reality."
74. Trinh, *When the Moon Waxes Red*, 32.
75. Tsing, *The Mushroom at the End of the World*, 27–29, 263.
76. Grisey, *Sowing Somankidi Coura*, 291–92, 299.
77. Tiquet in Grisey, 49.
78. Rodney, *How Europe Underdeveloped Africa*.
79. Cabral, *Return to the Source*, 39; and Chilcote, *Emerging Nationalism in Portuguese Africa*, 361.
80. Grisey, *Sowing Somankidi Coura*, 204.
81. Cabral, *Return to the Source*, 43.
82. Ukadike, "In Guinea-Bissau, Cinema Trickles Down."
83. Foster, "Marx's Theory of Metabolic Rift."
84. Cabral in Neves, "Ideology, Science, and People in Amílcar Cabral."
85. Davis et al., "Anthropocene, Capitalocene, . . . Plantationocene?"
86. Tiquet in Grisey, *Sowing Somankidi Coura*, 49–68.
87. Mukherjee, "Stereoscopic Vision in the Plantationocene."
88. Tsing, *The Mushroom at the End of the World*, 6, 162, 260.
89. Tomii, *Radicalism in the Wilderness*.
90. Winther-Tamaki, *Tsuchi*, 64.
91. Grisey and Touré, "Happiness Against the Grain," 30.
92. Glissant, *Poetics of Relation*; and Chen, *Asia as Method*, 223.
93. Trinh, *When the Moon Waxes Red*, 97.
94. Haraway, *Staying with the Trouble*.

CHAPTER 3. THERE IS NO COUNTRYSIDE

1. Maerkle, "Masao Adachi: Pt. I."
2. Harootunian and Kohso, "Messages in a Bottle," 73.
3. Sharp, "Interview."
4. Matsuda, *Fūkei No Shimetsu*, 308; and Marx, *Capital*, 1:716.
5. Andrews, *Dissenting Japan*, 65; Standish, *Politics, Porn and Protest*, 92; and Packard, *Protest in Tokyo*, 182.
6. Furuhata, "Multimedia Environments and Security Operations."
7. Furuhata, *Cinema of Actuality*, 145.

8. *Fūkeiron* practitioners were not alone in their pessimism. The artist Enokura Kōji stated in 1970 that "there is no blue sky and no black soil, just a stagnant sky and cold sidewalk." However, during an extended artist collaboration on land near Yokohama, Enokura discovered that "as the weeds were cut down, black soil gradually began to appear." Quoted in Winther-Tamaki, *Tsuchi*, 134.

9. Adachi in *The Anabasis of May and Fusako Shigenobu, Masao Adachi, and 27 Years without Images* (2011).

10. Tsing, *The Mushroom at the End of the World*, 5.

11. Tsing, viii.

12. In Klein, "Dancing the World into Being."

13. The music critics Aikura Hisato and Hiraoka Masaaki also assisted on the film.

14. From Nakahira's essay "Fūkei e no hanran," quoted in Prichard, *Residual Futures*, 100.

15. Harootunian and Kohso, "Messages in a Bottle." Nagayama wrote several books from prison, and Shindō Kaneto offers a dramatic account of his life in his 1970 film *Live Today, Die Tomorrow!* (its Japanese title translates as *Naked Nineteen-Year-Old*).

16. Harootunian and Kohso, "Messages in a Bottle," 73–74.

17. Harootunian and Kohso, 73–74.

18. Matsuda, *Fūkei No Shimetsu*, 11–12.

19. Adachi and Hirasawa, *Eiga-kakumei*, 290.

20. Furuhata, *Cinema of Actuality*; Terada, "Repletion"; Toscano, "Equator of Alienation"; and Ross, "Ethics of the Landscape Shot."

21. Nakahira in Prichard, *Residual Futures*, 100–8.

22. Nakahira, "Toshi: Kaisetsu," 139.

23. Nakahira, "Eugene Atget."

24. Prichard, *Residual Futures*, 84.

25. Nakahira founded *Provoke* with critic Taki Kōji, poet Okada Tadahiko, and photographer Takanashi Yutaka. Moriyama Daidō joined for the second and third issues. Nishimura Tamiko also worked as a darkroom printer at *Provoke*.

26. Prichard, *Residual Futures*, 97.

27. Prichard, 88.

28. By contrast, Nishimura Tamiko (b. 1948), a *Provoke* magazine darkroom printer, benefited from Japan Railways' promotional campaign that targeted solo travelers and women by journeying through the country photographing

chance encounters with women and children. Although her images also record modernization's effects on tradition, they also capture a sense of expanded personal freedom. Her road trip photobook, *Shikishima*, was published in 1973. Vermare and Martin, *I'm So Happy You Are Here*, 303.

29. Nakahira, "Gendai Eiga Jōkyō Jiten," 142. Nakahira composed these thoughts in his contribution to "A Dictionary of Keywords of Contemporary Film Practice" alongside essays by Matsuda and others.

30. Saito, *Karl Marx's Ecosocialism*, 16; and Saito, *Marx in the Anthropocene*, 4. See also Foster, "Marx's Theory of Metabolic Rift"; and Foster, *Marx's Ecology*.

31. Saito does acknowledge the work of Foster, Joel Kovel, and Paul Burkett.

32. For example, Kuruma Samezo, Yoshiro Tamanoi, and Teinosuke Otani.

33. Marx, *Capital*, 1:376.

34. Marx and Engels, *Collected Works*, 3:276, 273; Marx, *Capital*, 1:198.

35. For a comparable project, see Bert Winther-Tamaki's discussion of Endō Toshikatsu's 1997 installation of contaminated soil inside an incubator. Winther-Tamaki, *Tsuchi*, 200–4.

36. Saito, *Karl Marx's Ecosocialism*, 29–31.

37. Marx, *Grundrisse*, 489; Saito, *Karl Marx's Ecosocialism*, 66–67; and Saito, *Marx in the Anthropocene*, 22.

38. Harvey, "Between Space and Time"; and Saito, "Elasticity, Nature and Profit."

39. Gunning, "Before Documentary," 56.

40. Mészáros, *The Necessity of Social Control*, 49–50.

41. Matsuda, *Bara to Mumeisha*, 123.

42. The film also shares characteristics with Hani Susumu's social approach to documentary. Though he is usually associated with Ogawa Pro and Tsuchimoto Noriaki due to the social orientation of their work (see Chapter 2), Hani's attention to the atmospheric, affective qualities of everyday life, including in a little-known 1958 film portrait of Tokyo, surely influenced Adachi's and Matsuda's style. For more on this similarity, see Centeno-Martín, "Legacies of Hani Susumu's Documentary School."

43. Maerkle, "Masao Adachi: Pt. I."

44. Sharp, "Interview"

45. Hirasawa and Spigland, "REVOLUTION+1."

46. Furuhata, *Cinema of Actuality*.

47. Desjardins, *Outlaw Masters of Japanese Film*, 179.

48. Desjardins, 166.

49. Desjardins, 181.

50. Hayashi, "Marquis de Sade Goes to Tokyo," 275.
51. Hayashi, 269.
52. Saito Ayako quoted in Sas, "Pink Feminism?"
53. Rony, *How Do We Look?*
54. Furuhata, "The Actuality of Wakamatsu," 167.
55. Matsuda, *Fūkei No Shimetsu*; and Nakahira, "Toshi: Kaisetsu," 139.
56. Benjamin, *Selected Writings*, 258.
57. Matsuda, *Bara to Mumeisha*, 123.
58. Prichard, "Introduction to 'City as Landscape' (1970) by Matsuda Masao (1933–2020)."
59. Yoshida, "The Undulating Contours of Sōgō Geijutsu (Total Work of Art), or Hanada Kiyoteru's Thoughts on Transmedia in Postwar Japan."
60. Hanada, *Hanada Kiyoteru Chosakushū 3*, 150; and Marx, *Grundrisse*, 101.
61. Maerkle, "Masao Adachi: Pt. I."
62. Brecht also influenced Adachi's European contemporaries, whose leftist critique and formal reflexivity Nicole Brenez compares to *fūkeiron*. Brenez, "Peuple, Révolution, Paysage."
63. Hirasawa and Spigland, "REVOLUTION+1."
64. Marx, *Grundrisse*, 101.
65. Saito, *Karl Marx's Ecosocialism*, 106.
66. Saito, 110.
67. Marx, *Grundrisse*, 258.
68. Saito, *Karl Marx's Ecosocialism*, 111–12.
69. Harootunian and Kohso, "Messages in a Bottle."
70. Marx and Engels, *Collected Works*, 30:63; Saito, *Marx in the Anthropocene*, 19–20.
71. Berger, *Ways of Seeing*; and Williams, *The Country and the City*, 149.
72. Jackson, *Discovering the Vernacular Landscape*, 5–7.
73. Berger, *Ways of Seeing*; Casid, *Sowing Empire*; and Makdisi, *Romantic Imperialism*.
74. Nakahira, "Gendai Eiga Jōkyō Jiten," 142.
75. Moore, *Capitalism in the Web of Life*.
76. Saito, *Marx in the Anthropocene*, 108, 249.
77. Castree, "Socializing Nature," 3.
78. Saito, *Marx in the Anthropocene*, 108.
79. Ivy, *Discourses of the Vanishing*; and Robertson, "It Takes a Village."
80. Gavin, "Nihon Fukeiron (Japanese Landscape)," 219–31; and Marran, *Ecology without Culture*, 12, 43.

81. Watsuji, *Climate and Culture*, 29–31.
82. Watsuji, 3.
83. Marx, *Capital*, 1:381.
84. Steinhoff, "Doing the Defendant's Laundry."
85. Hirasawa and Spigland, "REVOLUTION+1."
86. Hirasawa and Spigland.
87. Maerkle, "Masao Adachi: Pt. II."
88. For more on Adachi's militant activities, see Eric Baudelaire's 2011 film *The Anabasis of May and Fusako Shigenobu, Masao Adachi, and 27 Years without Images*; and Philippe Grandrieux's 2011 film made with Nicole Brenez, *Il se peut que la beauté ait renforcé notre résolution* (*It May Be That Beauty Has Strengthened Our Resolve*)
89. Sharp, "Interview."
90. Yamagami is thought to have been protesting the fraudulent and politically influential power of the Unification Church, which had ties to Abe.
91. Hirasawa and Spigland, "REVOLUTION+1."
92. Maerkle, "Masao Adachi: Pt. I."
93. Women photographers such as Tokiwa Toyoko, Ishikawa Mao, and Ishiuchi Miyako turned their attention to military occupation too with a focus on the abuses of women, particularly around military bases in Okinawa, Yokohama, and Yokosuka.
94. Numerous photographers including Akagi Shūji have documented cleanup projects in Fukushima, their images of contaminated soil, bagged and sealed, testifying to the catastrophic environmental impact of the disaster as well as its lasting social trauma. See Prichard, "Seeing through the In/Visible."
95. Saito, *Karl Marx's Ecosocialism*, 97. See also O'Connor, *Natural Causes*; and Foster, "The Great Capitalist Climacteric, Marxism and 'System Change Not Climate Change,'" 9.
96. Saito, *Karl Marx's Ecosocialism*, 99–100.

CHAPTER 4. COMPANION PLANTING
IN WOUNDED LAND

1. Klein, "Dancing the World into Being."
2. Klein.
3. Wynter, "Unsettling the Coloniality of Being/Power/Truth/Freedom"; and McKittrick, *Sylvia Wynter*.
4. Tsing, *The Mushroom at the End of the World*, 27–29.

5. Mayer, "Centre."
6. Project description, 1991, Harvard Film Archive, Anne Charlotte Robertson Collection (hereafter HFA). Unless otherwise indicated, direct quotations are taken from this collection or my own transcriptions of Robertson's film soundtracks.
7. Harvey, *A Brief History of Neoliberalism*, 31, 37–38. See also Cosgrove and Karter, "The Poison in the Cure."
8. Little has been written about Robertson, though Scott MacDonald was an early champion of her work, and, more recently, Anjo-marí Gouws has written about Robertson's feminist representations of labor. MacDonald, *The Garden in the Machine*; MacDonald, *A Critical Cinema 2*; Gouws, "'I'm Washing My Dishes and Making a Movie'"; and Gouws, "Hearing and Seeing the In/Visible."
9. Getty Research Institute, *Maren Hassinger, Ulysses Jenkins, Barbara McCollough, et al. Oral History.*
10. hooks, *Feminist Theory from Margin to Center*, 88; Crenshaw, "Demarginalizing the Intersection of Race and Sex"; Anzaldua, *Borderlands/La Frontera*; Davis, *Women, Race & Class*; and Lorde, *Sister Outsider*.
11. Sedgwick, *Touching Feeling*, 1.
12. Sedgwick, 146, 149. See also Hawthorne, "'Reparative Reading' as Queer Pedagogy."
13. Sedgwick, *Touching Feeling*, 130.
14. MacDonald, *A Critical Cinema 2*.
15. Hansen, Bourgois, and Drucker, "Pathologizing Poverty."
16. MacDonald, *A Critical Cinema 2*, 217.
17. Quoted in MacDonald, 211.
18. Note, Spring 1979, HFA.
19. Marx, *The Machine in the Garden*, 226.
20. Letter to Jacob Goldberg, August 3, 2006, HFA.
21. Foucault, *The History of Sexuality*, 137–38.
22. Berlant, *Cruel Optimism*.
23. Reel 23, *A Breakdown (and) after the Mental Hospital* (September 1 to December 13, 1982).
24. Smith-Rosenberg, "Puberty to Menopause," 24.
25. Reel 23.
26. Lesage, "The Political Aesthetics of the Feminist Documentary Film"; Renov, *The Subject of Documentary*; Lebow, *The Cinema of Me*; and Warren, *Subject to Reality*.
27. Notebook, 1979, HFA.

28. For more on applying Marxist readings to mental disorders, see Busfield, *Managing Madness*, 130–39.

29. Bazin, *What Is Cinema?*, 13.

30. Lowder, "Email to Becca Voelcker," July 15, 2018.

31. Bozak, *The Cinematic Footprint*; Lovejoy, "Celluloid Geopolitics"; and Angus, *Camera Geologica*.

32. Scott MacDonald in conversation with author, February 2019.

33. Jacob and Roth, *The Amazing Decade*, 18; and Jones, *Body Art/Performing the Subject*, 15.

34. My exploration of Robertson's affinity with plants and animals may sound aligned to recent trends in new materialism, but the agency of other-than-human matter is not my focus. Rather, I am interested in Robertson's critique of anthropocentrism.

35. Worster, *Nature's Economy*, 311.

36. Clinebell, "Greening Pastoral Care"; and Brown and Hillman, *Ecopsychology*.

37. Born et al., "Effects of Sleep and Circadian Rhythm on Human Circulating Immune Cells."

38. Myers, "Exercise and Cardiovascular Health"; and Goldfarb, "Beta-Endorphin Response to Exercise."

39. Notes, April/May 1983, HFA.

40. Quoted in Rogoff, *Terra Infirma*, 124.

41. Quoted in Blocker, *Where Is Ana Mendieta?*, 18.

42. Dia Art Foundation, "Robert Smithson, *Spiral Jetty*."

43. Cadena, "Uncommoning Nature."

44. Quoted in Rogoff, *Terra Infirma*, 124.

45. For more on the scheme that brought Mendieta to the United States, see Shnookal, *Operation Pedro Pan and the Exodus of Cuba's Children*.

46. Casid, *Sowing Empire*.

47. Rogoff, *Terra Infirma*, 124.

48. Blocker, *Where Is Ana Mendieta?*, 12.

49. In the early hours of September 8, 1985, Mendieta fell from the window of her husband Carl Andre's thirty-fourth–floor apartment in Manhattan during a heated argument. In the murder trial that followed, Andre's defense weaponized stereotypes that reflected poorly on Mendieta and deflected attention from Andre. The Estate of Ana Mendieta told me that this context is not relevant to a discussion of her work. Following Helen Molesworth's lead, however, I see it as helpful in apprehending the scale of prejudice with which Mendieta contended. This said, I appreciate the value of viewing Mendieta in her own right and for this

reason place the context in an endnote and direct readers wishing to learn more to Hoffman, "Rear Window"; and Molesworth, *Death of an Artist*.

50. Rony, *How Do We Look?*, 5–6.

51. Johnston, "Women's Cinema as Counter-Cinema."

52. Rony, *How Do We Look?*, 18. Mendieta contrasts Laura Mulvey here, whose work within a predominantly white second wave context of feminist struggle left little room for female scopic enjoyment. See Mulvey, "Visual Pleasure and Narrative Cinema."

53. Orenstein, "The Reemergence of the Archetype of the Great Goddess in Art by Contemporary Women"; and Sjoo and Mor, *Great Cosmic Mother*.

54. Blocker, *Where Is Ana Mendieta?*, 19.

55. Trinh, *When the Moon Waxes Red*, 74.

56. Blocker, *Where Is Ana Mendieta?*, 34.

57. McCullough, "Bio."

58. Jackson, "'Know How to Do Something Different."

59. Quoted in Jackson.

60. Jacqueline Najuma Stewart discusses this insider/outsider positionality in Field, *L.A. Rebellion*, 286.

61. Bonner, "A Different Image," 163. See also Springer, "Black Women Filmmakers."

62. *L.A. Rebellion: Barbara McCullough on UCLA's "The View" (c. 1979)*.

63. Getty Research Institute, *Maren Hassinger, Ulysses Jenkins, Barbara McCollough, et al. Oral History*.

64. Quoted in Field, *L.A. Rebellion*, 3. For more on McCullough's relationship with New Hollywood, see Bonner, "A Different Image."

65. *L.A. Rebellion: Barbara McCullough on UCLA's "The View" (c. 1979)*.

66. Field, *L.A. Rebellion*, xii.

67. DeClue, *Visitation*, 2, 11.

68. *L.A. Rebellion: Barbara McCullough on UCLA's "The View" (c. 1979)*.

69. *L.A. Rebellion: Barbara McCullough on UCLA's "The View" (c. 1979)*.

70. *L.A. Rebellion: Barbara McCullough on UCLA's "The View" (c. 1979)*.

71. McKittrick, "Plantation Futures," 7.

72. McKittrick, 4.

73. Trinh, *When the Moon Waxes Red*, 148, 159.

74. Aguayo, *Documentary Resistance*, 109–10; and DeClue, *Visitation*, 9.

75. Tsing, "Unruly Edges"; and Haraway and Tsing, *Reflections on the Plantationocene*.

76. Wynter, "Novel and History, Plot and Plantation"; and McKittrick, "Plantation Futures," 8.

77. Bonner, "A Different Image," 163.
78. *L.A. Rebellion: Barbara McCullough on UCLA's "The View"* (c. 1979).
79. Geronimus, *Weathering*, 3.
80. Geronimus, 12.
81. Rony, *How Do We Look?*, 5.

CHAPTER 5. ON THE PICKET LINE, ON THE TELEVISION

1. Davis, *The Other Side of Empathy*, ix.
2. Davis, x.
3. Davis, 5–6.
4. Levine, *The Activist Humanist*, 11.
5. Johnston, "Poverty and Distribution."
6. For more on the *New Left Review*'s establishment with E. P. Thompson and Stuart Hall, see Moglen and Steinhouse, *Out of Apathy*.
7. Gallagher and Greenblatt, *Practicing New Historicism*, 60.
8. Gallagher and Greenblatt, 52, 65.
9. Bauer and Kidner, *Working Together*, 47.
10. For more on collective filmmaking in 1970s and 1980s Britain, see Friedman, *Fires Were Started*; Bauer and Kidner, *Working Together*; and Clayton and Mulvey, *Other Cinemas*.
11. Adamson, *Enduring Images*, 24.
12. Bauer and Kidner, *Working Together*, 54.
13. Bauer and Kidner, 67.
14. Bauer and Kidner, 47, 112, 143. For more on the Cinétracts project of 1968, see Adamson, *Enduring Images*, 46.
15. Bauer and Kidner, *Working Together*, 60.
16. Strikes, including those centered around women, also occupy an important place in histories of political cinema in the United States. See Aguayo, *Documentary Resistance*, 103–49.
17. Bauer and Kidner, *Working Together*, 60–61.
18. Macdougall, *The Corporeal Image*, 22–23; and Gaines, "Political Mimesis," 90.
19. Rony, *The Third Eye*, 5–6.
20. IG Farben, which used forced and slave labor to produce Zyklon B (the poisonous gas used during the Holocaust) was formed in 1925 from a merger of six chemical companies including Agfa, the film manufacturer.

21. Meier, "Cut-Flower Production in Colombia—A Major Development Success Story for Women?"
22. West and West, "Conversation with Marta Rodríguez by Dennis West and Joan M. West."
23. Demos, *Beyond the World's End*, 11,15.
24. Whyte, "Is It Colonial Déjà Vu?," 100.
25. Wright, "'The Devil Looks Like a Mounted Policeman.'"
26. Wright.
27. More recently, virtual reality has been described as an "empathy machine" by those who claim that its digital simulations can foster empathy. See Bollmer, "Empathy Machines."
28. Stoneman, "When Channel 4 Was Radical"; and Perry, "History, Landscape, Nation."
29. The Annan Report, officially called the "Report of the Committee on the Future of Broadcasting," reviewed the state of British broadcasting and made recommendations for the future of the industry.
30. Stoneman, "When Channel 4 Was Radical."
31. For a critique of socially oriented art practices in the early 2000s, see Bishop, "The Social Turn."
32. Trinh, *When the Moon Waxes Red*, 60. For more on claims of autonomy, see Kester, *Beyond the Sovereign Self*, 3, 20.
33. Davis, *The Other Side of Empathy*, 7. Elizabeth Dauphinée puts it similarly, arguing that "people become representations of their plights" in media representations of war and torture. Dauphinée, "The Politics of the Body in Pain," 142. See also Fassin, "Humanitarianism as a Politics of Life," 517; and Calain, "Ethics and Images of Suffering Bodies in Humanitarian Medicine," 280.
34. Winston, "The Tradition of the Victim in Griersonian Documentary."
35. Davis, *The Other Side of Empathy*, 2.
36. Aguayo, *Documentary Resistance*, 105, 132.
37. Gaines, "Political Mimesis."
38. Chouliaraki, *The Spectatorship of Suffering*, 2,8, 11; and Chouliaraki, *The Ironic Spectator*, 26.
39. Keenan, "Mobilizing Shame." The term "compassion fatigue" appears in Calhoun, "The Idea of Emergency," 34. See also Tester, *Media Culture and Morality*, 130; and Sontag, *On Photography*, 41.
40. Rangan, *Immediations*, 13–14.
41. McKittrick, *Sylvia Wynter*; Povinelli, *Geontologies*; and Yusoff, *A Billion Black Anthropocenes or None*.

42. Calhoun, "The Idea of Emergency," 33.
43. Calhoun, 55.
44. Foucault, *Discipline & Punish*, 200; and Rangan, *Immediations*, 101.
45. Rangan, *Immediations*, 67.
46. Rangan, 69–71; and Fassin and Pandolfi, *Contemporary States of Emergency*, 13.
47. Scarry, *Thinking in an Emergency*; and Calain, "Ethics and Images of Suffering Bodies in Humanitarian Medicine," 280. See also Campbell, "The Iconography of Famine."
48. Lissner, "Merchants of Misery." See also Plewes and Stuart, "The Pornography of Poverty," 23–27.
49. Rony, *How Do We Look?*
50. Rangan, *Immediations*, 94–96.
51. Calain, "Ethics and Images of Suffering Bodies in Humanitarian Medicine," 279.
52. Rangan et al., *Thinking with an Accent*, 5.
53. Rangan, *Immediations*, 99.
54. Waldman and Walker, *Feminism and Documentary*, 14–17.
55. For histories of Third Cinema, see Gabriel, *Third Cinema in the Third World*; Chanan, *Twenty-Five Years of the New Latin American Cinema*; Dissanayake and Guneratne, *Rethinking Third Cinema*; Ekotto and Koh, *Rethinking Third Cinema*; and Mazierska and Kristensen, *Third Cinema, World Cinema and Marxism*.
56. Solanas and Getino, "Towards a Third Cinema."
57. Bauer and Kidner, *Working Together*, 47.
58. Solanas, "Cinéma d'auteur ou cinéma d'intervention?"
59. Bauer and Kidner, *Working Together*, 109.
60. Cinema Action information sheet (1975) in Bauer and Kidner, *Working Together*, 111.
61. Espinosa, "For an Imperfect Cinema," 24–26.
62. For example, *Planas testimonio de un etnocidio* (*Planas, Testimony of Ethnocide*, 1970) documents the genocide of an Indigenous group and explores its economic and social contexts.
63. Silva, "Colombia."
64. Burton, *Cinema and Social Change in Latin America*, 25–34.
65. Bauer and Kidner, *Working Together*, 58, 65.
66. Bauer and Kidner, 109–11.
67. Bauer and Kidner, 109.
68. Glyn and Marris, "Seven Years of Cinema Action," 69.

69. For more on this debate in the discipline of art history, see Kester, *Beyond the Sovereign Self*, 20, 23–24.
70. Glyn and Marris, "Seven Years of Cinema Action," 69.
71. Glyn and Marris, 70, 80.
72. Johnston and Willemen, "Brecht in Britain," 104.
73. Glyn and Marris, "Seven Years of Cinema Action," 71.
74. Bauer and Kidner, *Working Together*, 66.
75. Dickinson, *Rogue Reels*, 264.
76. Johnston, "So That You Can Live," 12.
77. Nichols, "The Voice of Documentary," 18.
78. See Ulfsdotter and Rogers, *Female Agency and Documentary Strategies*; Warren, *Subject to Reality*; and Balsom and Peleg, *Feminist Worldmaking and the Moving Image*.
79. Price, "So That You Can Live," 15.
80. Aspinall and Merck, "So That You Can Live, II." The film's includes music by Robert Wyatt, Lindsay Cooper, and Scritti Politti.
81. Davies, *The Welsh Language*, 37.
82. Bauer and Kidner, *Working Together*, 61.
83. Aspinall, "This Sadder Recognition."
84. Williams, *Television*, 129–32, 136.
85. Karlin et al., "Problems of Independent Cinema," 33.
86. Wright, "'The Devil Looks Like a Mounted Policeman.'"
87. Arsenal–Institut für Film und Videokunst, "Nuestra Voz de Tierra, Memoria y Futuro."
88. Wright, "'The Devil Looks Like a Mounted Policeman.'"
89. Wright.
90. Nixon, *Slow Violence and the Environmentalism of the Poor*, 17. The futurity expressed in the film speaks to the Seventh Generation Principle, an Iroquois philosophy that evaluates present activities according to their effects seven generations into the future.
91. West and West, "Conversation with Marta Rodríguez by Dennis West and Joan M. West," 39–44.
92. Rodríguez, "Marta Rodríguez and Jorge Silva"; and Taussig, *The Devil and Commodity Fetishism in South America*, 92. My thanks to María Vélez-Serna for conversations about Marxism and Colombian cinema.
93. Povinelli, "Elizabeth Povinelli in Conversation with Kathryn Yusoff."
94. Rony, *The Third Eye*, 194–95.
95. Law, "What's Wrong with a One-World World?"; and McKittrick, *Sylvia Wynter*, 10.

96. Cadena and Blaser, *A World of Many Worlds*, 4.
97. Cadena, "Uncommoning Nature."
98. West and West, "Conversation with Marta Rodríguez by Dennis West and Joan M. West."
99. West and West.
100. Chanan, "The Changing Geography of Third Cinema," 385.
101. Nixon, *Slow Violence and the Environmentalism of the Poor*, 41.
102. Liboiron, *Pollution Is Colonialism*.
103. West and West, "Conversation with Marta Rodríguez by Dennis West and Joan M. West."
104. Aitken, *The Concise Routledge Encyclopedia of the Documentary Film*, 770.
105. West and West, "Conversation with Marta Rodríguez by Dennis West and Joan M. West."
106. Levine, *The Activist Humanist*, 7–8.
107. This process could be likened to that described in Rancière, *The Politics of Aesthetics*.
108. Waugh, *Show Us Life*, xiv.

CHAPTER 6. EXTRACTION IS STEALING, RELATIONSHIPS GIVE MEANING

1. Mitchell, *What Do Pictures Want?*
2. Demos, "The Agency of Fire"; and Demos, *Beyond the World's End*.
3. The Wretched of the Earth Coalition is among many voices criticizing contemporary climate activists who speak of unprecedented emergency for forgetting that the world has been "ending" for many Indigenous, working-class, Black, and Brown communities for generations. See The Wretched of the Earth, "An Open Letter to Extinction Rebellion."
4. The phrase "it is easier to imagine an end to the world than an end to capitalism" is attributed to both Fredric Jameson and Slavoj Žižek and inspires Mark Fisher's *Capitalist Realism*. For more on the compatibility and collaboration between critical theories stating that "there is no alternative" and capitalist imperialism, see Rockhill, "Imperialist Propaganda and the Ideology of the Western Left Intelligentsia." In the context of protest art in the Americas, Jennifer Ponce de León is one of several theorists who seeks to inscribe "the capacious and multiform capacities of movements from below" into art historical

narratives. See Ponce de León, *Another Aesthetics Is Possible*, 15. See also Reed, *The Art of Protest*.

5. Ross, *May '68 and Its Afterlives*, 20; and Adamson, *Enduring Images*, 5.

6. Hartman, "Dead Book Remains," 118.

7. Hartman, *Wayward Lives, Beautiful Experiments*, 301.

8. For a comparable theoretical intervention, see Aguayo, *Documentary Resistance*, 147; and DeClue, *Visitation*, 9.

9. Morrison, "Unspeakable Things Unspoken," 250.

10. Rhodes, "Whose History?"

11. Klein, "Dancing the World into Being."

12. Berger, *Why Look at Animals?*

13. Thanks to Debashree Mukherjee for helping me think through this with her presentation "Stereoscopic Vision in the Plantationocene."

14. Vizenor, *Survivance*.

15. Wynter, "Novel and History, Plot and Plantation," 99–100.

16. Sy, "Bungkalan as Natural Praxis," 65.

17. Sy, 76.

18. Camacho and Lien, "The Angry Christ (Plot and Plantation)."

19. Regencia, "Philippines 'Deadliest' Country for Environmental, Land Activists."

20. Camacho and Lien, "Offerings for Escalante."

21. Chen, *Asia as Method*, 223.

22. Dirlik, *The Postcolonial Aura*, 85–86, 98. Grant Kester emphasizes this mediation as a crucial component of much recent socially engaged art. See Kester, *Beyond the Sovereign Self*, 3.

23. Camacho and Lien, "Offerings for Escalante."

24. Crimp, "Mourning and Militancy."

25. Doing, "Phytograms."

26. My line of questioning here follows that developed by Anna Arabindan-Kesson in her recent consideration of how racialized identity, enslaved labor, and cotton were equated as resources for extraction in the nineteenth century. See Arabindan-Kesson, *Black Bodies, White Gold*, 3.

27. For more on non-chemical hand processing in experimental/artisanal cinema, see MacKenzie and Marchessault, *Process Cinema*; Knowles, *Experimental Film and Photochemical Practices*; and Zinman, *Making Images Move*.

28. Iyer, "A Pedagogy of Reparations," 183; Chakrabarty, "Provincializing Europe"; and Chen, *Asia as Method*, 2–3.

29. Camacho and Lien, "Offerings for Escalante."

30. Camacho and Lien, "Surviving Tiempo Muerto."
31. Mbembe, *Necropolitics*, 27; and Camacho and Lien, "Surviving Tiempo Muerto."
32. Camacho and Lien, "The Angry Christ (Plot and Plantation)."
33. Vaz and Brenner, "Press Release."
34. For more on animals in cinema, see Burt, *Animals in Film*; Chris, *Watching Wildlife*; Shukin, *Animal Capital*; Pick, *Creaturely Poetics*; Lawrence and Lury, *The Zoo and Screen Media*; and Ramos, *Animals*.
35. Vaz and Brenner, "Press Release."
36. Ana Vaz, notes on the film, in the press pack for *Cinemamultiversal* (2022).
37. Wynter and McKittrick, "Unparalleled Catastrophe for Our Species?," 11; and Berger, *About Looking*, 21.
38. Warren, *Subject to Reality*, 4; and Waldman and Walker, *Feminism and Documentary*, 13–19.
39. Cadena and Blaser, *A World of Many Worlds*, 4; and Escobar, *Designs for the Pluriverse*, 86.
40. Barua, *Plantation Worlds*, 11, 15–16.
41. Balsom, "'There Is No Such Thing as Documentary.'"
42. Escobar and Escobar, "É Noite Na América (Ana Vaz, 2022)."
43. Haraway, *Staying with the Trouble*, 78.
44. Sontag, *On Photography*, 14; Brower, "Trophy Shots"; Braddock, "Poaching Pictures"; and Ronan, "Capturing Cruelty."
45. Vaz in Picard, *Qu'est-ce que le réel?*
46. Vaz, "Director Q&A."
47. Haraway, *The Companion Species Manifesto*. A similar experience is described by Jacques Derrida in *The Animal That Therefore I Am*.
48. Escobar, *Designs for the Pluriverse*, 204.
49. Voelcker, "Interview."
50. Voelcker.
51. The Folk Memory Project, "About."
52. Ng, "Interview."
53. Ng.
54. Voelcker, "Interview."
55. Zhang, "In the Name of Memory."
56. Voelcker, "Interview."
57. Cai, "Interview."
58. Because the China Film Administration (part of the National Radio and Television Administration) determines whether a film can be screened in

commercial (or public) cinemas, many independent Chinese filmmakers withhold their films from the administration to preserve their creative rights and instead show their films in underground cinemas and festivals or online.

59. Aguayo, *Documentary Resistance*, 228.

60. According to Aguayo, asking this question is crucial because it "yields insight into the processes of privilege, exploitation, and marginalization that are masked by an uncritical approach to documentary representation as social change." Aguayo, *Documentary Resistance*, 16.

61. Aguayo, *Documentary Resistance*, 18.

62. Aguayo, 233.

63. Nixon, *Slow Violence and the Environmentalism of the Poor*, 17.

64. Lyons, *Vital Decomposition*, 62.

65. Nixon, *Slow Violence and the Environmentalism of the Poor*, 14–16; and Davies, "Slow Violence and Toxic Geographies."

66. Levine, *The Activist Humanist*, 8, 9, 11.

BIBLIOGRAPHY

Acosta, Alberto. "Extractivism and Neoextractivism: Two Sides of the Same Curse." In *Beyond Development: Alternative Visions from Latin America*, ed. M. Lang and D. Mokrani. Transnational Institute, 2013.

Adachi, Masao, and Gō Hirasawa. *Eiga-kakumei*. Kawade shobō shinsha, 2003.

Adamson, Morgan. *Enduring Images: A Future History of New Left Cinema*. University of Minnesota Press, 2018.

Aguayo, Angela J. *Documentary Resistance: Social Change and Participatory Media*. Oxford University Press, 2019.

Aitken, Ian. *The Concise Routledge Encyclopedia of the Documentary Film*. Routledge, 2013.

Allen, Lee. "Celebrate Sheep—Symbols of the Good Life for Navajos." *Indian Country Today*, September 13, 2018.

Andrews, William. *Dissenting Japan: A History of Japanese Radicalism and Counterculture, from 1945 to Fukushima*. Hurst, 2015.

Angus, Siobhan. *Camera Geologica: An Elemental History of Photography*. Duke University Press, 2024.

Anzaldua, Gloria. *Borderlands/La Frontera: The New Mestiza*. Aunt Lute Books, 1987.

Apter, David E., and Nagayo Sawa. *Against the State: Politics and Social Protest in Japan*. Harvard University Press, 1986.

Arabindan-Kesson, Anna. *Black Bodies, White Gold: Art, Cotton, and Commerce in the Atlantic World*. Duke University Press, 2021.

Arboleda, Martín. *Planetary Mine: Territories of Extraction under Late Capitalism*. Verso, 2020.

Arsenal–Institut für Film und Videokunst. "Nuestra Voz de Tierra, Memoria y Futuro." Conversation with Marta Rodríguez and Jorge Silva, 2019. https://

www.arsenal-berlin.de/en/berlinale-forum/archive/program-archive/2019/archival-constellations/nuestra-voz-de-tierra-memoria-y-futuro-1/.

Aspinall, Sue. "This Sadder Recognition: Sue Aspinall Talks to Raymond Williams about So That You Can Live." *Screen* 23, nos. 3–4 (1982): 144–52.

Aspinall, Sue, and Sandy Merck. "So That You Can Live, II." *Screen* 23, nos. 3–4 (1982): 157–60.

Balsom, Erika. "'There Is No Such Thing as Documentary': An Interview with Trinh T. Minh-ha." *Frieze*, November 2018.

Balsom, Erika, and Hila Peleg. *Feminist Worldmaking and the Moving Image*. MIT Press, 2022.

Barclay, Barry. "Celebrating Fourth Cinema." *Illusions* 35 (2003): 7–11.

Barnouw, Erik. *Documentary: A History of the Non-Fiction Film*. Oxford University Press, 1974.

Barrell, John. *The Dark Side of the Landscape: The Rural Poor in English Painting 1730–1840*. Cambridge University Press, 1983.

Barua, Maan. *Plantation Worlds*. Duke University Press, 2024.

Bauer, Petra, and Dan Kidner, eds. *Working Together: Notes on British Film Collectives in the 1970s*. Focal Point Gallery, 2013.

Bazin, André. *What Is Cinema?* University of California Press, 2005.

Benjamin, Walter. *Selected Writings*, Vol. 4. Edited by Michael W. Jennings. Harvard University Press, 1996.

Berger, John. *About Looking*. Bloomsbury, 2009.

———. *Ways of Seeing*. Penguin, 2008.

———. *Why Look at Animals?* Penguin, 2009.

Berlant, Lauren. *Cruel Optimism*. Duke University Press, 2011.

Bermingham, Ann. *Landscape and Ideology: The English Rustic Tradition, 1740–1860*. University of California Press, 1986.

Bishop, Claire. "The Social Turn: Collaboration and Its Discontents." *Artforum International* 44, no. 6 (2006): 178–83.

Blaetz, Robin. "Rescuing the Fragmentary Evidence of Women's Experimental Film." *Camera Obscura: Feminism, Culture, and Media Studies* 21, no. 3 (63) (2006): 153–56.

Blocker, Jane. *Where Is Ana Mendieta? Identity, Performativity, and Exile*. Duke University Press, 1999.

Boetzkes, Amanda. *The Ethics of Earth Art*. University of Minnesota Press, 2010.

Bollmer, Grant. "Empathy Machines." *Media International Australia* 165, no. 1 (2017): 63–76.

Bonner, Virginia. "A Different Image: Studies in Contrasts by Women Filmmakers of the L.A. Rebellion." In *Women and New Hollywood: Gender, Creative Labor, and 1970s American Cinema*, ed. Aaron Hunter and Martha Shearer. Rutgers University Press, 2023.

Borie, Maud, Mark Pelling, Gina Ziervogel, and Keith Hyams. "Mapping Narratives of Urban Resilience in the Global South." *Global Environmental Change* 54 (2019): 203–13.

Born, Jan, T. Lange, K. Hansen, M. Mölle, and H. L. Fehm. "Effects of Sleep and Circadian Rhythm on Human Circulating Immune Cells." *Journal of Immunology* 158, no. 9 (1997): 4454–64.

Bozak, Nadia. *The Cinematic Footprint: Lights, Camera, Natural Resources*. Rutgers University Press, 2011.

Braddock, Alan C. "Poaching Pictures: Yellowstone, Buffalo, and the Art of Wildlife Conservation." *American Art* 23, no. 3 (2009): 36–59.

Brenez, Nicole. "Peuple, Révolution, Paysage: A.K.A Serial Killer de Masao Adachi et Trop Tôt Trop Tard de Jean-Marie Straub & Danièle Huillet." *Krystalbilleder: Tidsskrift for Filmkritik*, no. 4 (2014).

Brower, Matthew. "Trophy Shots: Early North American Photographs of Nonhuman Animals and the Display of Masculine Prowess." *Society & Animals* 13, no. 1 (2005).

Brown, Lester R., and James Hillman. *Ecopsychology: Restoring the Earth/Healing the Mind*. Edited by Theodore Roszak, Mary E. Gomes, and Allen D. Kanner. Counterpoint, 1995.

Bruzzi, Stella. *New Documentary*. 2nd ed. Routledge, 2006.

Burt, Jonathan. *Animals in Film*. Reaktion Books, 2002.

Burton, Julianne. *Cinema and Social Change in Latin America: Conversations with Filmmakers*. University of Texas Press, 1986.

Busfield, Joan. *Managing Madness: Changing Ideas and Practice*. Routledge, 1989.

Cabral, Amílcar. *Return to the Source: Selected Speeches*. Monthly Review Press, 1973.

Cadena, Marisol de la. "Uncommoning Nature." *e-flux*, 65 (2015).

Cadena, Marisol de la, and Mario Blaser. *A World of Many Worlds*. Duke University Press, 2018.

Çağlayan, Emre. *Poetics of Slow Cinema: Nostalgia, Absurdism, Boredom*. Palgrave Macmillan, 2018.

Cai, Lou. "Interview: Zhang Mengqi and the '47 Km' Village: Embracing the Inherent Rhythm of the Land." *UK-China Film Collab*, December 10, 2023. https://www.ukchinafilm.com/self-portrait-47-km-2020/.

Calain, Philippe. "Ethics and Images of Suffering Bodies in Humanitarian Medicine." *Social Science & Medicine* 98 (2013): 278–85.

Calhoun, Craig. "The Idea of Emergency: Humanitarian Action and Global (Dis)Order." In *Contemporary States of Emergency: The Politics of Military and Humanitarian Interventions*, ed. Didier Fassin and Mariella Pandolfi. Zone Books, 2010.

Camacho, Enzo, and Ami Lien. "The Angry Christ (Plot and Plantation)." *Rosa Mercedes* 4 (2022). https://www.harun-farocki-institut.org/en/2022/05/13/the-angry-christ-plot-and-plantation/.

———. "Offerings for Escalante." The Courtauld Institute of Art, London, May 14, 2024. https://courtauld.ac.uk/whats-on/enzo-camacho-ami-lien-offerings-for-escalante/.

———. "Surviving Tiempo Muerto: Bungkalan and Peasant Resistance in the Philippines." Walker Art Center: Artist Op-Eds, April 2020. https://walkerart.org/magazine/amy-lien-enzo-camacho-bungkalan-peasant-resistance-phillipines-artist-op-ed.

Campbell, David. "The Iconography of Famine." In *Picturing Atrocity: Photography in Crisis*, ed. Geoffrey Batchen, Mick Gidley, Nancy K. Miller, and Jay Prosser. Reaktion Books, 2011.

Campt, Tina M. *Listening to Images*. Duke University Press, 2017.

Casey, Edward S. *Getting Back into Place: Toward a Renewed Understanding of the Place-World*. Indiana University Press, 1993.

Casid, Jill H. *Sowing Empire: Landscape and Colonization*. University of Minnesota Press, 2004.

Castree, Noel. "Socializing Nature: Theory, Practice and Politics." In *Social Nature: Theory, Practice and Politics*, ed. Noel Castree and Bruce Braun. Blackwell Publishers, 2001.

Centeno-Martín, Marcos. "Legacies of Hani Susumu's Documentary School." *Arts* 8, no. 3 (2019): 82. https://doi.org/10.3390/arts8030082.

Centeno-Martín, Marcos, and Michael Raine. "Tracing Tendencies in the Japanese Documentary Mode." *Arts* 9, no. 3 (2020). https://doi.org/10.3390/arts9030098.

César, Filipa. "Meteorisations: Reading Amílcar Cabral's Agronomy of Liberation." *Third Text* 32, nos. 2–3 (2018): 254–72.

Chakrabarty, Dipesh. "Provincializing Europe: Postcoloniality and the Critique of History." *Cultural Studies* 6, no. 3 (1992): 337–57.

Chanan, Michael. "The Changing Geography of Third Cinema." *Screen* 38, no. 4 (1997): 372–88.

———. *Twenty-Five Years of the New Latin American Cinema*. Channel 4 Television, 1983.
Chandler, David, and Julian Reid. *Becoming Indigenous: Governing Imaginaries in the Anthropocene*. Rowman & Littlefield, 2019.
Chen, Kuan-Hsing. *Asia as Method: Toward Deimperialization*. Duke University Press, 2010.
Chilcote, Ronald H., ed. *Emerging Nationalism in Portuguese Africa: Documents*. Hoover Documents, 1972.
Chouliaraki, Lilie. *The Ironic Spectator: Solidarity in the Age of Post-Humanitarianism*. Polity, 2012.
———. *The Spectatorship of Suffering*. Sage, 2006.
Chris, Cynthia. *Watching Wildlife*. University of Minnesota Press, 2006.
Clayton, Sue, and Laura Mulvey. *Other Cinemas: Politics, Culture and Experimental Film in the 1970s*. I.B. Tauris, 2017.
Clinebell, Howard. "Greening Pastoral Care." *Journal of Pastoral Care* 48, no. 3 (1994): 209–14.
Cosgrove, Denis. "Prospect, Perspective and the Evolution of the Landscape Idea." *Transactions of the Institute of British Geographers* 10, no. 1 (1985): 45–62.
Cosgrove, Lisa, and Justin M. Karter. "The Poison in the Cure: Neoliberalism and Contemporary Movements in Mental Health." *Theory & Psychology* 28, no. 5 (2018): 669–83.
Crenshaw, Kimberle Williams. "Demarginalizing the Intersection of Race and Sex: A Black Feminist Critique of Antidiscrimination Doctrine, Feminist Theory and Antiracist Politics." *University of Chicago Legal Forum*, no. 1 (1989): 139–67. https://chicagounbound.uchicago.edu/cgi/viewcontent.cgi?article=1052&context=uclf.
Crimp, Douglas. "Mourning and Militancy." *October* 51 (1989): 3–18.
Curtis, David. "Britain's Oldest Experimentalist . . . Margaret Tait." *Vertigo* 1, no. 9 (1999): 62–63.
Cwiertka, Katarzyna J. *Modern Japanese Cuisine: Food, Power and National Identity*. Reaktion Books, 2015.
Cwiertka, Katarzyna J., and Yasuhara Miho. *Branding Japanese Food: From Meibutsu to Washoku*. University of Hawaii Press, 2020.
Daney, Serge. "When Serge Daney Met Ogawa." In *Of Sea and Soil: The Cinema of Tsuchimoto Noriaki and Ogawa Shinsuke*, ed. Ricardo Matos Cabo. Sabzian, 2019.
Dauphinée, Elizabeth. "The Politics of the Body in Pain: Reading the Ethics of Imagery." *Security Dialogue* 38, no. 2 (2007): 139–55.

Davies, Janet. *The Welsh Language.* University of Wales Press, 1993.
Davies, Thom. "Slow Violence and Toxic Geographies: 'Out of Sight' to Whom?" *Environment and Planning C: Politics and Space* 40, no. 2 (2022): 409–27.
Davis, Angela Y. *Women, Race & Class.* Penguin, 2019.
Davis, Jade E. *The Other Side of Empathy.* Duke University Press, 2023.
Davis, Janae, Alex A. Moulton, Levi Van Sant, and Brian Williams. "Anthropocene, Capitalocene, . . . Plantationocene? A Manifesto for Ecological Justice in an Age of Global Crises." *Geography Compass* 13, no. 5 (2019): e12438.
d'Eaubonne, Francoise. *Le féminisme ou la mort.* P. Horay, 1974.
DeClue, Jennifer. *Visitation: The Conjure Work of Black Feminist Avant-Garde Cinema.* Duke University Press, 2022.
Demos, T. J. "The Agency of Fire: Burning Aesthetics." *e-flux* 98 (2019).
———. *Beyond the World's End: Arts of Living at the Crossing.* Duke University Press, 2020.
Denetdale, Jennifer Nez. "Representing Changing Woman: A Review Essay on Navajo Women." *American Indian Culture and Research Journal* 25, no. 3 (2001): 1–26.
Derrida, Jacques. *The Animal That Therefore I Am.* Edited by Marie-Louise Mallet. Translated by David Wills. Fordham University Press, 2008.
Desjardins, Chris. *Outlaw Masters of Japanese Film.* I.B. Tauris, 2005.
Dia Art Foundation. "Robert Smithson, *Spiral Jetty.*" 2019. https://www.diaart.org/visit/visit-our-locations-sites/robert-smithson-spiral-jetty.
Diawara, Manthia. *African Cinema: Politics and Culture.* Indiana University Press, 1992.
Dickinson, Emily. *The Poems of Emily Dickinson.* Edited by R. W. Franklin. Harvard University Press, 2005.
Dickinson, Margaret, ed. *Rogue Reels: Oppositional Film in Britain, 1945–90.* British Film Institute 1999.
Dirlik, Arif. *The Postcolonial Aura: Third World Criticism in the Age of Global Capitalism.* Westview, 1997.
Dissanayake, Wimal, and Anthony Guneratne. *Rethinking Third Cinema.* Routledge, 2004.
Doane, Mary Ann. "The Indexical and the Concept of Medium Specificity." *Differences* 18, no. 1 (2007): 128–52.
Doing, Karel. "Phytograms: Rebuilding Human-Plant Affiliations." *Animation* 15, no. 1 (2020): 22–36.
Dorsky, Nathaniel. *Devotional Cinema.* Tuumba, 2003.
Du Bois, W. E. B. *The Souls of Black Folk.* Bantam Books, 1989.

Ekotto, Frieda, and Adeline Koh, eds. *Rethinking Third Cinema: The Role of Anti-Colonial Media and Aesthetics in Postmodernity*. Lit Verlag, 2010.

Escobar, Arturo. *Designs for the Pluriverse: Radical Interdependence, Autonomy, and the Making of Worlds*. Duke University Press, 2018.

Escobar, Cristóbal, and Valeria de los Ríos Escobar. "É Noite Na América (Ana Vaz, 2022): Towards an Integral Politics of Animality." *Senses of Cinema*, no. 109 (May 2024). https://www.sensesofcinema.com/2024/film-and-the-nonhuman/e-noite-na-america-ana-vaz-2022-towards-an-integral-politics-of-animality/.

Eshun, Kodwo, and Ros Gray. "The Militant Image: A Ciné-Geography." *Third Text* 25, no. 1 (2011): 1–12.

Espinosa, Julio García. "For an Imperfect Cinema." *Jump Cut: A Review of Contemporary Media* 20 (1979): 24–26.

Estes, Nick, Melanie Yazzie, Jennifer Nez Denetdale, and David Correia. *Red Nation Rising: From Bordertown Violence to Native Liberation*. PM Press, 2021.

Eyman, Scott. *Print the Legend: The Life and Times of John Ford*. Johns Hopkins University Press, 2001.

Fanon, Frantz. *Black Skin, White Masks*. Pluto, 2008.

Faris, James C. *Navajo and Photography: A Critical History of the Representation of an American People*. University of New Mexico Press, 1996.

Fassin, Didier. "Humanitarianism as a Politics of Life." *Public Culture* 19, no. 3 (2007): 499–520.

Fassin, Didier, and Mariella Pandolfi. *Contemporary States of Emergency*. Zone Books, 2010.

Federici, Silvia. *Re-Enchanting the World: Feminism and the Politics of the Commons*. PM Press, 2018.

Field, Allyson, ed. *L.A. Rebellion: Creating a New Black Cinema*. University of California Press, 2015.

Fisher, Mark. *Capitalist Realism: Is There No Alternative?* O Books, 2009.

The Folk Memory Project. "About." https://thefolkmemoryproject.org/about.

Foster, Hal. "The Artist as Ethnographer?" In *Traffic in Culture*, 302–9. University of California Press, 1996.

Foster, John Bellamy. "The Great Capitalist Climacteric, Marxism and 'System Change Not Climate Change,.'" *Monthly Review* 67, no. 6 (2015): 9.

———. *Marx's Ecology: Materialism and Nature*. Monthly Review Press, 2000.

———. "Marx's Theory of Metabolic Rift: Classical Foundations for Environmental Sociology." *American Journal of Sociology* 105, no. 2 (1999): 366–405.

Foucault, Michel. *Discipline & Punish: The Birth of the Prison*. Translated by Alan Sheridan. Vintage, 1991.
———. *The History of Sexuality 1: The Will to Knowledge*. Penguin, 1998.
Freire, Paulo. *Pedagogy of the Oppressed*. Penguin, 2017.
Friedman, Lester D., ed. *Fires Were Started: British Cinema and Thatcherism*. Wallflower, 2007.
Fujii, Jinshi. "Yanagita Kunio and the Culture Film: Discovering Everydayness and Creating/Imagining a National Community, 1935–1945." *Arts* 9, no. 2 (2020). https://doi.org/10.3390/arts9020054
Furuhata, Yuriko. "The Actuality of Wakamatsu: Repetition, Citation, Media Event." In *The Pink Book: The Japanese Eroduction and Its Contexts*, ed. Markus Nornes. Kinema Club, 2014.
———. *Cinema of Actuality: Japanese Avant-Garde Filmmaking in the Season of Image Politics*. Duke University Press, 2013.
———. "Multimedia Environments and Security Operations: Expo '70 as a Laboratory of Governance." *Grey Room* 54 (2014): 56–79.
Gaard, Greta. *Critical Ecofeminism*. Lexington Books, 2019.
Gabriel, Teshome H. *Third Cinema in the Third World: The Aesthetics of Liberation*. UMI Research Press, 1982.
Gaines, Jane. "Political Mimesis." In *Collecting Visible Evidence*, ed. Jane Gaines and Michael Renov. University of Minnesota Press, 1999.
Gallagher, Catherine, and Stephen Greenblatt. *Practicing New Historicism*. University of Chicago Press, 2001.
Gavin, Masako. "Nihon Fukeiron (Japanese Landscape): Nationalistic or Imperialistic?" *Japan Forum* 12, no. 2 (2000): 219–31.
Geronimus, Arline. *Weathering: The Extraordinary Stress of Ordinary Life on the Body in an Unjust Society*. Virago, 2023.
Getty Research Institute. *Maren Hassinger, Ulysses Jenkins, Barbara McCollough, et al. Oral History*, Part 1 of 14, YouTube, May 9, 2016, https://www.youtube.com/watch?v=9VKGVAjEMnI.
Ghosh, Amitav. *The Great Derangement: Climate Change and the Unthinkable*. University of Chicago Press, 2016.
Gibson-Graham, J. K. *The End of Capitalism (as We Knew It): A Feminist Critique of Political Economy*. University of Minnesota Press, 2006.
Ginsburg, Faye D. "Indigenous Media: Faustian Contract or Global Village?" *Cultural Anthropology* 6, no. 1 (1991): 92–112.
Glissant, Édouard. *Poetics of Relation*. University of Michigan Press, 1990.
Glyn, David, and Paul Marris. "Seven Years of Cinema Action." *Afterimage* 6 (1976): 64–83.

Goldfarb, Allan. "Beta-Endorphin Response to Exercise: An Update." *Sports Medicine* 24, no. 1 (1997): 8–16.

Gómez-Barris, Macarena. *The Extractive Zone: Social Ecologies and Decolonial Perspectives.* Duke University Press, 2017.

Gordon, Andrew. *A Modern History of Japan: From Tokugawa Times to the Present.* Oxford University Press, 2019.

Gouws, Anjo-marí. "Hearing and Seeing the In/Visible: Anne Charlotte Robertson's Five Year Diary." In *Invisibility in Visual and Material Culture*, ed. Asbjørn Grønstad and Øyvind Vågnes. Springer International Publishing, 2019.

———. "'I'm Washing My Dishes and Making a Movie': Anne Charlotte Robertson and World-Making as Women's Work." *Camera Obscura: Feminism, Culture, and Media Studies* 35, no. 3 (105) (2020): 60–87.

Grant, Paul Douglas. *Cinéma Militant: Political Filmmaking and May 1968.* Wallflower, 2016.

Green, Rayna, ed. *That's What She Said.* Indiana University Press, 1984.

Grierson, John. "The Documentary Producer." *Cinema Quarterly* 2, no. 1 (1933): 7–9.

Grisey, Raphaël. *Sowing Somankidi Coura: A Generative Archive.* Archive Books, 2019.

Grisey, Raphaël, and Bouba Touré. "Happiness Against the Grain." *Camera Austria* 156 (2021): 25–36.

Gudynas, Eduardo. *Extractivisms: Politics, Economy and Ecology.* Fernwood Publishing, 2021.

Gunning, Tom. "Before Documentary." In *Documentary Film Reader: History, Theory, Criticism*, ed. Jonathan Kahana. Oxford University Press, 2016.

Hanada, Kiyoteru. *Hanada Kiyoteru Chosakushū 3.* Miraisha, 1963.

Hansen, Helena, Philippe Bourgois, and Ernest Drucker. "Pathologizing Poverty: New Forms of Diagnosis, Disability, and Structural Stigma under Welfare Reform." *Social Science & Medicine* 103 (February 2014): 76–83.

Haraway, Donna. *The Companion Species Manifesto: Dogs, People & Significant Otherness.* University of Chicago Press, 2003.

———. *Staying with the Trouble: Making Kin in the Chthulucene.* Duke University Press, 2016.

Haraway, Donna, and Anna Tsing. *Reflections on the Plantationocene: A Conversation with Donna Haraway and Anna Tsing.* Edited by Gregg Mittman. Edge Effects & University of Wisconsin–Madison, 2019.

Harootunian, Harry, and Sabu Kohso. "Messages in a Bottle: An Interview with Filmmaker Masao Adachi." *Boundary 2* 35, no. 3 (2008): 63–97.

Hartman, Saidiya. "Dead Book Remains." In *Grief and Grievance, Art and Mourning in America*, ed. Okwui Enwezor, Naomi Beckwith, and Massimiliano Gioni. Phaidon, 2020.

———. *Wayward Lives, Beautiful Experiments: Intimate Histories of Riotous Black Girls, Troublesome Women, and Queer Radicals*. Norton, 2020.

Harvey, David. "Between Space and Time: Reflections on the Geographical Imagination." *Annals of the Association of American Geographers* 80, no. 3 (1990): 418–34.

———. *A Brief History of Neoliberalism*. Oxford University Press, 2007.

Hawthorne, Sîan Melvill. "'Reparative Reading' as Queer Pedagogy." *Journal of Feminist Studies in Religion* 34, no. 1 (2018): 155–60.

Hayashi, Sharon. "Marquis de Sade Goes to Tokyo: The Gynaecological-Political Allegories of Wakamatsu Koji and Adachi Masao." In *The Pink Book: The Japanese Eroduction and Its Contexts*, ed. Markus Nornes. Kinema Club, 2014.

Hickel, Jason. *Less Is More: How Degrowth Will Save the World*. Penguin, 2020.

Hirasawa, Gō, and Ethan Spigland. "REVOLUTION+1: An Interview with Masao Adachi." *e-flux*, April 2023.

Hoffman, Jan. "Rear Window: The Mystery of the Carl Andre Case." *Village Voice*, August 7, 2020.

hooks, bell. *Feminist Theory from Margin to Center*. South End Press, 1984.

Hori, Hikari. *Promiscuous Media: Film and Visual Culture in Imperial Japan, 1926–1945*. Cornell University Press, 2017.

Iizuka, Toshio. "Email to Becca Voelcker." October 25, 2019. In possession of Becca Voelcker.

Iverson, Peter. *The Navajo*. Chelsea House, 2006.

Ivy, Marilyn. *Discourses of the Vanishing: Modernity, Phantasm, Japan*. University of Chicago Press, 1995.

Iyer, Usha. "A Pedagogy of Reparations: Notes toward Repairing the Film and Media Studies Curriculum." *Feminist Media Histories* 8, no. 1 (2022): 181–93.

Jackson, Elizabeth. "'Know How to Do Something Different': Interview with Barbara McCullough, Independent Filmmaker." *Jump Cut: A Review of Contemporary Media*, May 1991.

Jackson, John B. *Discovering the Vernacular Landscape*. Yale University Press, 1986.

Jacob, Mary Jane, and Moira Roth, eds. *The Amazing Decade: Women and Performance Art in America, 1970–1980*. Astro Artz, 1983.

Jesty, Justin. "Image Pragmatics and Film as a Lived Practice in the Documentary Work of Hani Susumu and Tsuchimoto Noriaki." *Arts* 8, no. 2 (2019). https://doi.org/10.3390/arts8020041.

Johnston, Claire. "So That You Can Live: Popular Memory." *Framework* 19 (1982): 12–16.

———. "Women's Cinema as Counter-Cinema." In *Notes on Women's Cinema*. SEFT, 1973.

Johnston, Claire, and Paul Willemen. "Brecht in Britain: The Independent Political Film (on *The Nightcleaners*)." *Screen* 16, no. 4 (1975): 101–18.

Johnston, Deborah. "Poverty and Distribution: Back on the Neoliberal Agenda?" In *Neoliberalism: A Critical Reader*, ed. Alfredo Saad-Filho and Deborah Johnston. Pluto, 2005.

Jones, Amelia. *Body Art/Performing the Subject*. University of Minnesota Press, 1998.

Jonsson, Fredrik Albritton. *Enlightenment's Frontier: The Scottish Highlands and the Origins of Environmentalism*. Yale University Press, 2013.

Jonsson, Fredrik Albritton, and Carl Wennerlind. *Scarcity: A History from the Origins of Capitalism to the Climate Crisis*. Harvard University Press, 2023.

Juhasz, Alexandra. *Women of Vision: Histories in Feminist Film and Video*. University of Minnesota Press, 2001.

Kagawa-Fox, Midori. "The Crucial Role of Culture in Japanese Environmental Philosophy." In *Japanese Environmental Philosophy*, ed. J. Baird Callicot and James McRae. Oxford University Press, 2017.

Kahana, Jonathan, ed. *Documentary Film Reader: History, Theory, Criticism*. Oxford University Press, 2016.

Karlin, Marc, Claire Johnston, Mark Nash, and Paul Willemen. "Problems of Independent Cinema." *Screen* 21, no. 4 (1980): 19–45.

Keenan, Thomas. "Mobilizing Shame." *South Atlantic Quarterly* 103, nos. 2–3 (2004): 435–49.

Kester, Grant H. *Beyond the Sovereign Self: Aesthetic Autonomy from the Avant-Garde to Socially Engaged Art*. Duke University Press, 2023.

Kimura, Michio. *Yamagata no mura ni akai tori ga tonde kita: Ogawa Shinsuke purodakushon tono nijūgonen*. Nanatsumori shokan, 2010.

Klein, Naomi. "Dancing the World into Being: A Conversation with Idle No More's Leanne Simpson." *YES! Magazine*, March 6, 2013.

Knowles, Kim. *Experimental Film and Photochemical Practices*. Palgrave Macmillan, 2020.

Konig, Regula. "Interview with Ogawa Shinsuke, Tokyo." In *Of Sea and Soil: The Cinema of Tsuchimoto Noriaki and Ogawa Shinsuke*, ed. Ricardo Matos Cabo. Sabzian, 2019.

Krauss, Rosalind. "Photography's Discursive Spaces: Landscape/View." *Art Journal* 42, no. 4 (1982): 311–19.
Krikorian, Tamara. "On The Mountain and Land Makar: Landscape and Townscape in Margaret Tait's Work." In *The Undercut Reader: Critical Writings on Artists' Film and Video*, ed. Nina Danino and Michael Mazière. Wallflower, 2002.
Law, John. "What's Wrong with a One-World World?" *Distinktion: Scandinavian Journal of Social Theory* 16, no. 1 (2015): 126–39.
Lawrence, Michael, and Karen Lury, eds. *The Zoo and Screen Media: Images of Exhibition and Encounter.* Palgrave Macmillan, 2016.
Lebow, Alisa, ed. *The Cinema of Me: The Self and Subjectivity in First Person Documentary.* Wallflower, 2012.
Lesage, Julia. "The Political Aesthetics of the Feminist Documentary Film." *Quarterly Review of Film Studies* 3, no. 4 (1978): 507–23.
Leuthold, Steven. *Indigenous Aesthetics: Native Art, Media, and Identity.* University of Texas Press, 1998.
Levine, Caroline. *The Activist Humanist: Form and Method in the Climate Crisis.* Princeton University Press, 2023.
Lewis, Randolph. *Navajo Talking Picture: Cinema on Native Ground.* University of Nebraska Press, 2012.
Liboiron, Max. *Pollution Is Colonialism.* Duke University Press, 2021.
Linebaugh, Peter. *Stop, Thief! The Commons, Enclosures, and Resistance.* PM Press, 2014.
Lippard, Lucy R. *Partial Recall.* New Press, 1992.
Lissner, Jorgen. "Merchants of Misery." *New Internationalist*, June 1, 1981.
Lorde, Audre. *Sister Outsider.* Crossing Press, 1984.
Lovejoy, Alice. "Celluloid Geopolitics: Film Stock and the War Economy, 1939–47." *Screen* 60, no. 2 (2019): 224–41.
———. "From Forests to Film: Chemistry, Industry, and the Rise of Nonflammable Film Stock." *Journal of Cinema and Media Studies* 62, no. 2 (2023): 151–56.
Lowder, Rose. "Email to Becca Voelcker." July 15, 2018. In possession of Becca Voelcker.
Lowe, Lisa. *The Intimacies of Four Continents.* Duke University Press, 2015.
Luca, Tiago De, and Nuno Barradas Jorge. *Slow Cinema.* Edinburgh University Press, 2015.
Lyons, Kristina M. *Vital Decomposition: Soil Practitioners and Life Politics.* Duke University Press, 2020.

MacKenzie, Scott, and Janine Marchessault, eds. *Process Cinema: Handmade Film in the Digital Age*. McGill-Queen's University Press, 2019.
MacDonald, Scott. *A Critical Cinema 2: Interviews with Independent Filmmakers*. University of California Press, 1992.
———. *A Critical Cinema 5: Interviews with Independent Filmmakers*. University of California Press, 2006.
———. *The Garden in the Machine: A Field Guide to Independent Films about Place*. University of California Press, 2002.
Macdougall, David. *The Corporeal Image: Film, Ethnography, and the Senses*. Princeton University Press, 2006.
MacKillop, Andrew. *More Fruitful Than the Soil: Army, Empire and the Scottish Highlands, 1715–1815*. Tuckwell, 2001.
Mackinnon, Iain. "Colonialism and the Highland Clearances." *Northern Scotland* 8, no. 1 (2017): 22–48.
———. "'Decommonising the Mind': Historical Impacts of British Imperialism on Indigenous Tenure Systems and Self-Understanding in the Highlands and Islands of Scotland." *International Journal of the Commons* 12, no. 1 (2018): 278–300.
Maerkle, Andrew. "Masao Adach: Pt. I." *ART iT*, April 27, 2016. https://www.art-it.asia/en/u/admin_ed_itv_e/qrzoxgokiylj4z8vnhfd/.
———. "Masao Adachi: Pt. II." *ART iT*, June 1, 2016. https://www.art-it.asia/en/u/admin_ed_itv_e/blga3uromicu6ehvjkfr/.
Makdisi, Saree. *Romantic Imperialism: Universal Empire and the Culture of Modernity*. Cambridge University Press, 1998.
Mann, Gregory. *From Empires to NGOs in the West African Sahel: The Road to Nongovernmentality*. Cambridge University Press, 2015.
Marran, Christine L. *Ecology without Culture: Aesthetics for a Toxic World*. University of Minnesota Press, 2017.
Martínez-Alier, Joan, Michiel Baud, and Héctor Sejenovich. "Origins and Perspectives of Latin American Environmentalism." In *Environmental Governance in Latin America*, ed. Fábio de Castro, Barbara Hogenboom, and Michiel Baud. Palgrave Macmillan, 2016.
Marx, Karl. *Capital: A Critique of Political Economy*, Vol. 1. Translated by Ben Fowkes. Penguin, 1976.
———. *Capital: A Critique of Political Economy*, Vol. 3. Translated by David Fernbach. Penguin, 1981.
———. *Economic and Philosophic Manuscripts of 1844*. Translated by Martin Milligan. Dover Publications, 2007.

———. *Grundrisse: Foundations of the Critique of Political Economy.* Translated by Martin Nicolaus. Penguin, 1993.
Marx, Karl, and Friedrich Engels. *Collected Works*, Vol. 3. Progress Publishers, 1975.
———. *Collected Works*, Vol. 30. International Publishers, 1975.
Marx, Leo. *The Machine in the Garden: Technology and the Pastoral Ideal in America.* Oxford University Press, 2000.
Matos Cabo, Ricardo, ed. *Of Sea and Soil: The Cinema of Tsuchimoto Noriaki and Ogawa Shinsuke.* Sabzian, 2019.
Matsuda, Masao. *Bara to Mumeisha: Matsuda Masao Eiga Ronshū.* Haga Shoten, 1970.
———. *Fūkei No Shimetsu.* Tabata Shoten, 1971.
Mayer, So. "Centre." *TinyLetter*, April 4, 2023. https://tinyletter.com/somayer/letters/centre.
Mazierska, Ewa, and Lars Kristensen, eds. *Third Cinema, World Cinema and Marxism.* Bloomsbury, 2020.
Mbembe, Achille. *Necropolitics.* Duke University Press, 2019.
McCullough, Barbara. "Bio: Barbara McCullough." https://web.archive.org/web/20230709122319/http://www.barbaramccullough.com/about-filmmaker-barbara-mccullough/.
McKittrick, Katherine. "Plantation Futures." *Small Axe: A Caribbean Journal of Criticism* 17, no. 3 (42) (2013): 1–15.
———, ed. *Sylvia Wynter: On Being Human as Praxis.* Duke University Press, 2014.
Meier, Verena. "Cut-Flower Production in Colombia—A Major Development Success Story for Women?" *Environment and Planning A: Economy and Space* 31, no. 2 (1999): 273–89.
Mekas, Jonas. "The Diary Film: A Lecture on Reminiscences of a Journey to Lithuania." In *Documentary Film Reader: History, Theory, Criticism*, ed. Jonathan Kahana. Oxford University Press, 2016.
Merchant, Carolyn. *The Death of Nature: Women, Ecology, and the Scientific Revolution.* Harper & Row, 1980.
Mészáros, István. *The Necessity of Social Control.* Monthly Review Press, 1972.
Million, Dian. "Felt Theory: An Indigenous Feminist Approach to Affect and History." *Wicazo Sa Review* 24, no. 2 (2009): 53–76.
Mirowski, Philip. *The Road from Mont Pelerin: The Making of the Neoliberal Thought Collective.* Harvard University Press, 2009.
Mirzoeff, Nicholas. "Visualizing the Anthropocene." *Public Culture* 26, no. 2 (73) (2014): 213–32.

Mitchell, W. J. T. *Landscape and Power*. University of Chicago Press, 1994.
———. *What Do Pictures Want? The Lives and Loves of Images*. University of Chicago Press, 2006.
Moglen, Seth, and Adam Steinhouse, eds. *Out of Apathy: Voices of the New Left*. Verso, 1989.
Mohanty, Chandra Talpade. *Feminism without Borders: Decolonizing Theory, Practicing Solidarity*. Duke University Press, 2003.
Molesworth, Helen. *Death of an Artist*. Podcast. Pushkin Industries, 2022. https://www.pushkin.fm/podcasts/death-of-an-artist.
Moore, Jason W. *Anthropocene or Capitalocene? Nature, History, and the Crisis of Capitalism*. PM Press, 2016.
———. *Capitalism in the Web of Life: Ecology and the Accumulation of Capital*. Verso, 2015.
Morrison, Toni. "Unspeakable Things Unspoken: The Afro-American Presence in American Literature (1990)." In *A Turbulent Voyage: Readings in African American Studies*, ed. Floyd W. Hayes. Rowman & Littlefield, 2000.
Mukherjee, Debashree. "Stereoscopic Vision in the Plantationocene." University College London, May 22, 2024.
Mulvey, Laura. "Visual Pleasure and Narrative Cinema." *Screen* 16, no. 3 (1975): 6–18.
Myers, Jonathan. "Exercise and Cardiovascular Health." *Circulation* 107, no. 1 (2003): e2–5.
Nakahira, Takuma. "Eugene Atget: Toshi e no shisen aruiwa toshi kara no shisen." *Asahi Camera*, November 1973.
———. "Gendai Eiga Jōkyō Jiten." *Kikan Firumu* 13 (December 1972): 99–152.
———. "Toshi: Kaisetsu." *Asahi Camera*, July 1971.
Neely, Sarah. *Between Categories: The Films of Margaret Tait*. Peter Lang, 2017.
Neves, José. "Ideology, Science, and People in Amílcar Cabral." *História, Ciências, Saúde-Manguinhos* 24, no. 2 (2017): 1–14.
Ng, Natalie. "Interview: Zhang Mengqi on Documentary 'Self-Portrait: 47KM 2020.'" Filmed in Ether, April 4, 2024. https://www.filmedinether.com/features/interview-zhang-mengqi-self-portrait-47km-2020/.
Nichols, Bill. "The Voice of Documentary." *Film Quarterly* 36, no. 3 (1983): 17–30.
Nixon, Rob. *Slow Violence and the Environmentalism of the Poor*. Harvard University Press, 2011.
Nornes, Markus. *Forest of Pressure: Ogawa Shinsuke and Postwar Japanese Documentary*. University of Minnesota Press, 2007.

Norrell, Brenda. "Diary of an Invisible Navajo Filmmaker." *Indian Country Today*, January 7, 2004.

Oberle, Bruno, Stefan Bringezu, Steve Hatfield-Dodds, Stefanie Hellweg, Heinz Schandl, and Jessica Clement. "Global Resources Outlook: Natural Resources for the Future We Want." United Nations, 2019.

O'Connor, James. *Natural Causes: Essays in Ecological Marxism*. Guilford, 1998.

Ogawa, Shinsuke. "Cinema giapponese degli anni '60." *Quaderno informativo* 41 (1972): 94.

———. "Documentary's Sense of Reality." *Gekkan Image Form*, June 1987. https://www.sabzian.be/text/documentary%E2%80%99s-sense-of-reality.

Ohnuki-Tierney, Emiko. *Rice as Self: Japanese Identities through Time*. Princeton University Press, 1993.

———. "Rice as Self: Japanese Identities through Time." *Education About Asia* 9, no. 3 (2004): 4–9.

Orenstein, Gloria. "The Reemergence of the Archetype of the Great Goddess in Art by Contemporary Women." *Heresies* 2, no. 1 (1978): 74–84.

Pack, Sam. "Indigenous Media Then and Now: Situating the Navajo Film Project." *Quarterly Review of Film & Video* 17, no. 3 (2009): 273–86.

Packard, George R. *Protest in Tokyo: The Security Treaty Crisis of 1960*. Princeton University Press, 1966.

Parrott, R. Joseph, and Mark Atwood Lawrence. *The Tricontinental Revolution*. Cambridge University Press, 2022.

Perry, C. "History, Landscape, Nation: British Independent Film and Video in the 1970s and 1980s." *Moving Image Review and Art Journal* 6, no. 1–2 (2017): 24–37.

Picard, Andréa, ed. *Qu'est-ce que le réel? What Is Real?* Post-éditions, 2018.

Pick, Anat. *Creaturely Poetics: Animality and Vulnerability in Literature and Film*. Columbia University Press, 2011.

Plewes, Betty, and Rieky Stuart. "The Pornography of Poverty: A Cautionary Fundraising Tale." In *Ethics in Action: The Ethical Challenges of International Human Rights Nongovernmental Organizations*, ed. Daniel A. Bell and Jean Marc Coicaud. Cambridge University Press, 2006.

Plumwood, Val. *Environmental Culture: The Ecological Crisis of Reason*. Routledge, 2001.

———. *Feminism and the Mastery of Nature*. Routledge, 1993.

Ponce de León, Jennifer. *Another Aesthetics Is Possible: Arts of Rebellion in the Fourth World War*. Duke University Press, 2021.

Povinelli, Elizabeth A. "Elizabeth Povinelli in Conversation with Kathryn Yusoff." Goldsmiths Centre for Contemporary Art, London, October 6, 2023.

———. *Geontologies: A Requiem to Late Liberalism*. Duke University Press, 2016.

Price, Derrick. "So That You Can Live: A Welsh Response." *Framework* 19 (1982): 14–16.

Prichard, Franz. "Introduction to 'City as Landscape' (1970) by Matsuda Masao (1933–2020)." *ARTMargins* 10, no. 1 (30 April 2021): 60–66.

———. *Residual Futures: The Urban Ecologies of Literary and Visual Media of 1960s and 1970s Japan*. Columbia University Press, 2019.

———. "Seeing Through the In/Visible: Akagi Shūji and the Limits of 'Environmental Restoration.'" *Japanese Studies* 43, no. 2 (2023): 153–69.

Rabinovitz, Lauren. "The Future of Feminism and Film History." *Camera Obscura: Feminism, Culture, and Media Studies* 21, no. 1 (61) (2006): 39–44.

Ramos, Filipa, ed. *Animals*. MIT Press, 2016.

Rancière, Jacques. *The Politics of Aesthetics: The Distribution of the Sensible*. Continuum, 2004.

Rangan, Pooja. "Audibilities: Voice and Listening in the Penumbra of Documentary; An Introduction." *Discourse* 39, no. 3 (2017): 279–91.

———. *Immediations: The Humanitarian Impulse in Documentary*. Duke University Press, 2017.

Rangan, Pooja, Akshya Saxena, Ragini Tharoor Srinivasan, and Pavitra Sundar, eds. *Thinking with an Accent: Toward a New Object, Method, and Practice*. University of California Press, 2023.

Raworth, Kate. *Doughnut Economics: Seven Ways to Think Like a 21st-Century Economist*. Penguin, 2017.

Raygorodetsky, Gleb. "Indigenous Peoples Defend Earth's Biodiversity—but They're in Danger." *National Geographic*, November 16, 2018.

Reed, T. V. *The Art of Protest: Culture and Activism from the Civil Rights Movement to the Streets of Seattle*. University of Minnesota Press, 2005.

Regencia, Ted. "Philippines 'Deadliest' Country for Environmental, Land Activists." Al Jazeera, July 30, 2019. https://www.aljazeera.com/news/2019/7/30/philippines-deadliest-country-for-environmental-land-activists.

Renov, Michael. *The Subject of Documentary*. University of Minnesota Press, 2004.

Rhodes, Lis. "Whose History?" In *Film as Film: Formal Experiment in Film, 1910–75* [Exhibition catalog]. Hayward Gallery, 1979.

Ritts Benally, Karen. "Thinking Good: The Teachings of Navajo Grandmothers." In *American Indian Grandmothers*, ed. Marjorie Schweitzer. University of New Mexico Press, 1999.

Robertson, Jennifer. "It Takes a Village: Internationalization and Nostalgia in Postwar Japan." In *Mirror of Modernity*, ed. Stephen Vlastos. University of California Press, 1998.

———. *Native and Newcomer: Making and Remaking a Japanese City*. University of California Press, 1991.

Rockhill, Gabriel. "Imperialist Propaganda and the Ideology of the Western Left Intelligentsia: From Anticommunism and Identity Politics to Democratic Illusions and Fascism." *Monthly Review*, December 2023.

Rodney, Walter. *How Europe Underdeveloped Africa*. Verso, 2018.

Rodríguez, Marta. "Marta Rodríguez and Jorge Silva." *Cinemateca: Cuadernos de Cine Colombiano* 7 (1982): 1–20.

Rogoff, Irit. *Terra Infirma: Geography's Visual Culture*. Routledge, 2000.

Ronan, Annie. "Capturing Cruelty: Camera Hunting, Water Killing, and Winslow Homer's Adirondack Deer." *American Art* 31, no. 3 (2017): 52–79.

Rony, Fatimah Tobing. *How Do We Look? Resisting Visual Biopolitics*. Duke University Press, 2021.

———. *The Third Eye: Race, Cinema, and Ethnographic Spectacle*. Duke University Press, 1996.

Ross, Julian. "Ethics of the Landscape Shot: A.K.A Serial Killer and James Benning's Portrait of Criminals." In *Slow Cinema*, ed. Tiago De Luca and Nuno Barradas Jorge. Edinburgh University Press, 2016.

Ross, Kristin. *May '68 and Its Afterlives*. University of Chicago Press, 2002.

Rouch, Jean. *Ciné-Ethnography*. University of Minnesota Press, 2003.

Ruby, Jay. *Picturing Culture: Explorations of Film and Anthropology*. University of Chicago Press, 2000.

Russell, Catherine. "'Playing Primitive: 'In the Land of the Headhunters' and/or 'War Canoes.'" *Visual Anthropology* 8, no. 1 (1996): 55–77.

Saito, Kohei. "Elasticity, Nature and Profit." In *The Unfinished System of Karl Marx: Critically Reading Capital as a Challenge for Our Times*, ed. Judith Dellheim and Frieder Otto Wolf. Palgrave Macmillan, 2018.

———. *Karl Marx's Ecosocialism: Capital, Nature, and the Unfinished Critique of Political Economy*. Monthly Review Press, 2017.

———. *Marx in the Anthropocene: Towards the Idea of Degrowth Communism*. Cambridge University Press, 2023.

Sas, Miryam. "Pink Feminism? The Program Pictures of Hamano Sachi." In *The Pink Book: The Japanese Eroduction and Its Contexts*, ed. Markus Nornes. Kinema Club, 2014.

Scarry, Elaine. *Thinking in an Emergency*. Norton, 2011.

Scheiner, Irwin. "The Japanese Village: Imagined, Real, Contested." In *Mirror of Modernity: Invented Traditions of Modern Japan*, ed. Stephen Vlastos. University of California Press, 1998.

Schneider, Tatjana, and Jeremy Till. "Beyond Discourse: Notes on Spatial Agency." *FOOTPRINT*, no. 4 (2009): 97–111.

Schulz, Amy J. "Navajo Women and the Politics of Identity." *Social Problems* 45, no. 3 (1998): 336–55.

Schweitzer, Marjorie, ed. *American Indian Grandmothers*. University of New Mexico Press, 1999.

Sedgwick, Eve Kosofsky. *Touching Feeling: Affect, Pedagogy, Performativity*. Duke University Press, 2003.

Sekula, Allan. "Photography between Labor and Capital." In *Mining Photographs and Other Pictures*. Nova Scotia College of Art and Design Press, 1983.

Sharp, Jasper. "Interview: Masao Adachi." *Midnight Eye: Visions of Japanese Cinema* 21 (2007). http://www.midnighteye.com/interviews/masao-adachi/.

Sharpe, Christina. *In the Wake: On Blackness and Being*. Duke University Press, 2016.

Shiva, Vandana. "How Economic Growth Has Become Anti-Life." *Common Dreams*, November 2013.

———. *Staying Alive: Women, Ecology and Development*. Zed Books, 1988.

———. *The Violence of the Green Revolution: Third World Agriculture, Ecology and Politics*. Zed Books, 1991.

Shnookal, Deborah. *Operation Pedro Pan and the Exodus of Cuba's Children*. University of Florida Press, 2020.

Shukin, Nicole. *Animal Capital: Rendering Life in Biopolitical Times*. University of Minnesota Press, 2009.

Silko, Leslie Marmon. *Yellow Woman and a Beauty of the Spirit*. Simon and Schuster, 1997.

Silva, Jorge. "Colombia: La Memoria Popular: Entrevista Con Martha Rodríguez y Jorge Silva." *Cine al Dia* 22 (1977): 18–22.

Simpson, Leanne Betasamosake. *As We Have Always Done: Indigenous Freedom through Radical Resistance*. University of Minnesota Press, 2017.

Singer, Beverly R. *Wiping the War Paint off the Lens: Native American Film and Video*. University of Minnesota Press, 2001.

Sitney, P. Adams, ed. "Poetry and the Film: A Symposium with Maya Deren, Arthur Miller, Dylan Thomas, Parker Tyler. Chairman, Willard Maas; Organized by Amos Vogel." In *Film Culture Reader*. Rowman & Littlefield, 2000.

Sjoo, Monica, and Barbara Mor. *Great Cosmic Mother: Rediscovering the Religion of the Earth*. Harper & Row, 1987.

Slobodian, Quinn. *Globalists: The End of Empire and the Birth of Neoliberalism*. Harvard University Press, 2020.

Smith, Ali. "Margaret Tait." LUX Online (blog), 2005.

Smith, Andrea, and J. Kehaulani Kauanui. "Native Feminisms Engage American Studies." *American Quarterly* 60, no. 2 (2008): 241–49.

Smith-Rosenberg, Carol. "Puberty to Menopause: The Cycle of Femininity in Nineteenth Century America." In *Clio's Consciousness Raised: New Perspectives on the History of Women*, ed. Mary S. Hartman and Lois W. Banner. Harper & Row, 1974.

Solanas, Fernando. "'Cinéma d'auteur ou cinéma d'intervention?' Table ronde avec Fernando Solanas." *CinémAction*, 1978, 60.

Solanas, Fernando, and Octavio Getino. "Towards a Third Cinema: Notes and Experiences for the Development of a Cinema of Liberation in the Third World (Argentina, 1969)." In *Film Manifestos and Global Cinema Cultures: A Critical Anthology*, ed. Scott MacKenzie. University of California Press, 2014.

Sontag, Susan. *On Photography*. Penguin, 1977.

Springer, Claudia. "Black Women Filmmakers." *Jump Cut: A Review of Contemporary Media* 29 (1984): 34–37.

Standish, Isolde. *Politics, Porn and Protest: Japanese Avant-Garde Cinema in the 1960s and 1970s*. Continuum, 2011.

Steinhoff, Patricia G. "Doing the Defendant's Laundry: Support Groups as Social Movement Organizations in Japan." *Japanstudien* 11 (1999): 55–78.

Stoever, Jennifer Lynn. *The Sonic Color Line: Race and the Cultural Politics of Listening: 17*. New York University Press, 2016.

Stoneman, Rod. "When Channel 4 Was Radical." *Tribune*, June 3, 2020.

Sy, Jose Monfred C. "Bungkalan as Natural Praxis: Peasant Agroecology in the Land Struggle in Hacienda Luisita, Tarlac." *Social Science Diliman: A Philippine Journal of Society and Change* 17, no. 2 (2022). https://journals.upd.edu.ph/index.php/socialsciencediliman/article/view/8763.

Szeman, Imre, and Jennifer Wenzel. "What do we talk about when we talk about extractivism?" *Textual Practice* 35, no. 3 (2021): 505–23.

Tait, Margaret. "Description of Land Makar." LUX Online (blog), n.d.
———. *The Hen and the Bees.* 1960.
———. *Lane Furniture: A Book of Stories.* 1959.
———. "Letter to Alan Fountain," September 26, 1983. Margaret Tait Collection, Orkney Archive, D97/37.
———. "Letter to David Curtis," Senior Visual Arts Officer, Film & Video, The Arts Council of England, February 25, 1998. British Artists' Film & Video Study Collection, University of the Arts London.
———. *Margaret Tait: Poems, Stories and Writings.* Edited by Sarah Neely. Carcanet, 2012.
———. *Origins and Elements.* Privately published by M. Tait, 1959.
———. *Personae.* Edited by Sarah Neely. LUX, 2020.
Taussig, Michael T. *The Devil and Commodity Fetishism in South America.* University of North Carolina Press, 1980.
Terada, Rei. "Repletion: Masao Adachi's Totality." *Qui Parle* 24, no. 2 (2016): 15–43.
Tester, Keith. *Media Culture and Morality.* Routledge, 1994.
Tomii, Reiko. *Radicalism in the Wilderness.* MIT Press, 2018.
Toscano, Alberto. "Equator of Alienation." *Taipei Biennial Journal*, 2012.
Totman, Conrad. *Japan: An Environmental History.* I.B. Tauris, 2014.
Trinh, T. Minh-Ha. *When the Moon Waxes Red: Representation, Gender, and Cultural Politics.* Routledge, 1991.
Tsing, Anna. *The Mushroom at the End of the World: On the Possibility of Life in Capitalist Ruins.* Princeton University Press, 2015.
———. "Unruly Edges: Mushrooms as Companion Species; For Donna Haraway." *Environmental Humanities* 1, no. 1 (2012): 141–54.
Ukadike, Frank. "In Guinea-Bissau, Cinema Trickles Down: An Interview with Flora Gomes." *Research in African Literatures* 26, no. 3 (1995): 179–85.
Ulfsdotter, Boel, and Anna Backman Rogers. *Female Agency and Documentary Strategies: Subjectivities, Identity and Activism.* Edinburgh University Press, 2018.
Vaz, Ana. "Director Q&A." Presented at the Open City Documentary Film Festival, London, September 7, 2022.
Vaz, Ana, and Fernanda Brenner. "Press Release: É NOITE NA AMÉRICA." Pivô, September 2022.
Vermare, Pauline, and Lesley A. Martin, eds. *I'm So Happy You Are Here: Japanese Women Photographers from the 1950s to Now.* Aperture, 2024.
Vizenor, Gerald. *Survivance: Narratives of Native Presence.* University of Nebraska Press, 2009.

Voelcker, Becca. "Interview: Mengqi Zhang." *Film Comment*, November 2019. https://www.filmcomment.com/blog/interview-mengqi-zhang/.

Voelcker, Becca, Jeremy Till, Tatjana Schneider, Christina Serifi, and Anthony Powis. "Positions: Other Economics: Changing Metrics and Values." Architecture Is Climate, 2023. https://architectureisclimate.net/foundations/.

Voyles, Traci Brynne. *Wastelanding: Legacies of Uranium Mining in Navajo Country*. University of Minnesota Press, 2015.

Waldman, Diane, and Janet Walker. *Feminism and Documentary*. University of Minnesota Press, 1999.

Waring, Marilyn. *Counting for Nothing: What Men Value and What Women Are Worth*. University of Toronto Press, 1988.

Warren, Shilyh. *Subject to Reality: Women and Documentary Film*. University of Illinois Press, 2019.

Watsuji, Tetsurō. *Climate and Culture: A Philosophical Study*. Translated by Geoffrey Bownas. Hokuseido, 1971.

Waugh, Thomas. "Acting to Play Oneself: Performance in Documentary (1990)." In *Documentary Film Reader: History, Theory, Criticism*, ed. Jonathan Kahana. Oxford University Press, 2016.

———. *"Show Us Life": Towards a History and Aesthetics of the Committed Documentary*. Scarecrow, 1984.

Wells, Liz. *Land Matters: Landscape Photography, Culture and Identity*. Routledge, 2011.

West, Dennis, and Joan M. West. "Conversation with Marta Rodríguez by Dennis West and Joan M. West." *Jump Cut* 38 (1993): 39–44.

Whyte, Kyle. "Is It Colonial Déjà Vu? Indigenous Peoples and Climate Injustice." In *Humanities for the Environment: Integrating Knowledge, Forging New Constellations of Practice*, ed. Joni Adamson and Michael Davis. Earthscan, 2016.

Willemen, Paul. *Questions of Third Cinema*. British Film Institute, 1989.

Williams, Raymond. *The Country and the City*. Vintage, 2016.

———. *Problems in Materialism and Culture*. Verso, 1980.

———. *Television: Technology and Cultural Form*. Wesleyan University Press, 1992.

Winston, Brian. *Lies, Damn Lies and Documentaries*. British Film Institute, 2000.

———. "The Tradition of the Victim in Griersonian Documentary." In *Image Ethics: The Moral Rights of Subjects in Photographs, Film, and Television*, ed. Larry Gross, John Stuart Katz, and Jay Ruby. Oxford University Press, 1991.

Winther-Tamaki, Bert. *Tsuchi: Earthy Materials in Contemporary Japanese Art.* University of Minnesota Press, 2022.

Worster, Donald. *Nature's Economy: A History of Ecological Ideas.* Cambridge University Press, 1994.

Worth, Sol, and John Adair. *Through Navajo Eyes: An Exploration in Film Communication and Anthropology.* 2nd ed. University of New Mexico Press, 1997.

The Wretched of the Earth. "An Open Letter to Extinction Rebellion." Redpepper, May 3, 2019. https://www.redpepper.org.uk/an-open-letter-to-extinction-rebellion/.

Wright, Emily. "'The Devil Looks Like a Mounted Policeman': 'Nuestra Voz de Tierra, Memoria y Futuro,' and the Cinema of Marta Rodríguez." *Kinoscope*, June 2019.

Wynter, Sylvia. "Novel and History, Plot and Plantation." *Savacou*, no. 5 (1971): 95–102.

———. "Unparalleled Catastrophe for Our Species? Or, to Give Humanness a Different Future: Conversations." In *Sylvia Wynter: On Being Human as Praxis*, ed. Katherine McKittrick. Duke University Press, 2015.

———. "Unsettling the Coloniality of Being/Power/Truth/Freedom: Towards the Human, After Man, Its Overrepresentation—An Argument." *CR: The New Centennial Review* 3, no. 3 (2003): 257–337.Yasui, Yoshio, and Noriko Tanaka, eds. *The Legendary Filmmaking Collective NDU and Nunokawa Tetsuro.* Cinematrix, 2012.

Yoshida, Ken. "The Undulating Contours of Sōgō Geijutsu (Total Work of Art), or Hanada Kiyoteru's Thoughts on Transmedia in Postwar Japan." *Inter-Asia Cultural Studies* 13, no. 1 (2012): 36–54.

Yusoff, Kathryn. *A Billion Black Anthropocenes or None.* University of Minnesota Press, 2018.

Zhang, Mengqi. "In the Name of Memory." Open City Documentary Film Festival, London, April 28, 2024.

Zinman, Gregory. *Making Images Move: Handmade Cinema and the Other Arts.* University of California Press, 2020.

INDEX

activism, 13, 23, 68–71, 125, 166, 194, 197, 213
Adachi Masao, 8*map*, 13, 100–118, 124–128
Adair, John, 60–62
aesthetics, 25, 40, 107–108, 117, 175–179, 182, 187. *See also* art; television
agriculture: aestheticization of, 49; and agri-business, 49, 67, 74, 86, 110, 150–153, 170, 196–199; traditional, 12, 19, 61, 65–66, 85–89, 94, 171, 189. *See also* food-sovereignty; Marx, Karl; organicism; soil
Aguayo, Angela, 54, 214
A.K.A. Serial Killer, 100–107, 103*fig.*, 110–113, 115–118, 122–124, 126, 204
alienation, 52, 81, 105–110, 117–120
ambivalence, 132, 138
American Newsreel, 13, 77
Amor, mujeres y flores, 168–178, 189–191
Angus, Siobhan, 23, 201
animals, 42–48, 61, 91, 144–145, 149–153, 204–209
Anpo, 77, 113
Anthropocene, 15, 74, 120, 206
anthropocentrism, 91, 150, 204–207
anthropology, 57, 60–61, 76, 181
anti-capitalism, 76, 107, 182
anti-colonialism: in Africa, 93–94; in Britain, 52, 166, 182–185; in general,
17, 21, 23, 46, 66–67, 74, 130, 154, 161; in Latin America, 188, 202; in North America, 57, 130, 152–154, 161
anti-pastoral aesthetics, 30, 100–103, 110, 129–131, 202
Anzaldúa, Gloria, 206
archives, 15, 27, 38, 81, 97, 132–135
are bure boke, 107–108
Ariyoshi Sawako, 12, 94
art: activist, 21, 95, 113, 150, 193, 200; history of, 17–18, 119; worlds, 130, 152, 155–156, 198
audibilities, 22, 54
audience: critical reception, 44, 51–56, 84, 187, 190–191; engagement, 9, 23–25, 58, 67–69, 198, 213; reach, 14, 113, 154, 162–163, 168–169, 172; screenings, 68, 95–96, 125, 145, 180, 213, 216
avant-garde. *See* aesthetics

back-to-the-land movement, 2–3, 9–12, 34, 67, 74, 82
beauty, 17, 35, 41, 47, 103, 158–160
Berger, John, 119, 205
biodiversity, 11, 19, 46, 73, 197
biopolitics, 22, 30, 46, 115, 139, 177
Birri, Fernando, 13, 37
Black Panthers, 13, 77
black-and-white film, 7, 35, 65, 77, 155

body: of filmmaker, 31–32, 59, 90–91, 132–33, 149–151, 158–160; land as, 2, 18, 130, 158–159; objectification of, 115, 139–141, 152–153
borders, 14–15, 70, 97, 151, 153
Bowman, Arlene, 8*map*, 28, 30, 41–47, 54–63, 85, 119
Brecht, Bertold, 117
British Broadcasting Corporation (BBC), 40, 174
bungkalan, 197–198, 201–203, 216

Cabral, Amílcar, 13, 69, 83, 92–93, 180
Cadena, Marisol de la, 20–21, 150, 189, 206
Calhoun, Craig, 176–177
Camacho, Enzo, 8*map*, 196–203, 208, 213, 214, 216
camera: colonial prohibition of, 12, 70; extractive use of, 9, 23, 56–60, 64, 73, 94, 207; in Navajo culture, 56–58, 63–64; political use of, 9, 18, 38, 59–61, 81, 192; techniques, 38–40, 54, 83–84, 90, 108, 123, 129; types of, 37, 65, 69–70, 135–136, 200
Campesinos, 186–187
Caora Mor Big Sheep, 49, 53
capitalism. *See* alienation; anti-capitalism; colonialism; extractivism; pollution; racism
Capitalocene, 15, 74, 120, 158
Carson, Rachel, 10, 12, 94, 147
Cauca Regional Council of Indigenous People, 188
celluloid, 24, 47, 50, 90, 143–145, 144*fig.*, 200–201
censorship, 12, 70, 210–211, 214
centers and margins: colonial, 30, 105, 175; reconfigured, 26, 61, 95, 96–97, 152, 185, 209. *See also* country and city; marginalization
Channel Four, 162–163, 168, 173–175, 185, 190

Chen, Kuan-Hsing, 96, 198
choreography, 31, 129, 155, 213
cinema: history of, 24–25, 51, 58, 111–112, 179; as venue, 94–95, 125, 145, 180, 214. *See also* Fourth Cinema; Hollywood; land: cinema; Third Cinema
Cinema Action, 8*map*, 28, 32, 167–168, 174–176, 178–186, 192
climate: breakdown, 3, 15, 29, 46–47, 99, 120, 129, 193; justice, 3, 19–23, 46, 132, 193–194, 215–216; and weather, 65, 71, 82, 85, 121–122
close-ups, 39–40, 60, 134, 169–171, 187, 207
Coconuco, 13, 187
Cold War, 10, 42, 68, 77, 101
collaboration, 65, 83, 114, 192, 197–198
collective filmmaking, 29, 32, 78, 155, 166, 170, 186–188
colonialism: in Africa, 12, 71, 73–74, 82, 92–93; clearances, 48–49; déjà-vu, 15, 47, 199; and epistemology, 12, 19, 21, 26, 171, 189; of Indigenous land, 42–43, 56–57, 61–62, 129; and language, 2, 52–54, 184–185, 208; in the Philippines, 196–204; settler, 17, 46, 52
color, 39, 116, 169, 202, 208–209
commons: agriculture, 48, 52, 197; documentary, 214
communism, 10–11, 101, 115, 179, 183
community gardening, 75, 146, 159, 196–198
companion planting, 133–134
consciousness raising, 145, 180, 202. *See also* feminism; Freire
consumerism, 11, 68, 89, 95–96, 101, 142
contamination, 103–104, 127–128, 131–136, 146
cooperatives, 14, 65, 69, 82–85, 91, 94, 166
cotton, 47, 93, 143, 201
counter-history, 27, 165–166
counterculture: in Europe, 166, 182–183; in Japan, 68, 77, 94, 113; in the US, 9–11, 23, 147

country and city, 3, 31, 45, 77–79, 85–89, 95, 106–110, 158, 164–165, 209. *See also* centers and margins
Crimp, Douglas, 199
crisis, 5, 19–20, 191–194, 199, 203
crofting, 47–50
Cuban cinema, 13, 25, 77, 93, 132, 149–154, 179
Cultural Association of African Workers in France (ACTAF), 71
Curtis, Edward, 56–58

dance, 32, 58, 95, 129–130, 133–134, 155, 210–213
Davis, Jade E., 32, 162, 175
day for night shooting, 208
d'Eaubonne, Francoise, 18
degrowth, 20, 72–73
demolition, 7, 213
Demos, T. J., 4, 171, 193
Deren, Maya, 39
diary, 22–23, 28, 131, 137–141, 146
Dickinson, Emily, 37, 146
Diné. *See* Navajo
distribution, 30, 32, 68, 94, 95*fig.*, 112, 167
documentary: colonial, 21–23, 44–47, 55, 57, 175–176; history of, 27, 70, 112, 157, 179–180, 195; industrial, 40, 63, 76; methods, 4, 44, 182–89, 209–210; participatory, 9, 60–62, 75–76; political, 43, 68, 105, 120, 153–154, 166, 175–178, 214; truth, 4, 22–23, 51, 53–55, 68, 90–91, 104
domesticity, 37, 67, 79, 138, 145, 167
Dorsky, Nathaniel, 40
Du Bois, W. E. B., 58
duration, 29, 65, 78, 147, 170, 192, 212
dùthchas, 47–48

earth (material). *See* soil
Earth Day, 10, 147
Earthrise, 9–10, 190

eco-feminism, 18–19, 130, 134, 145, 151–154, 161, 191
eco-intersectionality, 171
eco-therapy, 32, 146, 148*fig.*
ecological Marxism, 19, 31, 109
economic growth, 5, 9, 11, 19–20, 72–73, 99. *See also* gross domestic product
ecosystem, 10, 91, 129, 131–132, 145, 150, 171
editing, 83, 135, 138, 140, 143
Edo period, 87
education. *See* pedagogy
Eleventh Hour, The, 175, 185
emergency thinking, 5, 177
empathy, 32, 151, 162, 173–175, 192
enclosure, 48, 52, 74, 119
entanglement, 14, 30, 47, 102, 107–108, 118–119, 204
environmentalism: histories of, 85, 147, 190; as political movement, 9, 12, 103, 180, 197, 202. *See also* Earth Day; eco-feminism
Escalante, 198–200
Escobar, Arturo, 206, 209
Espinosa, Julio García, 180
ethics of representation, 9, 22, 28, 44–45, 61, 114, 170, 176
ethnography, 21, 51, 59–60, 70, 181, 206
experimental cinema, 14, 23, 54, 78, 130, 187
Expo, 101–102
extractive gaze, 23–27, 44, 57–59, 64
extractivism: Africa, 74, 82, 92–93; Brazil, 206; Britain, 3, 49, 164–165; China, 214; Colombia, 171, 181, 188–189, 191; concept of, 7, 9–12, 14–15, 18–19, 31, 46, 72, 214; Japan, 73, 110, 115; North America, 42, 129, 146, 150; Philippines, 197

factory, 12, 70, 82, 94, 167. *See also* strike
famine, 42, 193, 199, 210–213
Fanon, Frantz, 58
farm. *See* agriculture

fast food, 142
Federici, Silvia, 48
feminism: debates in and varieties of, 62–63, 133, 137–138, 145, 171; and filmmaking, 21–23, 27, 54, 150–154, 174; as historical approach, 27, 66–67. *See also* eco-feminism; labor: reproductive
fertilizer: artificial, 12, 71, 94, 110–111, 186; organic, 48, 67, 72, 88, 202
fieldwork, 76
film. *See* celluloid
film-poem, 34, 39–40, 53
first-person filmmaking, 56
Five Year Diary, 131–132, 134–149
Flaherty, Robert, 51, 112
flowers, 38, 136, 138, 146, 153, 168–190, 173*fig.*
Folk Memory Project, 210–11
food-sovereignty, 12–14, 71, 73, 81, 92, 92*fig.*, 197
Ford, John, 58
fossil fuel, 10, 15, 19, 72, 88, 136, 203
Foster, John Bellamy, 19, 109, 120
Foucault, Michel, 139, 177
Fourth Cinema, 25, 61
Freire, Paulo, 12, 13, 180, 202
fûkeiron (landscape theory), 101–112, 116–123, 127–128, 199
Fukuoka Masanobu, 12, 94
funding, 40, 69, 174, 190–191
Furuhata, Yuriko, 102, 107, 115
furusato, 88–89, 106
Furuyashiki, 67, 89
futurism, 4–5, 9, 27, 75, 99, 136, 198–199, 215

Gaia, 10
Gaines, Jane, 23, 169, 176
garden, 4, 29, 38, 52, 92, 122–123, 131–140, 146–149
gelatin, 144
gender. *See* eco-feminism; feminism; labor

genre, 78, 83. *See also* interdisciplinarity; landscape; television
geology, 1, 74, 129, 160
Geronimus, Arline, 160
Getino, Octavio, 13, 25, 179
Ghosh, Amitav, 5, 19
Glissant, Edouard, 96
Global North and South, 3, 21, 26–27, 31, 171, 216
globalization: cultural, 10, 88, 96, 121; food imports, 11, 73, 87, 199
Godard, Jean-Luc, 14, 125, 166–167, 183
grandmothers, 38, 41–44, 54–63, 183, 202, 211
Grierson, John, 40, 51, 53, 68, 86, 112, 174–176, 182, 188, 195
Grisey, Raphaël, 81, 91
gross domestic product (GDP), 72, 98, 101
Guedes, Ann, 166, 167, 182, 183, 185

Hammer, Barbara, 79
Hanada Kiyoteru, 117
Haneda Sumiko, 76
Hani Susumu, 76, 78
Haraway, Donna, 31, 207, 208
Hartman, Saidiya, 194, 195
Harvard Film Archive, 132
Heaven and Earth. *See Langit Lupa*
Highlands and Islands, 34, 48, 52
highway construction, 100, 132, 147, 155, 158–159, 205–206
Hokkaido, 18, 105, 116
Hollywood, 25, 58, 133, 157, 179, 208
humanitarianism, 71, 175, 177–178, 181, 187

identity, 16, 22, 28, 44–48, 52, 152–154, 176
ideology: extractive, 10, 20, 117, 189, 195; landscape, 17, 52, 77; nation or empire, 76, 86, 167
immediations. *See* Rangan
Independent Filmmakers Association (IFA), 174

individualism, 121, 132, 141, 166
industrial action. *See* strike
insider/outsider, 3, 21, 26, 45, 50–51, 56, 61, 107, 154–155, 206, 210
installation, 145, 207
interdisciplinarity, 21, 134, 216
internationalism, 13, 21, 71, 77, 96, 125, 183, 198
It is Night in America, 204–209, 207*fig.*
Iwanami Productions, 75–76, 78
Iyer, Usha, 27, 202

Japan National Railways (JNR), 89
Japanese Red Army, 126
Johnston, Claire, 152
Jōmon period, 87–88

Karlin, Marc, 166, 174, 179, 186
Karrabing Film Collective, 214
Kopple, Barbara, 176

La Fundación Cine Documental, 186
labor: manual, 47, 50, 78, 130, 137, 143, 169*fig.*; reproductive, 48, 63, 72, 79, 164, 171, 191; rights, 29, 70–71, 163, 167–168, 172; unionization, 179, 191. *See also* alienation; collaboration; colonialism; cooperatives; strike
Laing, R. D., 139
land: art, 17, 195; cinema, 4, 5, 7, 9, 14–24; dispossession, 21, 28, 56–57, 97, 155, 186–189; industrialization, 162, 199, 206; wasteland, 42, 48, 142; wounded, 129, 131–134, 151, 159–160, 202. *See also* enclosure; extraction; landscape; pollution; terra nullius; wilderness
Land Makar, 34–41, 36*fig.*, 47, 49–54, 211
landscape (concept), 17–18, 49, 52, 56, 86, 107, 119–124
landscape theory. *See fūkeiron*
landscape-portraits, 28, 38, 45, 130, 150, 210

Langit Lupa, 196–204
language, 2, 16, 52–55, 63, 98, 184–185, 208
L.A. Rebellion, 156–58
Las Hurdes, 187
leftism. *See* anti-capitalism; degrowth; labor; Marx, Karl; New Left
Leopold, Aldo, 11
Levine, Caroline, 29, 163, 191, 216
Lewis, Randolph, 44
liberation, 13, 65, 71, 76–77, 92–93, 125, 181–182
Liboiron, Max, 26, 191
Lien, Ami, 8*map,* 196–204
livestock reduction, 42, 61
Locke, John, 17
Long, Richard, 195
Los Angeles, 41, 43, 55, 58, 133, 154–159
Love, Women, and Flowers. See *Amor, mujeres y flores*
Lowder, Rose, 143, 201
Lowe, Lisa, 14

MacDonald, Scott, 136
MacDougall, David, 169
Mackenzie, Kent, 43
Magazine Mouth, 142
Magino, 67, 83
Mao Zedong, 79, 82, 89, 183, 209–211, 214
marginalization, 22, 30, 46, 53–54, 61, 117, 152, 155, 162, 168, 178, 185
Marker, Chris, 14, 166, 167, 175, 183
Marx, Karl, 9, 72–73, 108, 117–120, 122, 165, 186–187; theory of metabolic rift, 19, 31, 82, 93, 109–110, 112, 147
Marx, Leo, 139
Masayesva, Victor, 58
materiality, 24, 47, 130, 144, 204. *See also* celluloid
Matsuda, Masao, 101, 104–108, 112, 116–118, 120, 124
Mayer, So, 29, 131

McCullough, Barbara, 8*map*, 29, 32, 129–134, 154–161, 156*fig.*, 199, 213
McKittrick, Katherine, 15, 159
media. *See* audience; documentary; interdisciplinarity; materiality
Mekas, Jonas, 23
Melon Patches, 137–138, 138*fig.*
memory, 15, 47, 69, 97, 189, 194–195, 210–211. *See also* Folk Memory Project
Mendieta, Ana, 8*map*, 29, 32, 129–134, 149–155, 150*fig.*, 159–161, 171
Mészáros, István, 112
metabolic rift. *See under* Marx, Karl
migration, 14, 49, 65, 70–74, 81–83, 93–98, 97*fig.*, 105, 132, 185, 210
milltir sgwâr, 2, 16
Minamata, 12, 78
mining: coal, 2, 111, 165, 185; general, 57, 129; silver, 23, 47, 201; slate, 1–2, 185; uranium, 42
Mizoguchi, Kenji, 123
modernity, 29, 45, 57, 88, 94, 121–122, 158, 196, 205–210
Moore, Jason, 120
Moriyama, Daido, 113
Mukherjee, Debashree, 94
multi-generational relations, 38, 88, 158, 188, 214
music, 39, 106, 116–118, 158, 184, 198, 204. *See also* soundtrack
myth, 42, 85, 141, 153, 155, 157, 187–189

Nakahira Takuma, 104–109, 109*fig.*, 116, 127
Narita Airport, 77, 87, 88
National Parks, 1, 190, 205
nationalism, 2, 121, 185
nature: domination and despoliation, 16, 18, 42, 195, 199; rights, 19, 205
Navajo: culture and land, 42–43, 61, 63; language, 52; photography, 56–60, 64
Navajo Film Themselves, 60–62

Navajo Talking Picture, 28, 41–44
neocolonialism, 12, 71, 93, 188, 205
neoliberalism: in general, 9–11, 164, 194; Latin America, 25, 179; US, 132, 137
neorealism, 13, 40
New Left, 165, 182, 185
Nguyễn Trinh Thi, 199–200
Nichols, Bill, 53, 63, 183–184
Nippon-koku, 83, 88, 90
Nishikawa, Tomonari, 201–202
Nixon, Rob, 3, 188, 191, 215
non-fiction filmmaking. *See* documentary
nuclear power, 10, 34, 42, 48, 68, 127, 147, 200, 202
Nuestra voz de tierra, memoria y futuro, 171, 187–189, 202, 214

Ogawa Pro, 8*map*, 13, 28–30, 65–69, 72–79, 75*fig.*, 83–91, 94–102, 122, 212
Ogawa Shinsuke, 66*fig.*, 67, 75, 85, 212
oil crisis, 10
Okinawa, 11, 18, 101, 105, 127
organicism, 11–12, 29, 71–72, 81–82, 94, 133, 143, 147, 197, 201
Orkney, 34–41, 47–53, 50*fig.*, 201
Ōshima Nagisa, 105, 113
Ozu Yasujirō, 123, 217

paddy (rice), 7, 28, 84*fig.*, 85–87, 90, 99–100
painting, 17, 35, 52, 123
Palestine, 13, 125, 182
Pan-African solidarity, 13, 71
Paris, 13, 14, 65, 69–74, 81–82, 96, 116, 181, 183, 198
pastoralism, 4, 36, 63, 68, 83, 103, 106–107, 124, 161, 201
pedagogy, 67–68, 83, 98–99, 180, 202–203, 214. *See also* Freire
performance art, 18, 145, 149, 213
perspective. *See* insider/outsider; marginalization; positionality

pesticide, 10, 72, 81, 88, 147, 186
photography: activism, 13, 66, 81, 93, 102, 107, 190; extractive gaze, 18, 56–59, 94, 205, 207; history and theories, 4, 9, 116; material process, 23–25, 38, 47, 88, 143; slideshow, 23–24, 67, 70–71
phytography, 200–202, 201*fig.*
picturesque (aesthetics), 17, 52, 57
place: belonging, 18, 34, 40, 65, 87, 116, 210; displacement, 19, 48, 56, 77, 105, 151, 159, 186, 205
plantation, 17, 52, 65, 71, 74, 81–82, 93–94, 97, 130, 168–173, 196–203. *See also* Wynter, Sylvia
Plantationocene, 15, 74–75, 159. *See also* Tsing, Anna
plowing, 47, 49, 75, 82
Plumwood, Val, 19, 62
pluriverse, 206
police, 70, 77, 105–106, 116, 124–126, 136, 188
political mimesis. *See* Gaines, Jane
pollution, 11, 30, 72, 103, 129, 191, 202
pornography, 113–114, 177, 191
Portrait of Ga, A, 38, 39
positionality, 3, 23, 26, 44–46, 70, 96, 108, 162, 187, 210, 217–218
pottery, 16, 87–88
Povinelli, Elizabeth, 32, 189
Prichard, Franz, 107, 116
protest. *See* documentary: political; strike
Provoke: Provocative Materials for Thought, 107
psychology: antipsychiatry, 139; ecotherapy, 32, 146; medicine, 134–136, 138; women, 132, 139–140

racism, 43, 97, 157, 160, 171, 188–189, 191
Rangan, Pooja, 22, 30, 40, 46, 51, 54, 60, 162, 176–178
recycling, 94, 143, 201
Red Bus Film Screening Troup, 125–126
reenactment, 15, 57, 86–87, 189

reparative reading, 28–29, 134–136
reportage, 49, 114–117
representation. *See* documentary: political; eco-feminism; liberation; racism
reservation. *See* Navajo
resilience, 46–47
retreat, 2, 3, 11, 30
rice. *See* agriculture; paddy
ritual, 133, 153, 155–159
Robertson, Anne Charlotte, 8*map,* 28–29, 129–148, 150–155, 160–161, 207, 216
Rodríguez, Marta, 8*map,* 13, 25, 168–181, 186–188, 190–195, 197, 212, 214
romanticism, 3–4, 17, 120
Rony, Fatimah Tobing, 22, 30, 46, 57–60, 115, 152–153, 177
Rouch, Jean, 13, 181
Ryakushō: Renzoku shasatsuma. See A.K.A. Serial Killer

Saito, Kohei, 19, 31, 109, 115, 118–120, 127–128
salvage ethnography, 57
Sanjinés, Jorge, 190
Sanrizuka. *See* Narita Airport
screening. *See* audience; distribution; documentary: participatory; installation
seasons, 47, 92, 210
Sedgwick, Eve Kosofsky, 28–29, 134–136
self-portrait, 50, 60, 69, 209–113
self-sufficiency, 67, 74, 83, 91. *See also* cooperatives; food-sovereignty
S4C (Sianel Pedwar Cymru), 185
shakkei, 123–124
sheep: Navajo-Churro breed, 41, 42, 54, 61–63, 62*fig.,* 179; Scotland, 48, 49, 53
Shiga Shigetaka, 121–122
Shiva, Vandana, 19, 72
Shopping Bag Spirits and Freeway Fetishes: Reflections on Ritual Space, 156
silueta, 149–153

Silva, Jorge, 8*map*, 13, 25, 168–181, 186–188, 190–195, 197, 212, 214
Simpson, Leanne Betasamosake, 14, 32, 103, 129, 195
slow cinema, 29, 147
Smithson, Robert, 195
So That You Can Live, 163–168, 164*fig.*, 171, 174, 178, 180–185
social welfare, 132, 138, 146
soil: concept of, 16–18, 35, 66, 95, 152, 201, 215; damage, 19, 42, 110–111, 169; literacy and care, 21, 80–85, 90, 98, 146, 155, 197, 201
Sokhona, Sidney, 82–83
Solanas, Fernando, 13, 25, 179
Somankidi Coura, 8*map*, 30, 65–83, 80*fig.*, 91–92, 96–99, 98*fig.*, 137, 194, 197–198, 216
soundtrack, 21, 52–55, 116–118, 136, 145, 172, 204–205, 208. *See also* music; voice-over
species, 10, 21, 39, 61, 75, 98, 130–134, 149, 188, 194
Sprung, Steve, 166, 167, 180, 182, 183
strike (labor movement), 29, 70–71, 163, 167–168, 172, 176, 179, 191
students, 69, 104, 113, 124, 157, 183, 193
subjectivity, 22, 28, 63, 117, 130, 141, 142*fig.*, 150, 158
subtitles, 52–54, 169, 208
sugar, 196, 199, 200*fig.*
Sundial Carved with a Thousand Years of Notches, The: Magino Village Story, 83, 87, 90, 95

Tait, Margaret, 8*map*, 13, 30, 34–54, 63, 84, 90, 102, 175, 179, 210–211
Takamine Gō, 105, 127
television, 40, 83, 96, 155, 173–174, 185–186, 190
terra nullius, 17, 20, 32, 48, 155, 159, 197, 202

Third Cinema, 13, 25, 37, 125, 157, 179–181, 192, 198
Thoreau, Henry David, 11, 139, 146
time. *See* duration; memory; slow cinema
Tokyo, 3, 7, 65, 76, 89, 95, 101, 102, 106, 111, 124
Touré, Bouba, 13, 66*fig.*, 69, 70–74, 79–83, 93–98, 183, 198
tourism, 2, 34, 38, 49, 53, 59, 89, 106, 108
tradition. *See* agriculture: traditional; memory; Yanagita Kunio
translation. *See* language
trauma, 28, 43, 136, 151–156, 164, 176–177, 198, 209
Trevelyan, Humphry, 166–168, 174, 179
Trinh T., Minh-ha, 21–22, 36, 46, 51–56, 62–63, 83, 91, 97, 154, 155, 159, 175, 187, 190, 206
Tsing, Anna, 20–21, 31, 27, 72, 74, 91, 102–103, 107, 128, 131, 146
Tsuchimoto Noriaki, 76, 78, 101

unionization. *See* labor: unionization; strike
United Red Army, 115
University of California Los Angeles (UCLA), 55, 58, 157
urban space. *See* country and city

Vaz, Ana, 8*map*, 204–209, 215
Vietnam War, 68, 71, 77, 124, 182, 183, 199–200
view from nowhere, 23, 26, 44, 46, 63, 108, 189
village, 67, 69, 89, 98, 100, 165, 209–213
visual biopolitics. *See* Rony, Fatimah Tobing
voice-over, 38, 51, 55, 63, 105, 117, 136–140, 145, 184
Voyles, Traci Brynne, 42

Wakamatsu Kōji, 113–15, 125
Wales: identity, 16, 163, 166, 168, 183–184; land, 1–2, 6*fig.*, 165*fig.*, 217; language, 2, 3, 16, 184–185
Wang, Bing, 211
Waring, Marilyn, 72
Water Ritual #1: An Urban Rite of Purification, 155–157
Watsuji Tetsurō, 85, 121–123
weathering, 160
western (film genre), 58, 208–209
westernization, 73, 85, 101, 121–122, 177
Whole Earth Catalog, 11
Whyte, Kyle, 15, 47
wilderness: in Japan (*zaiya*), 11, 95; myth, 17, 34, 102
Williams, Raymond, 3, 16, 27–28, 43, 119, 165–166, 183–186

Winston, Brian, 22, 42, 175
Winther-Tamaki, Bert, 18, 95
Worth, Sol, 60–62
Wu Wenguang, 210
Wynter, Sylvia, 74, 130, 159, 196–197, 205

Xaraasi Xanne—Crossing Voices, 81

Yamagata International Documentary Film Festival, 67, 96
Yanagita Kunio, 68
yonaoshi, 87
Yusoff, Kathryn, 20, 73, 74

Zhang Mengqi, 8*map*, 209–214, 212*fig.*
zoo, 195–196, 204–208

Founded in 1893,
UNIVERSITY OF CALIFORNIA PRESS
publishes bold, progressive books and journals
on topics in the arts, humanities, social sciences,
and natural sciences—with a focus on social
justice issues—that inspire thought and action
among readers worldwide.

The UC PRESS FOUNDATION
raises funds to uphold the press's vital role
as an independent, nonprofit publisher, and
receives philanthropic support from a wide
range of individuals and institutions—and from
committed readers like you. To learn more, visit
ucpress.edu/supportus.

www.ingramcontent.com/pod-product-compliance
Lightning Source LLC
Chambersburg PA
CBHW051049230426
43666CB00012B/2627